Making School Inclusion Work

A Guide to Everyday Practice

Katie Blenk

with Doris Landau Fine

Brookline Books

Copyright © 1995 by Brookline Books

Cover photograph by Jack Foley, Foley Studios, Boston.

Library of Congress Cataloging-in-Publication Data

Blenk, Katie, 1954-
    Making school inclusion work: the Kids Are People School experience / Katie Blenk, Doris Landau Fine.
        p.   cm.
    Includes bibliographical references and index.
    ISBN 0-914797-96-4 (pbk.)
    1. Kids Are People School. 2. Handicapped children—Education (Early childhood)—Massachusetts—Case studies. 3. Special education—Massachusetts—Case studies. 4. Early childhood education—Activity programs—Massachusetts—Case studies.
I. Fine, Doris L. II. Title.
LC4032.M4B54 1995
371.91'09744—dc20   94-38275
                                                                     CIP

Brookline Books
P.O. Box 1046
Cambridge, MA 02238-1046

This book is dedicated to Alanna,
who touched our hearts in her fight to live
and taught us that all children,
no matter how significant their special needs,
are to be acknowledged and honored.
To Alanna and all the children
who have taught us how to live, learn and teach.
Thank you.

Alanna Thompson Roberge
Born August 15, 1990
Died May 12, 1991

We acknowledge with very much appreciation the contributions, support and enthusiasm of the Kids Are People School staff and parents. Without this strong positive support, the programs and experiences we describe in this book could not have come to pass.

A special thanks to Dr. Milton Budoff and Erica Schultz of Brookline Books for all they have done to make this book a reality.

TABLE OF CONTENTS

Foreword

With the advent of Public Law 94-142 in 1975, the federal government endorsed the principle that all children, regardless of ability or handicapping condition, have a right to an education in the least restrictive environment. Further legislation later expanded this concept to include children 0-3. Initially, many handicapped children were placed in substantially separate classrooms within the public school or in private specialized day programs. Some of these programs were and continue to be of very high quality, and many children have made dramatic and unexpected developmental progress as a result of these placements. Other specialized programs were remarkably poor and provided little more than "baby-sitting" services.

In recent years, there has been a rush toward "inclusion," the concept that children with special needs should be placed in the same classes as their age-appropriate typical peers. However, in many cases, this rapid shift toward the mainstreaming of all students has failed to take into account the essential basic principles that are critical to the success of this concept. So far, there has been little attempt on the part of public education to alter the standard curriculum and approach to teaching to insure successful inclusion.

Many school systems have covertly welcomed the idea of inclusion as a money-saving approach to the servicing of children with special needs. By placing all children in a regular class and providing support services within the classroom as opposed to a resource room or learning center, more children could theoretically be serviced by fewer specialists. However, due to a variety of factors — noisy larger classrooms, high pupil-teacher ratio, lack of specialized accommodations including computer support, and the failure of some students to learn effectively from the standardized curriculum — this approach often fails. Inclusion cannot be viewed as a money-saving approach to public education of the special child. Done effectively, inclusion is *at least* as expensive as the self-contained model. Placement of the challenged child in a regular class, without careful planning and adequate support services, is a major injustice to that child.

At the present time, most teachers have had little experience or training in working with special needs and are therefore ill-prepared to successfully integrate that student into their already large and busy classrooms. Some, in fact, are uncomfortable with these children, resulting in a suboptimal environment for the child and frustration on the part of the teacher. If inclusion is to be truly successful, school systems must require and provide special education training for all teachers; undergraduate and graduate education programs need to include courses in special education so that future teachers will be adequately prepared.

Presently, in order to place a child in a mainstreamed setting, it is not unusual to have a one-to-one aide specifically responsible for his teaching. Although aides are often well-meaning, they are rarely trained specialists. Thus, the child's educational opportunities may be limited and he remains de facto educationally isolated from his classmates. Social isolation can also be significant, particularly if the school has failed to place more than one similarly handicapped child in a regular class. In many cases, the handicapped child recognizes that he is different from his non-handicapped age-mates. He needs opportunities to socially interact with peers more like himself, as well as with typical children.

At the present time, therapists and specialists providing services to handicapped students within the public schools are often assigned unmanageable caseloads, significantly limiting much-needed individualized intervention to the students and essential consultation to teachers and parents. This situation is both frustrating for the conscientious specialist and of little benefit to the child. Adequate numbers of well-trained personnel must be available within any school system if the inclusion concept is to be successful.

This book tells the story of a school which began as a day care facility and which gradually and enthusiastically welcomed children with special needs. It is the story of this school's determination to provide the therapeutic services essential for each child's development, and to adjust the curriculum so that all children could successfully participate. Today, this school has grown from its day-care beginnings to a program that provides quality education and special services in an integrated setting throughout the elementary school years. Its history has been a stormy one, but its success suggests that the inclusion concept can work given the right environment.

There are no easy answers to the challenge of special education. Whether the concept of inclusion can be applied to, and adequately meet the needs of, all children remains to be seen. However, successful inclusion takes administrative commitment, creativity, financial resources, expertise, patience, parent and teacher support, and most of all, hard work and determination on the part of a dedicated and well-trained staff. This is the story of one school's experience with inclusive education. It deserves careful consideration and reflection.

October, 1994   *Margaret L. Bauman, M.D.*
                                                   Children's Neurology
                                        Massachusetts General Hospital

Preface

All children have the same basic needs: to be loved, cared for, listened to. They all experience similar feelings of joy with success and disappointment and frustration with failure. For children with special needs it is often more difficult to succeed and more common to fail. It may take enormous effort on the part of a child with special needs to accomplish what comes naturally to a child without special needs.

This book addresses the goals and practices required to allow every child, whether the student has special educational needs, knows little English or is poorly prepared for school, to be included in regular classes, with the expectation that the child's special needs — educationally, personally and socially — will be addressed with appropriate programs. In recent years, this concept has largely been directed toward integrating children with special needs in regular classes. We expand the concept to all students in the increasingly diverse classrooms of America.

In 1975 Congress passed the Education of All Handicapped Children Act, later renewed as the Individual Disability Education Act (119A). The earlier act, known as Public Law 94-142, endorsed the principle of all children's right to education in the least restrictive environment. Besides affirming a public commitment to the education of children with special needs, Public Law 94-142 led to the development of the concept of inclusion as the legal and moral standard for provision of educational services to children with special needs, as an expansion of this mandate to place students with special needs in the least restrictive environment. In 1986 Public Law 99-457, the Education of the Handicapped Amendment, expanded the SE standard for provision of educational and developmental services to infants and toddlers (ages 0-3 years). The concept of inclusion continues to develop in both public and private educational settings.

However, inclusion is not presently a universally accepted standard for the education of all children. In our experience at Kids Are People School, integrating children with a variety of special needs has been a positive experience for everyone involved. For example, children and adults learn to appreciate and accept differences in others. Parents of children with special needs see their children as capable of participating in regular education and receiving the special services they require, all in one setting.

The staff at Kids Are People School strongly believe that children with special needs and those without special needs grow and mature in many positive ways when integrated at the youngest possible ages. It is the responsibility, and should be the priority, of all educators and child care professionals to work toward a universal goal of integrated educational programs. Special services should be available and basic educational needs met for all children.

The purpose of this book is to show how inclusion works at Kids Are People School and to share with readers the experiences of the staff, parents and children over the course of several years.

Our goal is to clarify how to make inclusion work and when it doesn't work. We wish to show the benefits and challenges of this commitment to include *all* children, and to foster the desire in other professionals to integrate all children with and without special needs in regular school programs. By presenting the Kids Are People School model, we seek to help these professionals see how they can structure their programs to assure that all children are included.

In this book we have tried to be practical and specific in our presentation of the approaches that govern our practice, the organization of our classrooms, the resources we use, and the curriculum and methods we have created and utilize at our school to realize our goal of inclusion of *all* children in the program. Examples of these resources are to be found in Appendix 4. We hope this book will help to develop nurturing, accepting learning environments where we all grow together, helping, caring and sharing.

Fall, 1994   Katie Blenk
                                                                 Doris L. Fine

The Making of An Inclusive Program

This book talks about one particular program, one group of people, a set of standards this group has developed, and several years of experiences which brought us to the basis of our beliefs in what works best for children in education.

Kids Are People School has had a rocky road to our current place in the world of education.

In 1980, when we first started to include children with special needs in our program, there wasn't a word to describe what we were doing. Actually, it wasn't a situation where we said "We want to make our program inclusive." We were never *exclusive*. It never would have dawned on us to not accept a child *because* he had special needs. We simply took children into our program from the diversity of backgrounds an urban school provides. Thus, children from professional suburban families joined minority and majority students from the city.

The first child we knowingly took with special needs had started at Kids Are People as an infant and was not making developmental gains. We waited for a few months before talking to the parents about our concerns. We suggested an evaluation or at least a talk with their pediatrician. The parents followed through, but the pediatrician felt there was nothing to be concerned about. This particular child continued to develop very slowly. We waited another six months before talking to the parents again; this time the pediatrician agreed and had the child evaluated. The diagnosis which came back was Pervasive Developmental Delay. The parents were told the child should go to the local Early Intervention program and physical therapy services should be started. The mom came to talk to me about removing her child from our program. She stated that she didn't want him to leave and didn't know what to do. Two half-days of early intervention didn't seem like a lot of programming, plus she was going to have to quit her job to take care of her son. She also felt that given his special needs he'd be too much work for us. I told her that he could stay if she wanted, that the physical therapist could come to the school to do therapy, and that I didn't see how he could be extra work because we had already been taking care of him. She was happy; we were happy; there appeared to be no problems.

But there was a problem. Children with special needs were not supposed to be integrated with typical children. Word slowly spread that we at Kids Are People welcomed children with special needs and took the step of hiring therapists to give services to children who came to our program. The problem arose from the medical and educational community. Staff from Early Intervention programs called our parents and their doctors and told them that we were not a state-approved program and that we had neither the skills nor the right to work with these children. The children's medical personnel began calling me, often lecturing me about the needs of the children and the seriousness of what I had done. The medical community generally was appeased when they heard we had licensed therapists and staff.

Early Intervention continued its assault on us until we finally obtained a statement in writing from the State Department of Education that they had an interagency agreement with our licensing organization which allowed for preschools to have children with special needs.

Even the state child advocacy agency, the Office for Children, gave me a difficult time. One day early on in this process of inclusion, the licensor made a surprise visit. He observed a teacher working on basic skills with three children. We had hired her to give supportive tutoring work to a few children who were developmentally delayed. He asked what the teacher was doing. I said, "Oh, those children need a little extra work because they are behind in their basic skills." He said, "You can't do that! You don't have a Special Needs license." I said, "We are educators; that's what we do." He said, "Not without a Special Needs license." I told the teacher, "Stop teaching those children, it's illegal." The licensor said, "I'll send you a Special Needs license."

Interestingly enough, twelve years later I sat on the Task Force to revamp the special needs regulations. The Office for Children did away with the Special Needs license.

Other resistance to our inclusion approach came from a group of parents of typical children. A few parents somehow got the address of a child who had some behavior problems and sent an anonymous letter to the child's parents stating, "Your child should be in a special program for kids like him. He doesn't belong with our children." I was horrified. I felt so badly for the parents of this child. A letter went out from me immediately to all the parents stating, "Kids Are People School is dedicated to serving all children, especially children with special needs. If you have a problem with this, please find another program for your child. There is no negotiating on this."

A couple of parents left and the inclusionary process continued, but the battle with outside agencies did not end — things got worse.

Parents who had never had any hopes of an opportunity for their child to be educated with typical children started hearing about our school. Calls came in every day. Somehow, though it was never an official policy, we figured out that about one-third of the children at the school could have special needs. That seemed to be the proportion that the teachers could handle in their groups and still give quality care and education to all the children.

But many of the children with special needs were turning three or coming in at the age of three or older. This started us in a battle with the public school systems, because they were responsible for the children's education and had no intention of spending money for out-of-district placements to some small unknown preschool program. Fortunately, once they had seen their children included, the parents were determined not to allow the school system to segregate their children again.

And the state law was on our side: Chapter 766 states that children with special needs are entitled to an education in the least restrictive environment. We were by far the least restrictive environment around. This began a process of parents hiring lawyers and finding advocates to represent them at mediations between the school systems and ourselves. The battle was, and continues to be, uphill.

Things have certainly changed in the last fourteen years. At least superficially, the public school system supports inclusion. Two years ago the State Department of Education hired me as a consultant to a public school system to help them make their programs inclusive. At the same time, I looked at our kindergarten program and realized that we had seven, eight and nine year olds in it and had nowhere to place them except in a segregated public school program. I felt that we could not let them be segregated after they had made it in an inclusive program, so we decided to open an elementary school.

One year later, the elementary school is ending its first school year, and the battle for inclusion continues. This time the state department of education questions the correctness of a private school placement for children with special needs as being inclusive. It's amazing that the same organization could have hired me to help them create inclusive programs in the public schools. I guess different components of the state department of education have differing philosophies.

Even though inclusion has become a generally accepted form of education, there is a lot of controversy about whether it works or not, and mainly, *how to do it*. One of the biggest problems facing inclusion is that people are really *not* doing it right. If the current trend of forcing inclusion on educators who do not want to do it continues, and if programs which segregate the child within the classroom continue to be created as models of inclusion, then inclusion will fail.

We have written this book to show that inclusion can and does work, to help people who want to create inclusive programs do it right, and also to point out some general problems with the ways that children with special needs are educated, tested and treated. This book talks about what we have learned from the children over the last fourteen years. If we listen to the children, we can do things right.

CHAPTER ONE

The Children: Who Are They?

Kids Are People School is an urban educational program in Boston, Massachusetts. It is currently a multicultural, inclusive school for children grade six and under, starting with children as young as one month old. The philosophy at Kids Are People School has slowly developed over the years. Its main focus has always been threefold:

- that the children are safe
- that the children are happy
- that the children are growing, developing, and learning.

The children come from a wide range of backgrounds with varied cultures, experiences, home environments and abilities. They are white, black and Asian. They come from well-to-do, middle-class, and very poor families. There are children who are highly intelligent, children who are slow learners, and children who are cognitively challenged. Some of the children can run, jump, and dance; others can barely move a hand to communicate.

At our school children are encouraged to mature at their own individual pace. At different times each child may experience extremes of behavior, i.e., problems adapting to changes in their family or environment, transient medical problems, or developmental problems. In other words, every child is potentially a child with special needs.

A child's special needs can be defined as problems in the areas of behavioral, social-emotional, cognitive, gross motor, fine motor, or speech and language development. A child with a specific diagnosis such as blindness, deafness, neurological deficits, or chronic medical issues may experience problems in one or more of these developmental areas.

Because we feel that every child, at one time or another, could potentially be defined as a child with special needs, it is our belief that education should not be divided into normal vs. special needs programming, either in conducting programs or in staff training. Children with special needs can therefore be divided into three categories:

- Those with developmental delays or problems which may be outgrown or successfully treated.
- Those with a specific diagnosis with significant involvement, e.g., spina bifida, which will require ongoing attention and treatment.
- Those who fall into both of these groups.

It is not our intent to describe any particular disabling condition in depth, but to explain how any child with special needs can be included in educational programs. The children we describe on the next few pages have successfully been integrated into Kids Are People School. We introduce you to Marcus, Danielle, Esther, Afanwi, Sean, Lauren and Benjamin. These children represent a small sample of the young people who attend Kids Are People School. They were chosen because they are well known to the authors and their stories echo the needs and potential success of many young children.

Marcus

Marcus was born on June 19th, 1985, the first child of a healthy young couple in Boston, Massachusetts. At birth he was diagnosed as having spina bifida, a congenital defect of the spine which results in damage to nerves and muscles at and below the level of damage.

In Marcus' case, his lesion was low enough on the spine that he has feeling and motor control to the knee but no feeling in the lower portion of his legs. Marcus has some muscle weakness on the upper legs but from birth he has had movement at the hips. In addition to muscle weakness, he also had a mild case of hydrocephalus, requiring a shunt which originated in his skull and drained into his stomach. When he was 13 months old, this first shunt was upgraded to a new high-pressure valve which should remain in place until Marcus is six or seven years old. Marcus went home with his family at three weeks an alert, healthy and active baby boy with some limitation of movement in his legs.

Marcus entered Kids Are People School when he was 15 months old. On admission he could pull himself to sitting, sit independently and stand with the support of his leg braces. His language consisted of strings of word-like sounds, and he waved bye-bye and pointed accurately to body parts. Socially he was an engaging, lovable child who charmed both staff and children.

Initially, Marcus attended Kids Are People School five hours per day, five days per week. During the first year he received direct therapeutic services on a daily basis, with additional therapeutic activities carried out in the classroom. For example, on any given day Marcus could be observed laughing gleefully atop a green therapy ball, benefiting from social interaction with teachers and friends while gaining strength in his trunk muscles.

Marcus, age four years six months, has now been at Kids Are People School for three years. His language and cognitive abilities appear to be above average, eliminating the need for any additional services in those areas. As he progresses he continues to excel, moving ahead of many of his classmates. His dressing and eating skills are age-appropriate. However, mobility and toileting problems exist and will continue to be problematic in the future. Recently Marcus had bladder reconstruction to enable him to gradually have greater independence with his toileting. Currently, he is in diapers and catheterized twice a day.

Marcus' most significant gains have been in the motor skills area. With braces and crutches Marcus walks independently both indoors and out, fully participating in all school-related activities. He came to us a very bright, sociable, secure child. These interpersonal strengths and consistent attention to his therapeutic needs both at home and in school have been the foundation upon which Marcus has made such dramatic gains. Marcus has now been successfully integrated into a public school first grade program.

Danielle

Danielle was born on January 25th, 1986, the first child of a healthy young couple. She was born 10 weeks premature following a difficult pregnancy which required hospitalization for her mother. Her birth weight was two pounds, four ounces. She had low Apgar scores as well as significant respiratory distress which resulted in two days in an incubator. When she was three days old, an intraventricular hemorrhage resulted in a diagnosis of right hemiparesis, a form of cerebral palsy. Hospitalization continued for two months following birth. Danielle was discharged home on March 20, 1986, weighing five pounds, six ounces. Her developmental progress continued to be monitored through the hospital.

Due to significant delays in motor and language skills, Danielle, age twelve months (ten months corrected), was referred to an early intervention program in January of 1987. At that time she could sit independently, pull herself to a standing position, and roll to get around. Her speech and language skills consisted of vowel sounds and alert babbling. Formal cognitive/developmental assessment revealed Danielle to be a bright, alert and sociable infant, functioning above her age level in this area.

For the next six months, physical and occupational therapists made weekly home visits. In addition, Danielle's mother incorporated therapeutic exercises and activities into every aspect of Danielle's life.

In August of 1987, at age eighteen months (sixteen months corrected), Danielle entered Kids Are People School on a full-time basis. An engaging, pretty child, she demonstrated strength in social, emotional and cognitive areas. For example, she could easily complete a five-piece puzzle correctly, an advanced task for an eighteen month old child.

As a direct result of her right hemiparesis, Danielle had muscle weakness of her entire right side affecting movement and balance. While she was able to walk, balance and coordination were very poor, and she avoided using her right hand for any fine motor activity. Speech, language and eating skills were delayed due to oral motor weakness.

Danielle started at Kids Are People School with children ranging in age from fifteen months through thirty months, with whom she immediately clicked both socially and emotionally. Although Danielle received regular physical and speech therapy, from the beginning the staff felt the enormous and rapid gains Danielle made in motor and speech and language skills were directly related to her daily interaction with other children. This was enhanced by the teacher's integration of therapeutic exercises into classroom activities.

During her early years, Danielle was very cautious and self-protective when presented with motor activities. One year ago Danielle did not run, nor could she use any climbing equipment. She demonstrated a definite preference for left-handed manipulation of toys, consciously avoiding use of her right hand in most activities. Although Danielle still shows a left-hand preference for fine motor activities, she is willing and able to use both hands when engaged in gross motor games. For example, she can be seen hanging, holding on with both hands, from the top of the climbing structure or running freely through the room chasing her best friend Johann.

Although Danielle continues to have slight muscle weakness in the right side of her body, which no longer requires ongoing physical and occupational therapy, this weakness in no way defines who or what she can do or be.

She is now eight years old and, after attending Kids Are People School for three and one-half years, was successfully integrated into a public school first grade. She is a bright and creative child who fully participates in all classroom activities. Her language skills are age-appropriate and she no longer requires speech and language therapy. Imaginative play in the dress-up area is one of Danielle's favorite pastimes. From princess to monster to astronaut, Danielle's ability to role-play expresses her belief in her potential to be whoever she chooses to be.

Esther

Esther was born on April 19th, 1986, following a full-term pregnancy significant only in that her mother had several bouts of the flu in the first trimester. Initial Apgar scores were nine and ten respectively. Soon after birth Esther went home to her parents and 3 year old sister.

During the next six months Esther's development was marked by a poor sucking reflex; issues with eating resulted in an initial diagnosis of failure to thrive. Extreme hypersensitivity to a variety of sensory input caused Esther to be chronically irritable. She was sensitive to light, noise, wind and touch, resulting in incessant crying and inconsistent sleep patterns. In addition, from early infancy Esther's parents and doctors noted a possible hearing loss and extreme muscle weakness characterized by poor head and trunk control and weak uncoordinated movement of the arms and legs. In spite of all of these problems, Esther was playful with her family and indicated a strong and consistent social awareness of her environment.

Esther was referred for a series of evaluations at approximately six months. She was eventually diagnosed as having generalized hypotonia — extreme muscle weakness — with a tendency to respiratory illness and ear infections. Extensive testing, including chromosomal and blood evaluation, were within normal limits, eliminating a diagnosis of any particular syndrome.

From the beginning, both of Esther's parents spent an enormous amount of time and energy and used every possible resource to further their daughter's developmental progress. This was done with intensity, consistency and love. Besides the activities of the parents, from the age of four months Esther received ongoing physical therapy services through Boston Children's Hospital. She also received in-home, bimonthly occupational therapy.

Esther entered Kids Are People School when she was fifteen months old. She was immediately included in the infant-toddler group of nine children ranging in age from six months to two years. For the first year and a half Esther came to the program part time: five hours per day, five days per week.

On entry Esther had pervasive developmental delays. She was non-verbal but did respond to her name with facial expressions. Esther needed support to sit independently, had partial head control, and made no independent purposeful movement of arms or legs. Due to Esther's extremely poor attention span and language and motor delays, there was some question as to her potential for cognitive and general developmental progress. During the first year at school Esther's attendance was inconsistent due to respiratory problems, ear infections, and muscle spasms of the neck. These problems still exist but no longer interfere with her attendance.

When Esther was two years eleven months, she began attending Kids Are People School on a full-time basis: eight hours per day, five days per week. From the time of her initial placement, Esther received physical, occupational and speech and language therapy along with the regular educational program at Kids Are People School. Although the therapies were done on a consistent basis, the more important aspect of the program was the interaction with her peers. Additionally, her classroom teachers were able to integrate specific therapeutic goals into her daily activities. This integrated approach appeared to contribute greatly to Esther's very rapid developmental gains.

Esther, age eight years three months, has made tremendous gains. Although her muscles continue to be weak due to low tone, affecting the quality of her gait and balance, she walks independently. Articulation is still somewhat delayed, but expressive and receptive language are age-appropriate. Cognitively, Esther can identify colors and shapes and her letters and numbers, and she has begun to read. Her attention span has improved dramatically. For example, she can spend over twenty minutes working carefully on an arts and crafts project until it is completed to her satisfaction. Her social interactions are age-appropriate. She continues to have a warm, friendly nature which endears her to both adults and children.

Esther is an important member of the school and takes part in all school activities. She continues to receive physical, occupational, and speech and language therapies as part of her ongoing educational program.

Afanwi

Afanwi was born on January 12th, 1983, the fifth child of a healthy woman. Pregnancy had been normal, as was his birth. Developmental milestones were normal for the first year of his life, with Afanwi walking at nine months and his first real words evident at twelve months. Between eighteen and twenty-four months, Afanwi's mother and day care provider observed problems in several areas. Afanwi was not interacting socially; he had minimal eye contact and extreme sensitivity to human touch, except with his mother. As a result of severe behavioral problems at his day care program, Afanwi was forced to leave. At age two years six months, he was referred for a full developmental and educational evaluation to determine an appropriate program placement. The results of the evaluation, while inconclusive, suggested the possibility of pervasive onset disorder with secondary autistic-like qualities.

At age two years nine months, Afanwi entered Kids Are People School, where he remained until he graduated to a fully integrated first grade classroom in public school at age six years eight months. Upon his entrance at Kids Are People School, Afanwi was placed in a class of ten preschoolers, where he participated in all classroom activities. Gross motor skills were age-appropriate, but pervasive delays were evident in speech and language and fine motor skills. Of greatest concern to the staff was Afanwi's extreme avoidance of social contact with either staff or peers. Specific behaviors included total avoidance of eye contact, inability to attend to any activity for over thirty seconds, bizarre ritualistic behavior such as licking staff shoes, and self-stimulation in the form of rocking. At the time of entrance, Afanwi exhibited no independent self-help skills.

During his first two years at Kids Are People School, Afanwi received individual speech and language therapy five days per week. In the classroom, behavior modification was used consistently. Specific expectations included use of eye contact, modification to elimination of ritualistic behaviors, and progressive increases of attention to activities.

Gradually, over the course of the first three months Afanwi began to feed himself, became toilet trained, and began to make one-word utterances. Teachers observed that Afanwi made increased eye contact, and ritualistic behavior occurred less frequently. With the help of his friends, Afanwi's true personality and intellectual capabilities began to emerge. Over the years, ritualistic behaviors were eliminated and he became socially integrated in the classroom. It became evident the suggested diagnosis was inaccurate. The staff began to feel that Afanwi was a child with attention deficit disorder, a diagnosis which was confirmed by formal testing at age six.

As Afanwi matured, he demonstrated that he was a highly intelligent, creative, manipulative child. Problems with processing and poor attention, coupled with sensory integration difficulties, at times clouded the reality of just how capable he was. By age four, Afanwi could identify all his numbers, shapes and colors. He knew all his upper and lower case letters and the sounds they make. His favorite TV programs were the nightly newscasts; he paid close attention, appearing to understand much of what was reported, and could identify the various newscasters from each station.

Over the years Afanwi continued to receive weekly speech and language and occupational therapy. With time, Afanwi grew into an intelligent and capable child with a great sense of humor. Despite ongoing difficulties in the areas of fine motor skills, auditory processing, and sensory integration, Afanwi has grown to become a successful fourth grader in an integrated public school class.

Sean

Sean was born on January 31st, 1986, the second child of a healthy young woman. Pregnancy was reportedly normal and full term, but Sean's birth was complicated. Due to the fact that he was breech and the cord was wrapped around his neck, an emergency Caesarean section was performed. Sean was born with a high (above the knee) congenital amputation of the right leg. Despite the immediate and obvious trauma, Sean was normal in all areas of development from birth.

Sean was followed closely by physicians and therapists for ongoing treatment. At ten months he was fitted with his first prosthesis. From the beginning, his mother was an active participant in treatment which consisted of daily exercises encouraging Sean's normal development. He had age-appropriate developmental milestones including motor development. Socially, Sean matured into an engaging, verbal little boy who adapted well to the use of his prosthesis; in fact, he was walking with a walker at age 15 months.

Sean came to Kids Are People School at age two years seven months, a confident, capable, little boy who did not let his circumstances hinder his activities. He was monitored by the school physical therapist on a monthly basis, but otherwise participated fully in all school activities. With the exception of toileting he was independent in all self-care activities. In the classroom and playground, Sean easily kept up with his classmates including climbing, running and jumping. When he got tired, and sometimes because he knew the staff was encouraging him to bend his knees more, Sean would deliberately lock the knee mechanism on his prosthesis so it would not bend.

At age three years five months it was determined that Sean's prosthesis was too small, and he was fitted with a new one. His new prosthesis was designed differently from the old one and was intended to eventually give Sean more independence, specifically with toileting skills. In fact, the new prosthesis was designed with a suction cup which was improperly fitted, resulting in severe problems for Sean.

Initially Sean had difficulty walking due to the fact that the prosthesis was too long; also, the suction cup would loosen easily, with the result that the prosthesis would often fall off during walks to the park. Physically, Sean started falling spontaneously as he walked. His balance was poor, and he was easily knocked over by other children. This contributed to a loss of self-confidence and self-control which exhibited itself in different ways. Sean started refusing physical therapy, which had been increased to twice a week. He avoided participation in all activities requiring gross motor skills, including running with his buddies which had been a favorite activity. He had become a very unhappy little boy.

With time, the prosthesis was adjusted and Sean learned to use it more effectively. Although it is still far from perfect, most of Sean's self-confidence has returned. Although he is more cautious than in the past, he has begun to run and climb again and retains his balance more easily. In addition to the daily encouragement and support he has at home and in school, Sean continues to receive physical therapy twice a week in school. Although Sean has experienced some temporary reversals in his gross motor skills, he continues to thrive in all other areas, doing age-appropriate activities.

Lauren

Lauren was born on June 12, 1988, the first child of a healthy young couple. Lauren was born six weeks premature with postnatal complications. She remained in the hospital for five weeks due to apnea resulting from prematurity, but after five weeks was sent home a healthy baby. Her parents report that Lauren appeared to develop normally, and that they had no real concerns about her development until about eight months of age, when her mother noticed that she seemed quite weak. She couldn't really move around, and her hips rotated out, making her legs slack when she was on her back. Thus began several trips to a variety of specialists in several cities to determine what was wrong and what could be done to help Lauren. Lauren ended up in Boston, where specialists from an area hospital informed her parents that she had Rett's Syndrome, a rare condition with the following characteristics:

- It is only found in female children.
- There is normal development until between 3 months and 6 years, at which time the child stops developing and begins to lose abilities previously gained.
- There is no language.
- There is little attention to others, objects, or the environ-

ment.
- The child wrings her hands in a "hand-washing" fashion.
- The child eventually loses ground until she is no longer functioning in any area and her respiratory system eventually just stops working.
- It is rare for the child to live to adulthood.

Lauren was placed in Kids Are People when she was two years old. At the initial interview, we told her parents that we did not know anything about Rett's Syndrome. They said that most people didn't: it's very rare and there isn't a lot written on it. We told the parents we couldn't make any guarantees for Lauren other than that we would do our absolute best to help her. I remember the day I met Lauren. She was one of the most beautiful children I had ever seen. She made very little eye contact; she could bump herself sideways around the room a bit, and she fit most of the characteristics of a child with Rett's Syndrome, including no language and the wringing of the hands. But the thing I remember most was her huge eyes and her smile. From the moment I met her I was heartsick to think this beautiful little girl was probably going to die in the next few years. I had a brief moment of thinking, "I don't know if I can handle this, watching a child die." But I looked at the parents and thought, "*They're going to have to. I think we should help them.*"

Thus began a relationship with a child that has touched me more deeply than any I have known. I know it was initially because I did not want her to die, but Lauren and I clicked. She stole my heart, and I and most of the staff became determined to help her.

When Lauren started at Kids Are People, she was so weak she really could do little. Within a year of being with us she had a major seizure, and another a year later, but this has been followed by her doctors and is under control.

Over the course of the next four years, Lauren made very slow but steady progress in all areas, causing her doctors to eventually change her diagnosis to Pervasive Developmental Delay. Lauren today has extreme hypotonia (weakness of muscles) and chronic respiratory infections, but she can walk with assistance. She has a vocabulary, although she only puts two words together. She has a definite personality and is extremely social. She is very focused, and her attention has increased significantly even in the last couple of months. There is no way I believe she has Rett's Syndrome, and it has been a long uphill battle for her parents and myself to prove it to others. She is no longer the little girl I first met four years ago and looked so sadly at. At age six years, Lauren is progressing daily, and that's all that counts. She's moving forward, and that's the right direction.

Benjamin

Benjamin was born on April 16th, 1986, the first child of a healthy young couple. He was born a healthy, typical infant with no prenatal or postnatal complications. Benjamin entered the infant program at age 2 months. His overall development was typical until the age of nine months, when the staff referred him for an orthopedic exam because he was having a great deal of difficulty learning to crawl. The pediatrician felt there was no need for concern and denied a request for physical therapy. Ongoing observation was recommended. At age eleven months, the staff approached the parents again about Benjamin's motor development, especially weakness in the lower extremities. At this time, the pediatrician referred the parents for an orthopedic evaluation, and recommendation was made for physical therapy for strengthening. Physical therapy was given twice a week for six months, at which time it was terminated because his motor skills had improved significantly with the therapy.

What was much more significant about Benjamin was that at age 20 months he could correctly name shapes, the upper case letters of the alphabet, and the numbers one to five. By age two and a half he could identify all upper and lower case letters, shapes, some colors, the numbers one to ten, and many letter consonant sounds. By age three Benjamin was reading short sentences and sounding out words.

We had a difficult time toilet training Benjamin, not because he didn't want to be trained, but because he would be so focused on activities and learning that he would "forget to go." This and the birth of his younger brother caused him to act out a bit, but nothing significant enough to consider him a behavior problem.

When Benjamin was four and a half, he began to show signs of being bored: acting up, being in a dream world, not attending to task. Although it took all of us a few months to figure out what was going on, we eventually did. Benjamin, we knew, was highly intelligent, but we didn't know how intelligent. For several days running, when he was asked questions in the group, it would take him so long to answer that the teacher had to skip him and go back after others in the group answered. We finally figured out that Benjamin was so intelligent that he was thinking well above a concrete level and was analyzing all possible scenarios before answering the question. If the teacher were to hold up objects from the ocean for the class to identify, such as a piece of seaweed, and the answer we were looking for was 'seaweed', Benjamin would have already jumped way past seaweed as the answer to figuring out what classification this particular seaweed fell into, if it was part of the food chain for specific animals, and so forth.

Two of my favorite Benjamin stories are as follows.

I found a swallowtail caterpillar in the yard and brought it in to live at the school. I sat down with Benjamin's group (children age 4) and went through the whole process of how "the butterfly lays the egg, the egg hatches into a caterpillar, the caterpillar turns into a cocoon, and one day the cocoon breaks open into a beautiful butter-fly." Benjamin raised his hand. "Yes, Benjamin." "Actually, Katie, that's called metamorphosis." "Yes, it is, thank you, Benjamin."

When Benjamin was seven, the drama teacher sent the children home with the assignment to come in with an idea for a play next week. Each person would get up and discuss their idea. The day came and the teacher went around, and "dragons" and "princesses" and "Ninja Turtles" were all presented. Benjamin got up and said, "Well, there were these two paleontologists..." Teachers went run-ning for the dictionaries. Everyone looked at one another and the teacher said, "Good, Benjamin, explain to the children what these paleontologists do."

As you will read in the next chapters, it is as important to foster Benjamin's skills for his social and emotional well-being as it is to help a child put her braces on and off or give a child his daily asthma medicine.

Benjamin tested out at age six and a half in the *very* superior range of intelligence. He is more intelligent than myself and most of his teachers. He has a couple of peers a year older than him, and one six year old, who are as intelligent; he is also in a group of children that has several children with severe special needs. The makeup of his group is exactly what he needs to grow in all areas. Benjamin is a joy to teach, and it takes a teaching staff who is not afraid of reaching with Benjamin, not afraid of going the extra steps to challenge him, and who will honor him for who he is: one of the most delightful, enthusiastic learners we have had the challenge and joy of teaching. He is the perfect example of why all children need individualized education.

CHAPTER TWO

Teaching to Inclusion: How Do You Do It?

In early childhood programs as well as elementary schools, the keys to making inclusion work are the team of people running the program, and the structure of the classroom. Conversely, it is these two areas that often constitute the major barriers to inclusion.

THE STAFF

Regardless of the laws which require children with special needs to be included whenever possible, human nature, attitudes and prejudices come into play. All it takes is one adult who doesn't want children with special needs in their class to make inclusion fail. What goes on in the classroom, and the attitudes and working styles of the teaching team, are the real measure of inclusion. Inclusion will not work if the teacher is being forced to include children with special needs. If the administrators of the school philosophically disagree with inclusion, they can undermine it every step of the way: by not supporting the teaching staff, not funding necessary equipment, or not working with parents of typical children to help them to be open and accepting of the children with special needs. The flow of acceptance needs to be seamless, from the administration through teachers, therapists, parents and children — all working cooperatively to make the best educational program for all the children.

For a more complete discussion of the role of the staff in making true inclusion happen, see Chapter 4.

CLASSROOM STRATEGIES FOR INCLUSION

We have found that certain classroom strategies are essential for true inclusion to take place. They consist of the following.

Hands-On Center Teaching

It has been our experience, supported by a wealth of literature, that children learn best through the process of experience as opposed to lecture. When children are involved through their senses, their experiences are lasting. For example, a teacher can talk about the life cycles of a plant, but the difference in growing one's own plant and watching the changes is awesome. This is a simple example. A more difficult concept such as the heart pumping blood through our bodies can be presented through discussion, but a life-size body with removable parts gets the concept across to the children much more easily and engagingly. Touching, smelling, tasting and seeing goes beyond the learning process to become a life experience. Most young children picture the human heart as the shape of a valentine. An experiential lesson will leave a lasting impression of what we really have beating in our chests.

The classroom itself should be set up to have several learning center areas, stations, to foster this kind of experiential learning. The centers should include at least the following areas:

> Art area
> Water, sand, or other sensory manipulative area
> Large science area where hands-on experience can occur
> Computer areas (if possible, Logo should be part of this as a
>   great hands-on learning experience)
> Multicultural area
> Gross motor area
> Language arts area
> Mathematics/manipulatives area
> Library area
> Dramatic play area (which can change with curriculum sub-
>   ject matter)

For more information on setting up these centers and making them inclusive, refer to Chapter 5.

The concept of these learning centers is crucial to most other aspects of classroom strategies for inclusion. Even with one teacher and a group of 24 children, if there are interesting and challenging learning centers throughout the room, it automatically sets the stage for small groupings of children, child-directed activities, and cooperative learning in small groups. And it frees the teacher to move around the room to each center to assist, maintain control, even have extra time to work with small groups of children who may need extra help due to learning problems or physical challenges, or who are well above grade level and need more advanced instruction.

Child- And Teacher-Directed Activities

Children spend a great deal of time right through the teenage years at odds with themselves — they want to be in control, in charge, do it themselves. They're out of control, argumentative, demanding attention, and looking for external controls from the adults in their lives. Combining child- and teacher-directed activities is a great way to deal with this seesawing of emotions from children. While the teacher can set up activities (and there's no reason why the kids can't help when appropriate), it is very important for the teacher to disperse children's ideas throughout the curriculum. Teachers should search for springboard ideas coming from the children, and should include having the children help plan the curriculum. Idea-posting boards throughout the school are a way to incorporate and save ideas from children. When ideas come from children, you are automatically setting the stage for the children to be enthusiastic, cooperative and creative. Children who are non-verbal should also help make the choices; specific suggestions for helping these children express choices are included in the augmentative communication section in Chapter 8 of this book. Just because children are non-motoric or non-verbal does not mean they are retarded, and even if they are, it does not mean they do not have desires and preferences. They should be given every opportunity to participate in classroom choices. I cannot stress this enough: *wheelchairs and lack of language do not equal mental retardation.* This group of children is by far the most discriminated against because it's very easy to write them off — after all, what are they going to do or say about it?

I'd like the reader to imagine yourself unable to move your body and unable to communicate to anyone, but still the same person intellectually as you are as you read this book. Imagine being locked inside your own body. This is how I think Lauren feels day in and day out. People, if they care enough, try to guess at what she wants or needs. She can't even say, "My nose is itching me. Please scratch it." Imagine having a permanent itch on your nose and not being able to ask for help or to help yourself — to me this is the worst kind of torture.

Make sure when helping create child-directed activities that you ensure all the children get the chance to be choice makers. This is where caring and creativity combine to include all the children. Make sure, also, that the peers of children with special needs have been taught to solicit preference responses from their non-verbal friends, and the techniques necessary to elicit those choices.

The Teacher as Facilitator

I don't believe the best way to teach is to lecture. I do believe that facilitating education is the key to good inclusion and that good teaching is facilitating education. Facilitating education involves five steps.

Planning Activities. Planning activities which are fun, hands-on and open-ended but include curriculum goals takes work. However, it ends up making teaching easier in the long run because

- information learned from a hands-on activity tends to stay with the child because it is a life experience;
- if the activities are open-ended, it automatically leaves room for children's ideas to springboard off the original activity;
- if it's hands-on, it can usually be set up as a center for cooperative learning.

Presenting Material and Information. The key to facilitative education is introducing ideas and materials and then letting the children go at the project. The teacher doesn't lecture. He shares knowledge and then lets the children experience the learning so that it becomes their own knowledge. Reading and writing becomes a secondary but enriching part of learning, not a chore. The children tend to want to read and write about what they have learned. The seed of curiosity about specific topics has been started with the project's introduction and initial development. What happens is that the children come and say, "I want to write about this topic," and ask questions which allow the teacher to direct them to references to answer their questions. From there, they come back and share it with their classmates.

For someone with Lauren's issues, the teacher, after finding a way for Lauren to answer "yes" or "no", can then ask questions of Lauren to find where her interests lie. In our program, where kids have been together for years, the teacher can assign a friend to elicit the information from Lauren (more on this under Cooperative Education, below, and Communication, in Chapter 8). For Lauren, reference materials for more information on topics of interest should be in the form of computer programs, books and tapes on the subjects of interest. Friends would then work with Lauren in the listening library or computer area.

Grouping children. In center-based teaching, a very crucial component to facilitating education is grouping children correctly to set the tone for real learning to take place. Many things need to be taken into account. The complexity of the project will to some extent affect the grouping of abilities. If the project requires a great deal of complex problem solving, and children with significant cognitive delays are to be included in the group, then the group probably should also include the teacher and a mix of children with varying abilities. Sometimes a project can be done without the teacher, and the group should include at least one child who is capable of problem solving and getting the project completed.

The group should also have at least one child who is able and willing to make sure children who are non-verbal or non-motor are included. This child's skills would include knowing how the child with special needs communicates and how to elicit communication from him or her. Ideally, all the children should be willing and able to do this, but some children are more self-absorbed and just aren't as good at assisting. The teacher needs to make sure, whatever the project, that at least one capable, willing peer is in the group with any child with special needs who needs assistance.

Monitoring behavior. Just as important as making an activity interesting is monitoring behavior, so the teacher can ensure that

a) children stay on track,
b) problem solving is cooperative and fair,
c) all children are included in the project, and
d) materials and equipment are used correctly.

Once children get used to structured instruction and are focused around cooperative learning, monitoring behavior is easy for the most part, even with children whose special needs are totally behaviorally or emotionally based. In the right setting, behavior monitoring should involve the teacher asking "What's going on here?" when a problem or dispute erupts. Both sides should get to speak, but no matter what the problem appears to be from the viewpoint of the children, generally the next question should be "What is *supposed to be* going on?" Almost every time, kids will give the right answer, such as "We're supposed to be writing a story." The teacher's next question should be "Well, what do you need to do to get back to where you are supposed to be?"

The point here, again, is that the children are supposed to learn coping, communication, and problem solving skills *as part of* their academic learning. The teacher needs to facilitate this by having solutions to problems *come from the children* whenever possible. Of course, when physically or verbally aggressive children are in a group, obvious safety concerns sometimes make this impossible, but it should still be a goal of the program to work towards cooperative problem solving among the children.

Helping children come up with answers. An ongoing process that the facilitative teacher fosters is asking open-ended questions to help children think, create, and problem-solve. Open-ended questions should not always be used to get a specific answer, and answers children give which do not directly solve the problem or task presented should be considered for future projects. For example, if the children are working on a planting project, and the teacher asks "What do you think we need to make these plants grow?", the children might come up with water and soil, but not light. Not only should the teacher ask the children "What do you think would happen if the plant didn't have light?", but then a new experiment should be created to grow some plants without light. Children should have observation journals to record the differences in growth between plants given water, soil and light, and plants just given water and soil. New ideas such as "What would happen if we didn't give the plant soil?" should come from the first planting activity. The role of the teacher is to help the children come up with new ideas branching off the old one, and then to provide materials to try out their ideas and test their hypotheses. This is child-directed, teacher-facilitated, hands-on learning.

Cooperative Education

When people talk about cooperative education, it means children learning together and cooperating to get answers, solve problems, etc. To me, cooperative education is a very important component of inclusion. In our program it goes several steps further. Because many of the children have been together for years, and also because it is expected of the children from the day they enter the program, the children spend a great deal of time helping one another. In our program, cooperative education becomes a "child-teaching-child" process. This kind of child interaction, which at this point comes naturally in our program, can easily be incorporated into any program as long as the adults demonstrate the right attitudes. Children love to imitate and are very good at imitating details. Therefore, it is an important part of inclusion for adults to get out of the way whenever possible and let children cooperate and help one another learn.

There are people who feel that typical kids are losing out because of the children with special needs. What we have seen as a direct result of cooperative education and our peer tutoring program is that both groups of children are benefiting — and not just socially.

The typical children are learning the skills that good teachers need. They are learning:

- How to explain ideas to someone who doesn't understand.
- How to be patient.
- How to creatively get ideas across — when one method doesn't work, try another.
- How to change negative behaviors.
- How to persevere.
- How to organize ideas and materials and how to present activities.
- Compassion, nurturing and acceptance of differences.
- Positioning techniques.
- How to communicate using several different techniques non-verbally and verbally.

What these children are learning by working with their peers with and without special needs are life skills which are necessary to be successful in every career field. And these children are feeling good about themselves, accomplished, useful. It gives them a sense of pride. Working with their peers has caused a dramatic increase in cooperation levels in the program, a reduction of immature, selfish behaviors, an increase in the desire to learn, and a decrease in time-out use and other disciplinary techniques. We see the children responding more readily and appropriately to questions such as "How do you think that makes the other person feel?" or "What do you think the right thing to do was?" The children have become much more thoughtful and considerate. Behavioral problems are at a minimum, even though there are several children placed here because of their behavioral problems. In addition, children become watchful and protective of their friends and are right there informing the teacher if there are any problems occurring.

Teachers have to share attention among all the children, so it really makes sense to nurture cooperative education as the method to give the most to all the children. We do believe also that children have a way with one another that is different from child-adult interactions. Kids tend to get more out of each other, and they tend to socialize more often and try harder. The motivation for Lauren to get a response from her friends appears to be much stronger than with adults. In addition, peers are always available and helpful to one another. They relate differently to their peers. We have seen students with severe developmental delays responding with awareness and alertness to questions from other students, whereas they may simply stroke the adult's arm and smile, unresponding.

Furthermore, Kids Are People is a year-round, full-day program, since we originated as a full-day early childhood day care program. We feel the twelve-month consistency has been good for all the children. We don't have to start in September setting new limits, with new teachers and with children who have missed out on therapies and structure for ten weeks. Parents and children can take time off from school any time during the year. And if there is any chance the typical children are missing out because of their peers with special needs (which we do not at all believe), this time is made up in the additional 69 days of school each year and the extended daily hours. Also, the children don't have to adjust to a new set of adults in the summer or in September. Whenever possible the teacher moves with the class, which leads to a discussion of multi-aged classes as a key to successful inclusion.

Multi-Aged Classrooms

Multi-aged classes are the most important factor to making inclusion work at the elementary school level. No matter how much adaptation you do to the curriculum to help integrate a child, if he/she is the only one doing first grade work in fourth grade, it's very obvious. *I cannot stress enough that inclusion allows those children in that class to feel their learning experience is not unusual because other children are doing the same work.* If it is obvious that some children in the class are always doing easier work (what fourth graders would label as "baby work"), then no matter what adaptations you do to the curriculum, those children are still segregated within the class. If, however, classes are set up as multi-aged classes, nothing is very obvious other than adaptive equipment — which is a fact of life.

In these classes, everyone is doing different things in small groups throughout the day. It doesn't matter that Benjamin and a peer are doing eleventh grade spelling games on the computer, if Lauren is at another computer with a friend doing a different spelling game. The point is all four children are doing spelling. It doesn't matter that in the multi-aged 1st-3rd grade class some children are doing a shared reading experience with big books and a teacher, while other children are in the library researching a project on environmental pollution — they are all doing reading.

There is no room for differences of any kind when a classroom is set up by chronological age with desks lined up and the teacher directing all activities. This isn't just speaking to children with special needs, it's speaking about the educational system's need to force children to be the same. Groups of 24 children sitting at desks in classrooms all across this country are being taught by standards that were set up years ago, dictating that this and only this is first grade work. This is what we'll teach, and don't learn it too slow or you'll be left behind and labeled. Don't learn it too fast or you'll be bored and eventually labeled as a behavior problem or, worse, emotionally disturbed. Educational curriculum is currently designed for the middle group within the one-year age span.

Benjamin is representative of extremely bright children whom the system fails. As detailed in his case study in Chapter 1, by the time Benjamin was two he knew all of his letter names and sounds, and by three he was reading. When he left Kids Are People to go to kindergarten, an in-depth report went with him stressing how extremely intelligent Benjamin was and how important it was for him to be given special projects and work at his own level. The report was ignored. By December of his kindergarten year, the public school thought Benjamin exhibited emotional problems and recommended observation by the school psychologist. Benjamin was "withdrawn", "not focused on his work," "living in a dream world", "had no friends" and was having "toileting accidents." When his parents called us and asked me to help, I went to the team meeting. The teacher went on and on about all of Benjamin's negative behaviors, never once saying anything positive. The child she was describing sounded disturbed and in trouble and was not the child who had left our program. I asked, "Did you read our report?" The answer was "I'm sure I did, but it has little to do with what's going on now." I said "OK., what are you working with the children on academically?" She said "Letter sounds." I said "Well, I guess if I was Benjamin and knew all my letter sounds by age two, I'd withdraw into my own world too."

In my opinion this was one of the worst cases of irresponsible behavior towards a child I had ever seen, because this school had the information ahead of time — they just ignored it. At this point, even though I'm not enamored of testing, I suspected Benjamin by standardized test definition was probably at genius level. I recommended to the parents that in order to help them to get the school to change Benjamin's curriculum, they should have an IQ test done. If we had it in a psychological report, then we could force these educators to listen to us about Benjamin's needs.

When Benjamin was tested he was six years and three months old. The results of the testing showed Benjamin to be in the "very superior" range, with reading skills above eighth grade level and spelling skills above sixth grade level. In arithmetic Benjamin scored at about a third grade level because he didn't know how to add a column of three 2 digit addends. He had never been shown this. After he was shown once how to do it, his score jumped considerably. The test results also showed that Benjamin felt different from his peers and isolated.

This story of Benjamin very clearly demonstrates the need for multi-aged classrooms where curriculum is not determined by chronological age according to some nebulous dictate that six year olds are only able to learn certain concepts. Benjamin is not the only child like this. In multi-aged classes children experience a variety of learning experiences from other children who know many different things. Each child has a unique ability and knowledge base. Socially, someone like Benjamin needs young children around him as peers; academically, he needs more advanced students so he doesn't feel different and is challenged.

At the time that Benjamin left Kids Are People we did not have an elementary school. It was specifically because of Benjamin and a few of his friends that we started the new elementary school. Benjamin is currently enrolled in our school in a multi-aged classroom and has just turned eight. He is working on eleventh grade algebra and geometry, and his "social problems" are nonexistent. The fact that Benjamin is eight and doing eleventh grade math brings me to another component of inclusion — individualized education for all children.

Individualized Education

At Kids Are People we do individualized education for all the children, not just the children with special needs. We feel the biggest problem in education today is setting curriculum by age-graded levels: "First-grade work is first-grade work and that's what first graders should learn." This philosophy totally discounts children as individuals with different abilities, experiences and learning styles. For someone like Benjamin this clearly did not work. His failure in public school was wholly due to the fact that he knew too much and was bored, and they did not adjust their curriculum to his academic levels — even when they had been told in advance!

Right now we have another child who is a six year old reading at a fourth grade level. No intelligent person is going to expect us to keep her from moving forward. Yet that is what happens in classrooms all across the country: age-graded curriculum holds some children back and is over the heads of other children.

In multi-aged classes, children work in small groups at their own level, where they can be challenged by children who know more and be helpful to children who know less.

I have seen children as young as two and a half bored in toddler rooms, looking longingly at the preschool rooms, interested in the older children and in their educational materials and equipment. Exceptions need to be made, with parent permission, for these children to move into the preschool room early — anything less is unfair. Of course, I have seen parents push for their children to move early into an older group when the child wasn't at all ready. So common sense always needs to be used when determining programming around individual children.

Individualized education is difficult to do in a typical classroom with 25-30 children. In consulting to a public school with large class sizes, I was able to convince the teacher to do more center-based teaching in small groups using cooperative learning techniques. The teachers found that this method did give them more free time, even in a class of 20 or more students, to work with individual children who needed additional work.

Low Child-to-Teacher Ratio

Small group size is very important for quality education, and absolutely necessary for individualized education. It takes a classroom teacher a lot longer to find out where each child is academically and socially and what their learning styles are in a class of twenty-five students. It also is very difficult to facilitate cooperative, child-directed activities in a large class. Planning activities for so many children and individualizing these activities for each child's needs becomes almost impossible with the high numbers in public school classrooms. Class size in an inclusive program should be between twelve and fifteen, depending on the makeup of the group, and no more than twenty children with two teachers.

In the Kids Are People elementary school, group size is one to twelve, with additional non-assigned teachers to facilitate inclusion. This results in a ratio of about 1 to 8, with children working in groups of 3 and 4 most of the time. At the preschool, the ratio is at the most one teacher to ten children (ages three to five), and sometimes one to five depending on the makeup of the group.

CHAPTER THREE

When Inclusion Doesn't Work

There are several circumstances which can prevent inclusion from working. These are the major issues.

I. Forced Inclusion

Forced inclusion of children with special needs into classrooms whose teachers don't want them is probably the worst injustice we can do to our children.

> Over the last several years of lecturing on inclusion some teachers and administrators have expressed their feelings to me in public. That they "feel sorry for those kinds of children but I don't want them in my [school, class, etc.]. I can't work with them. I don't want to. I shouldn't have to. I was doing just fine teaching normal kids. I didn't go to school for that. I don't see why I'm being forced to do this. If I wanted to teach those kids I would have studied that."

I've heard it so many times, put in so many different ways, that I really think the Powers that Be must stop and think about what they are doing. Making laws and getting court orders demanding integration is all fine and good, but the real inclusion takes place in individual classrooms, with individual teachers who want these students in their classes and will actively work to make them a meaningful part of the learning community, supervised by administrators who will support their efforts.

In our opinion, and historically, prejudice does not just disappear. People who do not want to work with children with special needs are scared, ignorant or prejudiced — and no matter what we do, some people who are prejudiced are hateful. Children with special needs disgust them. One person actually told me they feel physically ill when they are around people with special needs. These are facts and are part of human nature.

I myself have told these people they shouldn't teach children with special needs. In my opinion, they shouldn't be teaching children at all if they are so lacking in compassion. But after several conversations of this nature, my beliefs that everyone should integrate have changed. I believe all children who can be beneficially included should be. If about ten percent of the population has special needs, then ten percent of the classroom should be integrated.

But these students should be sent to the wonderful, caring, nurturing teachers and administrators who can foster the best of what inclusion is all about. Let these people do it. Give them the education, the equipment, the support and the finances to do it so that our children with special needs get the programs they deserve. If legislators and politicians continue on their course of forcing resistive, prejudiced educators into integrating, we foresee that 5 to 10 years down the road the research will show that inclusion didn't work. And the research will be right!

Integrating children with special needs and making it work takes a very special group of dedicated, mature, committed people. People who think about the children as being part of their life, not just a job. People who work so hard they don't have time to look at the clock and are exhausted at the end of every day. People who spend time and energy trying creatively to find ways to access activities and communication, better ways to position children, ways to encourage real bonding between the children without special needs and their peers with special needs.

People as dedicated as these are not only difficult to find but have a high burnout rate. Inclusion at its best is very hard work. This burnout is a serious problem. It makes *critical* the necessity of supportive administrators, and also of more realistic staffing patterns and collaborative teaching efforts so inclusion can really happen.

Besides needing special people as teachers, the teachers need an administrator who isn't just supportive of inclusion but firmly believes in the concept and will do everything possible to make the best educational environment for *all* the children. This requires a lot of hands-on support and intervention on the part of the program administrator. To make decisions about children's programs the administrator must know the children and their needs, be available to help with discipline problems, and provide support for therapeutic and equipment needs, creative classroom adaptations, and so forth. The basic piece that makes inclusion work is teamwork, not only by teachers, therapists and administrators, but also by the children and their parents. Everyone needs to attempt communication and cooperation united in a common atmosphere of acceptance and a common goal of learning and growing together.

II. The Child Who Shouldn't Be Included

So are there any children who shouldn't be included? From the viewpoint of the children, probably not. All children with special needs can benefit at least socially from inclusion. Except for those who are so severely mentally retarded that they are not aware of their environment or the people around them, children with special needs will benefit just from the interaction with typical kids. Given a proper climate, the typical children will benefit from the experience of acknowledging the reality of severe mental retardation and perhaps reach an understanding which will open their minds as adults to compassion and acceptance.

Children who Cannot Respond to Stimuli. Notwithstanding this point, we don't know what children who are severely mentally retarded and do not respond to stimuli could get from inclusion. We don't know because there's no way to measure change if the child makes no responses. These children are probably not children to integrate. If the child can't learn or respond, then inclusion isn't appropriate. But it is very important to realize that some children may "appear" as if they can't learn or respond. Never write off a child. They just might surprise you.

I do think that if a child can respond socially even some of the time, then inclusion should be tried for at least a year. A few months is not enough for children with severe retardation.

Children with Severe Emotional/Behavioral Problems. Careful evaluation needs to be used in determining whether children with severe behavior problems should be included. The main characteristics this child displays are a total disregard for authority, and violent, dangerous behaviors which jeopardize the safety of the child and his/her peers. Now there is a big difference between a child who is seriously dangerous and one who is merely disruptive to the group, disobedient and sometimes unsafe. It takes a teacher with a sense of fairness, compassion, and a strong sense of self to determine the difference.

In our opinion the difference is quite obvious. Sometimes it's hard for teachers to step back and examine what is really going on. Some of the best teachers I have known have had children in their class whom they didn't like. For one reason or another, the kid just rubbed them the wrong way — nothing he or she could do was acceptable. Good teachers acknowledge that they have personal feelings such as these. Teachers are just people and don't always like or get along with every child. For a lot of teachers it feels wrong not to like every child, so they blame the child, not being honest about the real reason a child is so difficult.

The same is true the other way. I have seen children antagonize teachers, where the teacher loses all sense of control with the entire group because of one child who doesn't like the teacher. These problems should be dealt with immediately. Responsible teachers should admit their feelings to the administration. The administration should be grateful for their honesty before things get too far out of hand, and respond appropriately by removing the child to another group and *not* acting negatively towards the teacher. Since kids are people too, we have to accept that all teachers and kids are not good matches and act swiftly before the child, the teacher or both feel like failures.

When is a child too disruptive for inclusion? It's hard to give specific rules because each child, teacher and group is different. However, these are some guidelines.

1. *If the teacher and child are a bad match, another inclusive setting should be tried for three to six months to be really fair to the child.* It is important that the child's experiences from the last classroom do not set the child up to fail again. The new teacher should not be allowed to be biased by the previous teacher, and the new teacher needs to be aware that the child will most likely respond initially in terms of what he or she learned from the last experience in the classroom. Three to six months will not only be enough time for the child to act out anger and frustration but will be enough time for the child, if inclusion is going to work, to settle down and start making changes.

2. *Is the group a poor choice for that particular child?* Besides the child and teacher being a poor match, sometimes the makeup of the group could be a bad match.

The group is a bad match for a child to join if, for example, the child has Tourette's Syndrome and there are several children in the group who have behavior problems which include inappropriate vulgar language, sensitivity to name-calling resulting in aggressive behavior, or inappropriate sexual acting-out behavior. A child with Tourette's Syndrome could really upset the delicate balance of behavioral appropriateness which is being worked on in the group. This is not to say a child with Tourette's Syndrome should not be included — it's just very important not to include the child in the wrong group.

Another example of a "bad" match for a child and a group would be a child who is extremely aggressive being put in a group that has a child who had recent surgery, or brittle bones such as with Osteogenesis Imperfecta (abnormally brittle bones from birth). The need to keep these children safe must be of primary focus, so a physically aggressive child most likely should be included in a different group.

These are some examples when a child could have a negative

impact on the functioning of the group, or the group have a negative impact on a child, making the two a bad match. A child who is severely withdrawn and shy, or who is very sensitive about some physical challenge, could do very poorly in a group with a child who is critical and deliberately verbally abusive to others. If this kind of behavior can't be controlled within the group, the child who is insecure could easily withdraw even more. Careful consideration should be given to placement of each child. Other considerations when deciding on the appropriate class for a child are:

> a. Is the child the only one who is physically challenged? If so, this could really affect the child emotionally. A child who is physically challenged needs peers who are physically challenged to identify with as much as he or she needs typical peers.
> b. Will this particular child upset the functions of the group?
> c. Will any member of the class upset or decrease the current functioning level of the child?
> d. Is the group too large to continue giving the quality attention to all the members of the class if this child is added?
> e. Is the group currently too needy for the teacher to be able to give to the new child all that she or he requires?

3. *Is the program inflexible, set up in such a way that the child has to conform at all costs?* If this is the case, often children with behavior problems cannot make it. A child with severe behavior problems often can't conform easily; that's why he is seen as a child with behavior problems. Explosive behavior is often set off by rules being so rigid that the child can't feel that he has any say in what happens to him. This is not to say that clear, specific rules with clear, specific consequences should not be made. It is absolutely crucial to the functioning of the group that rules be set with consequences. But whenever possible, it is just as important to make sure that the child has choices and that it is up to the child to make the right ones.

It is equally important to try and help the child maintain a sense of dignity and not be embarrassed. Whenever possible, if the teacher can help the child make the right choice and prevent an explosive outburst, the teacher is preventing the child from getting out of control and ultimately from embarrassing himself. The more often this desirable outcome can occur, the more likely it is that the child will make changes.

Aggressive, out-of-control behavior can't always be prevented no matter how sensitive the teacher is. Sometimes a child with emotional/behavioral problems needs to act out. The goal is to direct that negative behavior in a way that no one gets hurt, including the child, his peers, and the teaching staff. When this kind of behavior arises, it is best to remove the child as soon as possible for three reasons: 1) to prevent the other children from getting hurt, 2) to prevent the children from witnessing the behavior for future imitation, and 3) to help the child feel safe from embarrassment. It's one thing to get completely out of control with an adult, but it's very difficult to feel good after losing control in front of your entire class. When this happens it's hard for the child to rejoin the group without feeling bad about himself.

In addition, the teacher or administrator should not force an apology on the child. The adult disciplining the child should help the child to come to the conclusion that an apology would be appropriate. The adult should say things like, "What do you think you should do now?", or even, "I know if you had hurt me, I'd feel better if you said you were sorry you hurt me." If you can lead the child to making a decision to apologize, you are really helping the child to grow, but it should be the child's own decision in the end. A forced apology may not be sincere, and often children will say "I'm sorry" just to try not to have to accept responsibility for their actions. Our favorite is the child who smacks someone across the face and immediately begins to proclaim it was "just an accident."

A program which is so inflexible that all the children have to always do what the teacher says and everything is teacher-directed is definitely not a place for a child with a behavior problem. It probably isn't that great for any children. But children with behavior problems will be set up to lose in a classroom where the teacher's word is law and no negotiating ever takes place. Children need to learn how to compromise, and this is a major weakness of children with behavioral problems. So an inflexible classroom, without a lot of choice and child-initiated activities, would not be an appropriate setting. Of course, again, clear and consistent limits and consequences need to be set in a more appropriate setting.

4. *Was enough time taken to give the child a real chance to make it in the class?* Often a program will say they'll try a child out for a couple of weeks. That just doesn't seem fair. It says something about the program itself and the expectations it has for children. At Kids Are People, we have two sets of expectations, very low ones and very high ones. Our low expectations are around who the child is that is coming to us. In other words, we don't expect the child to have any set of abilities in social skills, self-help skills, motor skills, or verbal skills. But we have high expectations for what we feel even the most delayed child is potentially capable of. We just don't write children off based on professional assessments or even parent reports.

In general, behavioral/emotional problems come from an issue of lack of internal control on some level. The reasons for these can range from environmental to chemical imbalances. *Whatever the cause of the behavior problems (often not identified), the issues are the same: helping the child to act appropriately and make responsible decisions.* I have seen kids who are so out of control and have failed so many times, having been dismissed from several programs, that by the time we get them, their own expectations of themselves are very low and they expect to fail. It is impossible to undo what has been done, or even get a real impression of how the child might begin to behave, unless there is enough positive time in the new group setting.

We have seen kids come in and do everything negative they could think of to see if we'd let them stay. We consistently tell kids that we don't like what they did but we love *them*. This is crucial at the beginning with children who have severe behavior problems. They don't trust us, they don't trust themselves, and they are sure they are awful people. When time after time they see us setting firm limits on what is not allowed, but still being caring to them, they really can start to relax and say "Well, maybe what I'm doing is bad, but I'm not." They can then think about changing their behavior to become a real part of the community which is accepting of them. But this all takes a lot of time, and can't be done in a few weeks. Some kids will even be perfectly behaved the first month. It takes time to lead the child in the right direction of change.

We once gave a child two years, because when he wasn't acting out he was such a wonderful person that the glimpses of goodness kept us going through the bad times. He wasn't just well behaved. At the times when he was behaving well, he was a loving, caring child who was incredibly supportive to the children in the school who were physically challenged. If we had had a room which was a safe place for him to punch the walls, he probably could have stayed with us.

But part of the problem with an inclusive program is getting and keeping parents of children without special needs. To have a room such as was needed for this particular child would set the stage for parents of typical children, at initial interviews and later, to not want their children in the program. They have to really think about whether they want their child(ren) with children who are so out of control that a room such as described is needed for them. And parents fear that the staff might put their child in such a room.

This particular child was so violent when he did get out of control that it took two adults to hold him down and often not before he had bitten, scratched, kicked or punched us. A child who is so violent that he jeopardizes everyone's safety really should not be included even though it benefits him or her. The overall group has to be considered at this point.

5. *Were several techniques tried in order to help the child grow in a positive way in the group?* Sometimes things that work with most children just don't work with certain children, and good teachers will try a variety of techniques to help a child make changes. But some teachers are set in their ways of how things should be done and believe that children should conform. These kinds of teachers are not teachers who should work in inclusive classrooms.

Another thing which can happen even with the best team is a staff and child getting into a habit of how they respond to a given situation. For example, with a child who consistently lies, you would at the onset identify this behavior to the child and explain about the effect lying has on how people respond. But teachers can get so used to a child who chronically lies that the teacher never believes the child. It can develop into a really negative situation which often becomes cyclical. Often a team doesn't realize the situation has even developed, because it becomes a habit not to believe in the child and the child never expects anyone to believe her so she continues to lie.

It's very important for the team to gather to assess progress and analyze problems. This is often easier in a small program. It should be the job of the administrator to be observant of techniques which aren't working and not only point them out but, hopefully, have some helpful suggestions for alternative techniques. This is not to say that the teaching staff should not also evaluate interactions, but sometimes it really takes someone else to step back and to identify that there is a problem. Self-evaluation is a difficult thing; it's hard to be objective about ourselves. A good teaching team isn't going to have problems with this. They're going to agree there's a problem and generally are happy the administrator sees they're trying but having a difficult time. Mature, responsible teachers want help and are grateful if the administrator is aware, never mind cares.

Mature staff is a key element of an inclusive program, especially a program which has several children with behavioral/emotional problems. Maturity is never a matter of age, it's a perspective on children and one's own role in the program. If a teacher takes it personally that a child spit in her face, slapped her, etc., then she isn't going to be effective at encouraging change with that child.

Now, this doesn't mean that anyone enjoys this kind of interaction with a child. Very firm limits need to be set. In our program, if a child does anything violent to a teacher or seriously attempts to hurt himself or another child, he is removed from the room to the office and punished; his parents are informed for carryover at home. But in an inclusive program with children who exhibit severe behavioral/

emotional problems, teachers need to expect that this kind of behavior can, and most likely will, occur. A good teacher will try and prevent these behaviors as much as possible, but when they occur, the mature teacher doesn't take it personally because he realizes it doesn't matter who was dealing with the child at that time. Anyone would have been slapped or spit on. It wasn't personal.

6. *Did the child make significant changes, and are the benefits to the child outweighed by the danger to others or the progress of the group as a whole?* Especially in the case of children with behavioral/emotional problems, if significant changes are not evidenced by the end of the first year in an inclusive program, the placement is probably not working. If close evaluation of how the program functioned is made, most likely the team will find an inordinate amount of time was spent in disciplining that particular child to the point where the other children are losing out. If this is the case, then the goal of inclusion for this child may be counterproductive for this group. If the team tried several techniques, the child was receiving ongoing therapy to help him/her deal with behaviors, and nothing has worked, it may be time to look at a more therapeutic setting with daily individual and group counseling. But before this is recommended, the team needs to make sure the child was dealt with fairly and appropriately and the class itself was the right mix for this child.

Taking children who have serious emotional/behavioral problems into an inclusive program is a huge responsibility for the entire staff and should not be done lightly. It takes a special group of people to have the necessary enormous patience, emotional and physical strength, deep love for all children, and belief in the right of each child to be given a chance. Without a very strong, supportive administration, it is almost impossible for the teachers to do it alone. It requires a complete team approach including therapists, parents, teachers, administrators and peers.

I don't believe every team of teachers can do a good job of it or should do it. These kids are by far the most difficult to include, and a team needs to know when to give up and get a more restrictive type of setting and when to keep trying. And the team needs to be mature enough to emotionally accept that they did their best and, in certain cases, their best was not enough to turn the child's life around.

If attempting inclusion of children with severe behavioral/emotional problems, it is important that there be more than one child with this kind of special need, because these children are usually very bright, very aware and very sure that they are different from others. They need to see that others get the same limits set in the same way for the same behaviors.

Also, although confidentiality is an important concern in programs, it is important to deal with the concerns of the parents of typical children. Their concerns have to be addressed and acknowledged, especially if their child has been hurt or is picking up negative behaviors. We make it clear to parents from the start that their complaints won't get another child removed from the program, but that every attempt will be made to make changes necessary to protect their child or eliminate negative adopted behaviors.

It is crucial, too, that the team of adults be clear with the typical children about expectations for their behaviors in specific circumstances. They should explain to the children why a particular child may be acting a certain way. The team needs to enlist the help of the typical children in setting limits with the children with behavioral/emotional problems. The team has to give the children ways to express their feelings about how they are being treated.

And at all costs, the child with behavioral problems cannot be allowed to become a scapegoat for all problems which occur in the classroom. Teachers need to see that discipline is handed out fairly and not always assume it was the child with behavioral problems who started problems. We have seen kids blame a child who wasn't even in the room. They were assuming the teacher would openly believe that if there was a problem this particular child would have to be involved.

If this begins to happen, the child's teacher needs to evaluate his ongoing responses to the child with behavioral problems to make sure he has consistently been fair to the child. And the group as a whole needs to be talked to about accusing someone falsely and how seriously unfair that is.

If a program cannot actively involve all parties in the goal of making inclusion work for children with behavioral/emotional problems, the program should refrain from providing services to children with these kinds of special needs.

III. People Aren't Really Integrating the Children.

Currently, there is a very strong push to force inclusion. In some ways this is great because it is opening doors for children with special needs to get appropriate programs. However, many schools feeling the pressure to include are making programs which aren't really including all children and calling it inclusion. There are several ways that cities and towns can look like they are answering the call for inclusion, get away with giving less-than-appropriate programs, and say they are "doing inclusion."

One Child Is A Pioneer. Schools who do this are really behaving criminally — and it happens a lot. They take one child who is physically challenged, place him or her in a school, and say, "We are doing inclusion in our school." This is no different than saying "We are a multicultural program — we have a black child in our school." It is *so* unfair for a school to make one child a pioneer. Children need typical peers, but they also need peers with similar special needs to identify with. It is so important for the children to see that they are not the only ones who have to struggle with the challenges facing children with special needs. It's like anything. It's easier to do something or accept problems if others are facing the same issues.

I know one school district which has thirteen children in wheelchairs, one in each of thirteen schools. They therefore say thirteen of their schools are inclusive. What is wrong with these people? Why can't they see how flawed their thinking is? I don't know how many times I've heard administrators say of a child in a wheelchair, "Oh, he's not the only child with special needs. We have children with speech problems too!" I can't believe how completely ignorant these comments are. Children with special needs need to have peers with *similar* special needs so they have someone else attempting the same hurdles.

Why are adults so unaware when it comes to children? Adult support groups — for DES, cancer, death of a spouse, alcohol abuse — exist all over the country, people with similar problems supporting one another. Why doesn't this rule of thumb apply to children with special needs? This is so sad, but it's because children with special needs are often seen as not having feelings and/or working minds. All it would take is for the adults who make decisions on programming to be required to spend one day in a wheelchair and unable to talk. I believe a lot of programs would change if this was a requirement. It takes empathy to do a good job of inclusion. The government can mandate inclusion, but they can't force people to feel for and identify with these children. Anyone setting up an inclusive program, or already running one, who does not look at every situation and say several times a day, "If I were this child in this circumstance how would I feel? What would I need? What can I change to include this child?" isn't doing his job.

Child-Specific Aides. When a child is assigned an aide, which is a common practice today in programs calling themselves inclusive, the majority of the time the child is segregated within the classroom. If a child is so involved that she needs an aide, the aide should be assigned *to the class* to help manage setup of activities, do feeding tubes, get children in and out of equipment, put on and off braces and facilitate interaction among the children.

Assigning an aide to a child results in the adult getting in the way — becoming a gatekeeper. The key to inclusion is the quality of the interaction between the children. If an aide's only job is to work with one child, that aide is going to be hovering over the child. Part of quality inclusion is that children with special needs can foster their own inclusion. In a good inclusive program, children with special needs reach out to the typical children independently whenever possible, and the typical children reach out to the children with special needs.

In addition, in a classroom where an aide is assigned to an individual child, the teacher often interacts infrequently with the child, seeing it as the aide's job. The unspoken message to the children is that that particular child is different because the teacher doesn't interact with her.

I have also seen aides be so overly protective — almost possessive — of their assigned child that their attitude, tone of voice and body language when other children approach give the message that the child with special needs is so different that she needs an adult for protection. As this kind of response continues, the typical children attempt less and less interaction with the child with special needs. Having to get by an adult to get to a child is just too intimidating.

This isn't to say that if a child has a severe behavior problem, has extreme medical needs or is in need of a lot of adult input to make it through a day, that an extra adult isn't necessary and helpful. Any classroom can use an extra set of hands whether the classroom is inclusive or not. But the teacher or aide should be part of a team for the entire class. Make sure, furthermore, that no adult ever unconsciously gives the message that a child with special needs is different or should be treated differently from the rest of the children in the class.

Staff is willing but doesn't understand how to integrate. There are wonderful, talented, caring teachers who never thought when they were training that they would be teaching children with special needs. Not having any training in special needs education, and understanding that most times it's more work to teach children with special needs, these teachers have difficulty envisioning how they will give quality care and education to all the children — but they are willing to try.

These people are willing and want to work in inclusive programs and to set up the classroom as inclusive. But then the children arrive, and the child in the wheelchair is left sitting around a lot. He is the last one set up at every activity. The teacher or an aide gives everyone their class assignment and then goes to assist the child with special needs on an assignment he can do.

This scenario is especially true of the elementary classrooms where children are seated at desks and the teacher directs the lessons. The classroom setup alone is going to lead to segregation within the class for the child with special needs. *Traditional classroom setups are not conducive to inclusion.* It is very important, even though staff are willing to run an inclusive classroom, that they are also willing to change teaching methods and classroom setups from what they are traditionally used to. If these changes are not made, then true inclusion, even with the most willing staff, will not be happening for the children.

Misleading willing teachers into thinking that dramatic changes will not take place and that inclusion doesn't take more work is setting the stage for frustration and failure, for the teacher and the children with special needs.

So, training is needed to orient these teachers to the working philosophy of inclusion. And continuing support for the teacher *must* be provided — intensively during the first weeks at least; on call by the teacher in succeeding weeks — without a sense of stigma experienced by the teacher when she calls for consultation.

CHAPTER FOUR

The Staff: Who's Running This Show?

An inclusive program begins with an integrated staff. Staff configuration varies from program to program but will essentially be made up of administrators, teachers, and occupational, physical, and speech therapists. In some states a special needs coordinator is required. All programs must have a health care consultant or nurse on call. But regardless of the staff configuration, a firm belief in, and commitment to, the benefits of an inclusive program should be the primary educational philosophy of the group.

The organizational management of any program requires carefully orchestrated communication between administration, staff, and parents. This is particularly true of an inclusive program. There are meetings, documents and continuous communications with a variety of medical, community and educational agencies when including children with special needs. Depending on the complexity of a child's problems, communication concerning the child may need to increase significantly. The degree and quality of this interaction contribute in many ways to a child's social, emotional, intellectual, and physical well-being.

One of the keys to a successfully integrated program is the staff's recognition that most problems which may arise in a program can apply to *all* the children at one time or another. Some of the problems included below will be more intense and chronic for a child with special needs than for a child without special needs, but none of them are exclusive to the children with special needs.

- physical limitations relative to mobility in the program
- dependent toileting
- withdrawn behavior
- aggressive/impulsive behavior
- medical considerations
- more individualized curriculum development
- special diets

- meeting special positioning or equipment needs
- remembering individual therapy/medical schedules
- education of entire group concerning the special needs of their peers
- self-esteem, positive image, issues for all children (understanding differences)
- safety issues
- teacher/therapist communications
- parent/teacher/therapist communication

Clearly, the smooth operation of an inclusive program requires a complex team approach in which consistent, direct, and sensitive communication is the primary element. The role of each person on the team is specific and defined by his or her training, background, and assigned position in the program. Although the staff have their assigned responsibilities, *integration of roles is the key to success.* Ideally, respect, trust, and a sense of humor will guide daily events and activities.

There is no typical day in an inclusive program. However, in the following pages we address universal crucial areas of concern when integrating children with special needs.

Social/Emotional Issues

One of the staff's major concerns is that every child be included in all activities, on time, with the group. Thus, staff members must consider the physical limitations of a child in their care when planning activities. In our experience, all activities can be modified to include all children. A child who cannot move his legs can be encouraged to dance with his group by moving his arms and head to the music. If an activity cannot be modified to include all children, it should be eliminated from the curriculum.

Both at home and in school, Marcus prefers activities which he can do with ease. He loves the computer, art, sand and water tables, and dress-up. He tends to avoid difficult gross motor activities, but with an adult's determined encouragement, he will push himself. For example, Marcus does not jump at the chance to go to the playground. Once there, however, he joins in with his friends swinging, sliding and climbing.

Marcus' avoidance of a difficult activity is a natural response for any child. In his case, his fears are based on a realistic appraisal of potential physical dangers. Walking to the playground on snow or ice, crutches slipping on wet leaves, or even a sudden rainstorm all present risks for Marcus. Once at the playground, Marcus' physical safety concerns are compounded by many social and emotional issues. He prefers to be independent yet knows he must be assisted on most of the equipment. Because the sandbox is a safe and comfortable place which Marcus can get to on his own, it is usually his first choice. He enjoys playing on the tire swing, but it requires an adult's assistance, and Marcus is very sensitive to the issue of requiring extra adult help for many activities. He often waits in anticipation that the teacher will notice that he needs help rather than ask for it.

Children with severe and chronic special needs face a lifetime of dependence on others for a range of basic skills that most of us take for granted. In fact, this lack of assertiveness is a very real issue for many children with special needs. This needs to be taken into consideration when working with these children by encouraging them to feel comfortable asking for help. One of the most important jobs of the staff is to teach all children who can ask for help that when it is necessary it is okay to do so without feeling bad.

Children with significant physical limitations and other kinds of problems want to participate fully in all classroom activities. Their desire to join in may sometimes be overshadowed by their realistic anxieties concerning physical safety, embarrassment at appearing "different," and concerns about needing more help than their friends. Staff sensitivity to these issues, plus specific knowledge of how to best help each child, will result in success for both staff and children.

Special Positioning

One of the most important parts of the staff's job is to be aware of optimal benefits for each child. For a child with an attention problem, it is important that the child be located close enough to the teacher that she can draw his attention back into the activity. For example, a gentle touch on Afanwi's arm with a redirection such as "And Afanwi has an A in his name" would bring Afanwi right back into the activity concerning the letter A.

For Marcus it is very important that his crutches be placed within reach so that he is free to move around the room independently, whenever he wants. All the children in the program are allowed to sit in the adaptive chairs and to use the walkers and crutches of the other children. The important issue is to have the children learn what it is like to use this equipment, but also to return it to their friend who needs it to be mobile.

More specific positioning issues would include the teacher knowing that a child with cerebral palsy has weak muscles on her right side and avoids use of her right hand. For example, Danielle did everything possible to avoid using her right hand for the first six months at Kids Are People School. Placing puzzle pieces, Legos, and bristle blocks in a location that forces Danielle to use her right hand is beneficial for increased muscle strength and coordination of her right hand.

Something as simple as having a child who needs the therapy chair moved up to the table in the middle of his/her friends, automatically increases stimulation to the child, involves the child in conversation even if he/she can't speak, and prevents segregation within the classroom. Choice of therapeutic equipment (chairs, walkers, etc.) which creates accessibility, e.g., the chair that will fit at the table with the other children, is crucial for socialization at meals and table activities.

Sometimes equipment needs for a child can cause segregation or difficulty with activity participation. This is the time for creativity. For example, no child with a wheelchair, crutches or a walker can get around outside after a major snowstorm. As all young children love going out and playing in the snow, the staff have to think of a way to enable participation for a child with a serious physical impairment or even a broken leg. An inexpensive sled with safety belts and a back for support will do the trick, and the child is then being treated "special" in a good way which will make his friends want to join in his play.

Self-Care Issues

A great deal of time is taken up by self-care issues. Teaching young children how to dress and feed themselves, as well as toilet training and hygiene, is a major task. In an effort to help children move towards independence, a great deal of focus must be placed on self-help skills. For all children this is a complicated issue that must be dealt with in a sensible and sensitive way. For some children with special needs, independent self-care may never be a reality, and then other issues come into play. We next discuss the major areas of self-help skills and the problems which arise when working with children.

Eating. The questions parents ask most frequently about their child concern food. "Does he/she eat at school?" "Why can't I get him to eat at home?" "How do you cook your macaroni and cheese?" Getting children to eat is a universal problem for parents and teachers. Combine this with teaching children to feed themselves, and one can envision a table of six year olds with spaghetti flying, milk spilling, and orange hands, faces and walls. While all this is going on, add to the group a couple of children who have motor challenges, and the teacher might just want to go to lunch and not return. However, organization, patience, and a few specific techniques can free up the teacher to assist any child who needs help. One of the methods we use is the rule that no one can begin eating until everyone has their food and drink. While the teacher dishes out the food, one child can make up a story for the group. This entertains the children while the teacher is busy; it helps the children to be creative, to think in a logical fashion, and to attend. It also encourages positive self-image by having the child successfully talk in front of a group. This method works well with all groups of children. For groups of younger children, one teacher would direct a story or singing time while the other teacher dishes out the food.

To encourage eating skills for children who cannot feed themselves, we put pieces of food on the tray of their chair or table as well as spoon-feed them. We encourage the child to bring food to his or her mouth. This is good for hand-to-mouth coordination and oral stimulation as well as fine motor skills. Specific equipment designed to assist the child who has fine motor problems can be used, such as scoop bowls, plates with suction, or spoons bent at an angle for better control. The staff must above all remember that whatever methods or equipment are used, eating time is also a very social time and is a great opportunity to help all the children to interact in a positive, helpful way which encourages independence both in social skills and feeding.

If a child has a feeding tube, we feel it is important not to segregate him during the feeding process. We have one child sit and talk to him until the feeding is done. Different children do it on different days, but it is always a child from his own class. Feeding tubes can be strange and scary to typical children when they first see a child with one. *Staff need to explain the purpose and need for the feeding tube to the children in the group.* Children often identify with one another and may be concerned that they might need a feeding tube, braces, wheelchairs, etc. All of this needs to be explained to the children.

Dressing. Probably the most frustrating part of being a teacher of young children is teaching them how to dress themselves, especially when there are ten children in a group. Two lost mittens, one broken shoelace, five boots on the wrong feet, and the entire outside walk time has been used up.

Many things can be done to facilitate the process. A large bead attached to Esther's coat zipper enabled Esther to learn to zipper. Attaching mittens to the jackets limits the chances of children putting them on the wrong hand. Footprints on the floor for comparison with boot bottoms help the child to figure out which foot his or her boot goes on.

For a child with motor problems these skills are more difficult and sometimes impossible to master. The point to remember is to keep the child involved. If the child can't help the teacher at all with dressing, then doing something such as putting the child's hat in his lap and saying "You can hold the hat for me," then thanking him for his help, is a way of keeping the child involved. If the child has some capability, having him work on putting his hat on while the teacher does the rest is still having the child work on helping. The point is to not make the child feel bad, helpless or dependent. In fact, it is less work for the teacher to help a child who can't dress himself than it is to continually remind the child who can dress himself to stop wrestling with his friends, stop jumping off the table, stop feeding the rabbit Legos and please put your coat on now!

Toileting. Programs which restrict entrance to children who are not toilet trained will have a very difficult time becoming integrated. Many children with special needs will never be toilet trained because of motoric issues or severe cognitive delay. For programs which accept infants and toddlers, it is second nature to change diapers. Performing the task of diapering older children is not an issue for the adult. What does become an issue is being sensitive to the older child's feelings. It is difficult for an older child to deal with the fact that she still wears diapers while all her friends are toilet trained. For Marcus it became an issue when he was age three. All his friends were toilet trained, and we positively reinforce children in the group for getting and staying trained. A big deal was made about "big boy" or "big girl" pants. Praise was showered on the children for staying dry. Marcus began to feel bad because it was the first skill in his life that he was not able to master. What we did was talk to his mom about getting him "big boy" pants to wear over his diapers. We matched the praise around getting "big boy" pants with moving from the toddler group and becoming a big preschooler. This alleviated the problem and helped Marcus not to feel so different from his friends.

Toileting is one area that does take more time. This situation with Marcus brings into focus just how difficult the future can be for children such as Marcus as they grow older. Considering what Marcus will have to deal with, the few extra minutes of time spent cleaning and changing him becomes a special time to talk with him instead of a burden.

Toileting is one of the few major issues that need to be addressed with Sean each day. Although he is toilet trained, in order for Sean to use the toilet his prosthesis must be removed. This takes additional time, but the more important issue, again, is sensitivity to Sean's feelings. Sean has actually used the time to get attention from his friends by making them laugh when he moves his leg without the prosthesis. He looks different and funny to his friends, and Sean, instead of feeling bad, has found a way to deal with his difference and share it with his friends. For his friends, it is not as scary to see Sean with no lower leg because Sean is not ashamed or scared. It actually takes the teacher of the older groups a lot less time to get through daily toileting, because the other children are so independent in toileting skills, than it does the infant and toddler groups.

It is very important to be sensitive to the right of privacy for older children who cannot be toilet trained. They may want not to be part of a group for this routine process due to their embarrassment.

In the end, helping the child who needs help, be it an infant or a seven year old, is just part of the job; it becomes a habit and is not a hassle. It's the little extras that we do to help the children that make the job rewarding. In helping the children, the staff help themselves to grow and learn. There is a very real appreciation for life and for the things we all take for granted everyday, simple things like walking and talking, dressing and eating.

Medical Considerations

There are a variety of medical issues which need to be addressed on a day-to-day basis in an inclusive program. From food allergies to asthma, from colds to insect bites, the staff who work with young children often find themselves attending to medical concerns. For programs which accept children with special needs, there are often more medical issues to deal with, many of which are a routine part of everyday life working with children.

Medical and Food Allergies. Often programs have children with special needs and do not realize it. The child with life-threatening asthma, or serious allergies to food or insect bites, needs special attention. Being aware of allergies and dispensing medication is a serious responsibility for all teachers. Communication is very important so that the wrong medicine is not given, the wrong dosage is not given, the medicine is in fact given at all. Keeping medication in a child-safe place in the program, keeping it well labeled and having more than one person check the label against the child's name, insures the safety of all the children.

It is quite easy to remember to medicate a child who has medicine every day of his life; it is much more difficult to remember medicine for a child with a transient illness. We feel that since we have so many children to watch out for and the parent needs to only think about his own child, *it is a good idea for the parent to help by calling to remind the teacher at the time the medicine is to be dispensed.* Most of the time this is not necessary, but that one day when the art project becomes sand play, the water table becomes a wading pool and the classroom becomes a carnival, the teacher could surely use a reminder from the parent.

Remembering to prepare a special lunch on days that the program is serving a lunch which includes foods a child is allergic to, requires informed teachers, cooks and grocery shoppers. Helping the child not to feel different or the other children not to feel jealous because he is eating a different lunch is also necessary. Because some children are allergic to a number of foods, it is impossible to completely delete all of them from the school menu and still serve a variety of nutritious meals to the rest of the children. It is important that the administration as well as the classroom team have all of this information in case the regular teacher is not in school. It is necessary to plan for special meals around the child. Often the parent is glad to provide the meals and help the staff. This too takes extra time but, more importantly, takes consistent planning and forethought.

Surgical Issues. Young children at one time or another may require surgery, be it for tonsillitis, ruptured appendix or broken bones. Whatever the case, if the child is to recover quickly and get right back into the swing of daily school life, some compromise may be needed by the child's program to assist in the process.

Often children with severe physical impairments will require surgery to progress motorically. For example, Marcus has had surgery a number of times. Marcus' surgery for his hip and ankles required the staff to consider several issues. Of utmost importance was Marcus' safety. When Marcus returned to school with casts on both his legs, our number one priority was to protect his ankles. They had to heal properly so he could eventually go from full-length braces to short leg braces and enjoy the freedom he has strived so hard for.

Obviously we could sit Marcus in one corner of the room and keep the other children away from him — but there would be no sense in Marcus returning to school and being segregated. It was important to plan for Marcus so he could participate in activities with his friends while he was healing. Many interesting table activities were set up in safe areas with his friends away from the flow of traffic, e.g., computer, art, sand and water play, etc. With Marcus' help, we explained to the group the importance of not bumping or pushing Marcus. *We expect the children to help their friends.* Two year olds and up can understand what being "gentle" means. It is important to talk with the children and trust them but to also set strict limits around safety issues for everyone's well being.

Although having a child back at school right after surgery is a liability, a good program is not going to focus on the potential harm. Instead, the staff will generally rise to the occasion because of their love and concern for the child. Fear is very quickly replaced by sympathy and respect for the child in pain, and the desire to get her right back into the mainstream of life.

Another concern is the safety of the staff. When Marcus had surgery on his hips and returned to school in a spika cast weighing eighty pounds, it was important for the staff to be trained in how to move him so they would not hurt themselves or Marcus.

Additionally, Marcus could not be moved from place to place. It was very important for the teacher to be aware of what Marcus was doing so that he had toys, as well as his friends interacting with him.

Healthwise, it was important that Marcus be turned several times each hour and cleaned carefully. While this took a great deal of time, energy, and planning, looking at Marcus unable to move, being so good-natured and uncomplaining, made the extra work seem insignificant. Again, his friends were told why Marcus could not move and that it would be really wonderful if they would help him by bringing him toys and playing with him. Of course this suggestion made Marcus the center of attention for the eight weeks he was confined to the body cast.

Marcus also had surgery to reconstruct his bladder and sphincter, hopefully to enhance independent toileting in the future. He returned to school with a tube connected to a bag to collect his urine while he healed. The tubes were quite long, and if they knotted or got a bend in them the urine could back up and make Marcus quite sick. This was in our opinion the most serious safety issue we had dealt with. Besides being sure that the tubes did not get accidentally pulled out, the thought of Marcus getting sick because of us was quite unsettling. Not only did the teacher check the tubes periodically, the administrator and therapists also did. All teachers were told what to look for to ensure his safety, even if they were just walking by Marcus. *While it may seem unrealistic to expect a director to check on the child, there will be times, if a program has children with serious problems, that everyone must be hands-on with the situation on an ongoing basis.* The commitment to serving children with special needs really has to start at the top. It is a full-time, one hundred percent commitment that takes more worry, more planning, more patience, and more love, but will be the most wonderful experience of your life.

ADMINISTRATION OF THE SCHOOL: THERE'S NO MIRACLES GOING ON HERE

Kids Are People has a life of its own. I look around some days and can't believe what I see the children doing for one another — naturally, voluntarily, because they are friends. Of course some days I look around and I can't believe what they're doing *to* each other, but that is a different story.

I love my job. It's too demanding, I'm working too many hours, I'm under a great deal of stress and there's not enough hours in the day. I've taken one vacation week in the last two years — but I love my job.

I love it because I get to be a part of miracles every day. They are hard-won miracles but they are *our* miracles, the kids', the parents', the staff's and mine. The day Lauren said my name for the first time, I sat down at my desk and cried. I called her mom to tell her, and I sounded so upset when she answered the phone that she thought Lauren had had another seizure.

One day a couple of months ago, I was battling it out once again with a team from a public school system who wanted to move a very fragile little girl out of our program, not because she was ready to move, not because they had a better or equal program for her, not for any reason except money. In the middle of this meeting which consisted of eleven professionals, the educational specialist from the public school yelled at me, "You know there's no miracles going on at Kids Are People School!" I leaned across the table and said very calmly, "Yes, there are. And it's the hard work of my staff and kids that are creating miracles. The kind of miracle that has gotten this child to where she is now. Don't you tell me there aren't miracles going on there." Little did she know that I had considered just shutting her up a miracle — but small miracles I see as big miracles. Lauren saying my name will last me a lifetime.

The first day Marcus took steps was another moment of glory for us. The kids have taught me most of what I know, either directly or because I had to investigate options, create methods or learn new techniques to help them.

But some of the things I learned from the children I couldn't find in books. For example:

Lauren taught me that no matter what, even if everyone around me disagrees, I need to give children a chance. I have to believe in the children and try to get through to them.

Afanwi taught me that even a two and a half year old can fool an entire team of professionals. Evaluations *are* only a minute window on a child's life and ability.

Esther taught me that intelligence is in the eyes. That even though some children can't walk or talk, it doesn't mean they aren't intelligent. And even if they aren't intelligent, they still have feelings. Esther and a couple of her friends taught me that there are many ways to communicate without talking.

Marcus taught me it doesn't matter whether you walk, crawl, wheel or are carried; as long as you get there, that's all that matters.

Benjamin taught me that the moment we adults decide that this is what first graders "should learn," we are closing the world off. What any child "should learn" is what they as individuals are capable of.

And the typical friends of these children — what did they teach me? They taught me that children are better integration specialists, better therapists, better counselors and better teachers than any adult can ever be. But we must create the opportunity for their gifts to be of value to other children.

Of course running Kids Are People has given me many stress-filled days too.

The absolutely hardest part of my job is dealing with people who get in the way of what we are doing at Kids Are People School. There are two categories of people who do this on an ongoing basis: outside agencies and internal members of the community

Outside Agencies

To give some idea of the complexity of our existence as a private-sector school, consider the many agencies we deal with during a normal school year: state agencies that license us and pay for welfare-eligible and/or emotionally disturbed students; city agencies concerned with the building space and the public schools; private agencies concerned with child advocacy, social services, and home health care; and parent organizations with various concerns. Just responding to the requirements and issues posed by these organizations leaves us with a very full plate. On the next pages I discuss the issues of concern in our contacts with these agencies.

Licensing and Accreditation. For the most part the public agencies are great resources and are really there to help. We at Kids Are People hate to be evaluated as much as anyone, but evaluation is an important fact of life and should and can be done in the least painful way possible. If you do what is required and have all the paperwork and requirements fulfilled, you'll get licensed and accredited, eventually.

Advocacy. The biggest hassles and the most time spent comes from advocating for the rights of children with special needs. It is the most stressful, time-consuming and annoying part of my job. Not because of the children and families, but because of the irresponsible, manipulative and immoral actions I have seen taken against children with special needs. Here are some examples.

- A school told a parent that her child was too dangerous and she should have her child evaluated. Meanwhile, it was their suggestion that the child stay at home and they would send work home for the mother to do with the child. This is illegal!
- A public school psychologist gave a psychological report to a child's advocate prior to the IEP planning team meeting. When the meeting took place and the advocate used the report to help get the child a private school placement, the psychologist said that the report was wrong. When the advocate said, "What are you saying? It's right here, I'm quoting your report!", the psychologist said, "Oh, I hit the wrong button on my computer. I have set phrases I use and I just punch in names, scores and dates." So much for individualized, never mind *accurate*, evaluations of children!
- After evaluating a very fragile child in our program, a public school psychologist said that she felt the child shouldn't be moved from our school. But when we got to the team meeting she said, "She'll probably do OK if she is moved." After the meeting the psychologist came up to me and said, "I'm sorry, Katie, but our jobs are on the line these days. Besides, I know you'll win it at mediation anyway." Which isn't the point. Things have gotten really bad when a public school system is telling a psychologist what to say. Up until this point you could at least expect the psychologist to be there for the kids. So do I blame the psychologist? Absolutely not; she needs a job just like the rest of us.
- One public school system has set up a retrieval system where if a school's special education coordinator retrieved (yes, that is what they are calling it) a child from a private placement, the coordinator's home school would be given

$10,000.

These are just a few examples of what is going on in this state. It makes me so angry because it only has to do with money, not children and their needs.

Advocating for children takes more than caring and integrity these days. For our particular program, because we are a private school, fighting for children to be placed with us has become more of a chess game than a meeting of a team to determine the best possible programming for an individual child.

Currently, most cities and towns say they are integrating children in the public school. But as discussed in Chapters Two and Three, saying it and doing it are two different things. There are some good inclusive models in the Massachusetts public schools. But they are few and can service few children.

Today when we go to an IEP planning meeting, if we say the child has made gains and is progressing, the public school representatives automatically say great — then she's ready to go to public school. If we say the child is progressing slowly, then they say what difference does it make if we move her? It is so rare these days that the meetings actually focus on the child. In fact, in the last two years I have only been at one meeting where the public schools recommended that the child remain with us. It generally doesn't matter what the circumstances are of the particular child; the goal from the point of view of the public school is to "retrieve" the child. Somehow the public schools feel the money* is theirs. It isn't. It's all of our money from taxes. And if they cannot or do not provide the quality education our children with and without special needs deserve, then the money should go to private programs which will do it. The current opinion of the Powers that Be is that public education is the only option.

The fact is that it costs money to run quality programs, and it costs a lot of extra money to run quality inclusive programs.

If public schools continue to be housed in run-down, dark, dank, inaccessible buildings (which many are), if teachers continue to have tenure regardless of the job they do, if programs continue to be without new materials, supplies and equipment to the point where teachers have to bring in their own Xerox paper, then private programs will continue to outperform them. Parents will continue to be dissatisfied, and children will continue to lose out.

If public schools continue to assign 50 to 75 children with special

---

* The monies involved in an out-of-district placement for the child must be paid by the school district in which the child's family resides.

needs to one therapist, then children aren't going to receive their services. Teachers can't teach without books, materials, and equipment. Therapists can't do therapy with a huge caseload; evaluations and reports are all that get done.

The way the IEP planning meetings are set up now, the public school has a team leader, psychologist, speech therapist, educational specialist, physical therapist, occupational therapist, and nurse. In cases where the child is already in our program, a representative from Kids Are People would attend the meeting with reports from the teacher and therapists who currently know and work with the child. The parents and their advocate would attend to represent the child.

Given this scenario, if each person makes a recommendation for placement, the team will always recommend the public school because of the number of public school representatives. It wouldn't matter what the child's needs were, or whether or not the public school had an appropriate placement equal to or better than ours. Given one vote per participant, the representatives from the public schools outnumber all others and can therefore say the team recommended the placement.

Not only is this unfair to the child, it's inappropriate. As discussed in Chapter Seven, evaluations are a minute window of time in a child's life and a snapshot of her abilities. It's really inappropriate for a team of people — some of whom have never met the child and the rest evaluated her for an hour — to have more say than her parents or the teaching team who works with her day in and day out.

At one such meeting, a representative from the state child welfare agency, the parent, the early intervention program who had worked with the child before us, our representative, and the child's advocate all recommended that the child remain at Kids Are People, due to the child's fragile physical and emotional health. The public school people recommended that the child go to a public school program. Of the public school representatives, only two had ever met the child. The team leader tried to say that *the team* recommended the child go to the public school, when in fact five different parties recommended the child stay at Kids Are People and only the public school representatives wanted the child moved. This was the most blatant case of the team meeting only being about money and not being for the child.

The argument over private vs. public education will continue for a long time and is really a political issue, but *children* are being caught in the middle. Child planning meetings need to change; the focus needs to be on the child and not politics; only one representative from each program should have a vote as a member of the team, to be fair to all parties and to focus on the child's and family's needs.

Public school personnel need to be honest and professional, and feel safe to state what they really think a child needs, without threat of retribution if they honestly do not feel it will be in the best interest of the child to be moved. The focus on decision of placement needs to be around that particular child.

At one meeting, the team was discussing whether or not the child needed to continue her program through the summer. The psychologist said he felt the child needed it for maximal benefits to the child, but that if it was recommended then any child in the future could have it recommended and summer programs would have to be created. His point of view was obviously a political/financial point of view and had little to do with the needs of that particular child. This kind of issue needs to be removed from team meetings. Only discussion about the needs of one child, the focus of the meeting, is relevant at that meeting.

Parents and Advocates. Wanting a specific kind of education for a child and getting it are two different things. Parents need to know that not only do they have rights, but there are advocates out there willing to help fight for the rights of children. If parents don't question the placement of their child, the public school will make the decision for them. If parents do not raise concerns about what they feel their children need, no one will do it for them. Parents have to be their child's first and strongest advocate. And parents need to investigate what the laws are around education and parent rights. Often when I talk with parents and they tell me what was done to their child, I hear things that I can't believe. And the more I talk to parents, the more I find out that they do not know they have *any* rights. Laws differ from state to state but are generally there to help families and protect children. Pamphlets on parents' rights under the law can often be obtained from the state department of education or from the local school.

Intent and specifics around the laws often need to be interpreted. This is where advocates can come in handy. There are lists of advocates available in most areas. Parents must ask other parents or professionals whose judgment they trust for recommendation of an advocate. Some advocates charge per hour; some are funded publicly.

Funding. Money issues are the part of the job I hate the most, generally because we seldom have any and when we do it's already owed to someone.

Funding for children with special needs often goes hand in hand with advocacy. When the child's Individual Education Plan is signed, the team meetings are over, and the child is in our program — often we still don't have the money. Some school departments pay us on time. The speed of payment is generally directly proportional to the attitude of the funding source toward our program. If the source feels that we are a quality program, and understands that we depend on our funding to get by week to week, then we often get our money for our services in a timely fashion. If our funding source is annoyed that the child is placed with us, then often we do not receive payment for months after the child is in our school.

In addition, funding sources fight desperately not to pay us for retroactive services in cases when parents placed their child with us because the public school system did not give her an appropriate program. In one case we had a child for three years without being paid for our services. When the parents won a hearing indicating that Kids Are People was the appropriate placement for this child, the hearing officer awarded the parents back payments for the time the child was with us. Ultimately these have to be paid, but further issues often arise to delay it.

Agencies who fund us make us give the service before paying us. For example, for children in our program whose slots are paid for by the welfare department, we have to provide a month's worth of services and then bill for them. We then receive the payment seven to eight weeks later. This kind of intermittent cash flow just makes things more difficult. Plodding through month after month is the only way, but it can be done.

The added costs we carry for our children with special needs include:

- Increased payroll due to increased number of teachers for small groups.
- Loss of revenue due to decrease in group size.
- Increase in equipment costs.

    Many children with special needs require a variety of materials and equipment to make their environment accessible and to adapt curriculum. This includes but is not limited to: chairs
    tables
    prone standers
    special computer equipment
    special computer programs
    feeding utensils
    writing utensils
    toileting chairs
    therapy equipment

Sometimes Medicaid or insurance will pay for equipment,

but often the wait of six months to a year is too long. Responsible programs generally foot the bill, because often the equipment request is deferred or rejected.

- Increase in rent for additional space for therapies (no, not all therapies can be done in the classroom).
- Staff training.

Staff training is an ongoing issue in our program. Besides formal training and staff meetings, a great deal of my time is spent on supervising the teaching staff. The majority of the issues I spend time on relate to our inclusion practices. How do we include this child in that activity? Is that the best position for that child? Is that the best equipment to use? Can we make something better? He/she can't do that; what can we do to find a way so he/she can? This is an ongoing daily issue. Inclusion isn't a set thing; it's a daily evaluation process of procedures, care and education within the classroom for each particular child.

- Time and money spent on report writing, evaluations, team meetings, and mediations.
- Salaries for therapists.
- Time and money spent on parent support and training.

An enormous amount of energy is spent on dealing with parents of children with special needs. The staff and I spend 50 to 100 percent more time listening to, solving problems with, meeting with, and training parents of children with special needs in comparison to the amount of time spent on parents of children without special needs. Parents of children with special needs did not wake up one day and say "I think I'll have a child with special needs." Generally speaking this child has turned their life upside down. They often live in a constant state of uncertainty of what the future holds, wavering between hope and depression. They need a great deal of support and encouragement.

This is not to say that the parents of the "typical" children do not need a lot of energy and support — life is often crazy for them too. But for programs considering becoming inclusive, the staff need to realize that inclusion will place huge demands on their time that did not previously exist.

Social Services and Medical Personnel

State Agencies. A great deal of time is spent dealing with outside agencies trying to get what I need for the children. Below are some of the issues I need to address with outside agencies on a weekly basis.

Medication needs. Children on a variety of medications often need medicines changed or dosages increased. For example, with a diagnosis of hyperactivity or attentional problems, as the children grow, they often need increases in medication. Staff need to be aware of behavioral changes to keep medical personnel informed.

Medical needs. Some examples are children with chronic disease such as diabetes, children with seizure disorders who need careful monitoring, or even a child with a feeding tube which gets infected.

Child evaluations. A lot of time is spent trying to set up a child's evaluations. Sometimes children can't be seen for months. Often a child may need to be evaluated for such things as augmentative communication, seating, hyperactivity, etc. It's to the benefit of our program to follow through and have these evaluations set up as soon as possible to help make changes for the child.

Equipment, braces and therapies. Children outgrow wheelchairs and braces, and we have adaptations and casting done right at our school. This takes a lot of extra time, but we get what we need for the children a lot faster. And from what we have observed from several children who have come to us from other programs, what we do is the exception, not the rule. We have had children arrive in wheelchairs with their knees almost in their faces. And we have found out that the children got their wheelchair two or three years before and no one ever had it adjusted as the child grew. Parents don't always know to even question if an adjustment needs to be made. But school personnel should consider it part of their job to evaluate equipment and brace changes. When I see a child in a wheelchair which hasn't been adjusted in three years, the message is loud and clear: the system didn't work for this child; someone didn't care and didn't do their job. In addition, if you then have the child looked at by a physical therapist, most likely you will find tightness in joints where there shouldn't be any and weakness in parts of the body where therapy could have helped strengthen the child.

Time and time again this is what we find, because once the child was put in the wheelchair, often therapy stopped. *It is crucial to the health of children in wheelchairs that the wheelchair be seen as a method of getting around some of the time and that the child be stretched, walked, made to bear weight on his limbs whenever possible.* Without this, muscles shorten, bones get brittle, scoliosis can develop, and the child's health is put at risk.

These things don't need to be done all the time by a therapist. But parents and classroom staff need to be trained how to do them, and the importance of these exercises on a daily basis to the overall well-being of the child needs to be stressed.

It is part of the administrator's job to make sure the staff is trained, therapies are being done, and classroom positioning and in-class therapies are done consistently. As administrator of the program, I see it as my responsibility to ensure that brace needs, equipment needs, wheelchair adaptations and adjustments are taken care of in the school program.

All programs considering inclusion need to determine who will be responsible for follow-through in monitoring the children's equipment needs and seeing that these needs are met. It needs to be someone with knowledge and enough influence to be able to follow through. It is also important that teachers be told to inform the designated person if they notice equipment wear or braces or equipment getting small, fitting or functioning poorly. Staff may also need to be taught what too small means for braces or wheelchairs — sometimes they look okay but aren't.

Home Needs. A lot of time is also spent on helping parents obtain equipment or services within the home. Some equipment can travel back and forth with the child. And since no one is going to pay for two wheelchairs, therapy strollers or walkers for one child, the program has the choice of footing the bill on less expensive items or sharing. We often will purchase equipment because of the huge delays in getting equipment once it is determined a child needs it. In addition, we have equipment we use at the school which the school owns and is for the use of several children, such as therapeutic potty chairs, a variety of walkers, computer equipment, programs, and switches, and a variety of therapeutic chairs, therapy equipment, and eating and writing utensils.

Parents want to have many of these things at home too. Part of our job is to help the parents get such equipment as therapeutic potty chairs, therapeutic bath chairs, etc.

We have found agencies which are willing to come right to the school and fit children for walkers, braces and wheelchairs. This has been extremely helpful to us and has gotten the children what they need in a very short time. Every program should identify such resources in their area.

An issue for all programs is helping families through crises. These include but are not limited to:

- Charges of child abuse against the parent or another indi-

vidual connected to the child.
- Homelessness — several children live in shelters or in some cases aren't even in shelters.
- Parental job loss.
- Parental chronic illness.
- Death of a loved one.
- Divorce.
- Setting up family counseling, play therapy.
- Helping families deal with prejudice. Several children we work with have been of color and started school elsewhere as the only minority child in their school. Issues of racism have come up when the children and teachers have interacted with the child in a consistently negative way, setting the child up to fail. When the child comes into our program, which has a varied cultural mix, problems simply disappear.

These are issues most administrators have to deal with on an ongoing basis. Many become even more serious when a child with special needs is involved because additional stress on the family can lead to lack of follow through on the part of the family in addressing the child's needs. School and home follow-through in addressing a child's special needs is critical to the health and well-being of the child; any breakdown could be detrimental and in some cases life-threatening.

Having discussed these concerns, it becomes quite obvious that there is an enormous amount of interaction between our program and outside agencies so we can give the best care to the children we service. The major problems with outside agencies are the slowness with which they respond to these issues and the attitude that things can't be done.

The ongoing attitude at our program is, "Why can't we?" "How can we?" This should be the theme for the nation in educational reform. Too many people over too many years have relied on the attitude of "It can't be done." That attitude is the safest, easiest way to be lazy and do the least possible to get through the work week without looking lazy. I wish I could just blame it on a lack of creativity and imagination, but it isn't, and it may just be the problem underlying American society at this point in time.

And this is not to say that we never have these issues within our own program. We do. As I stated at the beginning of this chapter, my biggest frustration as administrator of Kids Are People School is anyone getting in the way of us doing what is best for the kids in our program. Internal members of the community can also do this.

Internal Members of the Community

I have a wonderful teaching staff, and over the years, with the exception of a few people, the staff we have had have been great for kids. Our teachers work longer hours than most and year-round, and I'm sure the pay isn't more. But what I think we have going at Kids Are People School is a common bond among the staff to help the children. For the most part there is a feeling of unity, of working towards the goal of really making inclusion work. There is a wealth of energy, knowledge and ability among our staff. And despite the long hours and mediocre pay, I continually see several things coming from these people. I see pride and joy when a child achieves even a small goal. I see enthusiasm for teaching. I see respect and humor in dealing with the kids. And I see sadness, frustration and worry when something's going wrong in a child's life. On the rare occasion I see anger, annoyance and impatience — generally when a child is wasting everyone's time acting out. But mostly I see the love and compassion with which our staff guide these children.

I see them looking tired at the end of the day and I worry about burnout. I see them frustrated when I walk in at the one moment their group falls apart. I see annoyance at times when I tell them about what they should be doing at that moment with a particular kid and I know they're thinking "I was getting to that, but I had to do this." And I know that what they were doing was important, but the child still in her wheelchair was more important, and it's my job to point it out even if it annoys them. And I'm sure I should find more time to praise them, but often we have just enough time to fit everything in and point out what we need to do in the future.

I really don't know how we do all that we do. There is always an unending list of things to do, and I know how hard we all work. I know we are as good as we can be at making inclusion work, and I know we are driven by it. So I'm never sure if our model can work in most other schools. Many times I've been told "Well, you people can do it that way. You're private — you make all the decisions. We can't do it. It's the nature of a public school." And I don't know whether only a small group of people driven by the same goals can make it work at its best and make it look easy. Or whether school-based management will be one of the keys to changing around public school education and inclusion. All I do know is my staff, hand-picked and trained by me, work incredibly hard with constant input from me on a daily basis.

Also, I intervene with children who are acting out and disrupting the group. I don't know how much time other principals have to put into this, but if children with severe behavioral problems are going to be included, there needs to be that kind of direct attention from the senior staff at the program. I'm talking about being willing to physically jump in and prevent injury to a child or teacher, because this is the reality. Are the administrators going to find the time on a daily basis to hold a physically abusive ten year old for 30 minutes while he tries to spit, bite, kick and punch? And are they going to have a close enough hands-on relationship with the children and staff to understand the child and help the teacher to see it wasn't a personal attack on him or her?

Having said all of this, there are some administrators, teachers or therapists who are just bad for the program. I think quality inclusive education can work if the administrator is hands-on and the program is small enough. But what makes a teacher, therapist or administrator bad for the program? Well, I guess I can only talk about our program.

For our program, if a teacher is sickly it would be almost impossible for him or her to make it here. For this job, especially with elementary school aged children who are physically challenged, you need to not only be healthy but have a ton of energy and strength. In addition, due to the nature of the behavioral/emotional problems of some of the children, a teacher who is out sick a lot can really upset the balance of the group that consistency makes possible. In fact, any time teachers are out it is definitely difficult for the entire program. It is so hard to find appropriate substitutes that we have very strict policies.

For example, teachers are supposed to come in unless they are *really* sick. A headache or cold doesn't do it. Plenty of notice is required if teachers want time off, and calling in sick on a Monday or Friday is really frowned upon (because we find it hard to believe). These policies may seem a little harsh and even uncaring, but our teachers can't leave their work on their desk, and there are so many children with medication needs, medical problems, allergies, and special needs that we can't just call up a temp agency to replace a teacher. No one could do it but another member of the staff. While we do have extra staff, and it's not uncommon for me to work with a group, someone who is sick a lot would impede the smooth running of the program. For the most part, after staff have worked in our program long enough, they see how difficult their day is if other staff are out sick. I know that if a teacher who has been with us for a while calls in sick, he or she is really sick.

Another teacher who would not be good for our program is a lazy teacher: someone who does the minimum to get by, never initiates, just puts in the hours. That kind of attitude would be picked up by the rest of the staff and wouldn't be tolerated by peers. The reason for this is that we all depend on one another to help when things are going wrong, to support us when issues around the program are overwhelming. In reality the program functions as a team. Materials, rooms, equipment are all shared; no one has "their own space." So if someone's not holding up their end — for example, leaving an activity center messy, or letting their group destroy equipment — it affects all other groups, it doesn't just upset me. Therefore, a teacher who is doing the minimum and never helps out will be identified right away and will either change or leave. We have a one-month probation period in which we or the new teacher can determine if the job isn't right for them. And as I stated before, these teachers work incredibly hard and don't have the time, energy or patience to do someone else's work.

Though we have an intensive interview process, periodically we'll have someone who's not a good match for our program because they are prejudiced against children with special needs. As hard as it is to imagine this could happen — it has. Often it's a particular child they are biased against, but sometimes it's more than just a bad match. In our program we have some children who are significantly involved, and some of the issues a teacher has to deal with can be unappealing. They can include constant drooling, vomiting, diarrhea, using a feeding tube, gagging up phlegm, or chronic constipation requiring massaging the stomach to help the child go. These are just a few issues, but they are ongoing parts of every day in caring for these children, and it isn't easy.

The unprejudiced teacher sees beyond these issues to the child. But even if you love the child, drool still feels like drool when it's dripped all over your leg, and it's not the greatest feeling. For the teacher who just can't stomach it, you'll notice him constantly doing everything possible to avoid interacting with that child even if the child is assigned to his group. He'll get other people to change her, feed her, hold her while he "deals with the rest of the group." He seldom talks directly to the child, but about her, segregating her within the group by always pointing out to the group why he can't do this or that because he *has* to do something for the child with special needs.

In addition, body language always tells the whole story. Watch the faces of the prejudiced teachers, and this is no exaggeration: they'll actually look disgusted or as if they are cringing while they are caring for the child. They seldom cuddle the child or touch the child in a caring way and often do not initiate conversations with the child. They go about doing the chores necessary to care for the child without talking.

A critical point about children who are non-verbal: *it is crucial as part of inclusion that the child be talked to as if he understands everything that is being said.* If there is no way to really determine how much the child understands, then it is imperative that you treat the child like he understands everything. To do less than this is to exclude the child from valuable interactions. A teacher who continually doesn't talk with the child as if he understands, you automatically know has prejudged the child and has determined that the child is incapable of understanding. The same is true of talking about the child right in front of him. Don't assume the child doesn't understand — he might, and it could be harmful for him to hear certain things. So watch body language and interactions between teacher and children — some teachers are not cut out to work with certain children.

I personally feel that if a teacher is interacting in these ways, I wouldn't want her working with any of our children. I feel that all of our staff should be able to work with any of the children if necessary.

Another teacher who isn't right for an inclusive model is one who lacks common sense. I think a wealth of common sense is one of the main attributes of a good teacher. I don't think any person who lacks common sense should be teaching in any program. But for our program it is especially necessary for people to use their heads and to be able to make split-second decisions. It can be a matter of life and death in some circumstances. And people who lack common sense often aren't safe with the children. Between children with serious behavioral/emotional problems, children with serious medical issues including severe diabetes or seizure disorders, and children who mouth everything in sight, you can't have a teacher who isn't aware at all times, able to react immediately, and thinking ahead about potentially dangerous situations. Accidents will happen, but preventable ones shouldn't.

And lastly, a teacher who is self-centered, immature and irresponsible is the worst kind of teacher for an inclusive program. This job really demands giving of yourself heart and soul, and if a teacher is always focused on what she needs, what's easier for her, or ever takes a child's behavior personally, then that person will not have the best interests of the children in mind. You can't be focused on your personal problems when you're trying to get a non-verbal, socially delayed child to interact with a group.

As difficult as it is to know when to let a child go, it's equally difficult to let a teacher go; but the best interest of all the children and the staff must be considered. I have found that parents get very attached to their child's teacher, and they hate change, especially sudden change. Over the years we have had staff leave suddenly for various reasons, and parents have a very difficult time dealing with it — much more so than the children. At our school parents have gotten really spoiled because teachers often stay for years and with the multi-aged setup, a child often has the same teacher for more than one year. Parents forget that if their child was in public school she would have a different teacher every nine months.

Having any teacher leave suddenly is very stressful, especially a well-liked teacher. Teachers may leave for a variety of reasons: they have personal problems or life changes, they find the requirements and expectations too demanding, they burn out, whatever. What parents don't realize is that getting mad about a teacher leaving doesn't help the situation.

Often we have to "try out" several people before we hit on someone who is a good replacement. The inclusive model is a much more physically and emotionally demanding program to work in, and there is so much to remember. In addition, often the parents of children with special needs are very demanding of the program staff. It's rare for us to hear from the parents that we are doing a good job. After several years I realized that parents are generally happy if we aren't hearing from them; and they will let us know whenever they are unhappy. I know it's not just our program. I hear this all the time from teachers and administrators from other schools.

Sometimes, because you don't want a changeover in staff, you keep people on who aren't that great and you work with them trying to overlook the problems. But it almost never works. A teacher is either good at working in an inclusive program or they're not, and the program will survive if a person leaves. Parents seem to forget that the person they liked so much for their child was hired and trained by us. But eventually they adjust to a new teacher, and life goes on.

It's also just as important to know when to let a great staff member leave when they first approach you. Offering more money, different hours, whatever, doesn't work. Even if the person stays, they often don't do the same quality job and eventually leave anyway, often without a lot of notice. The demands of the job burn people out quickly, and if they are sensible enough to know it's time for something new, then let them go; otherwise you're just prolonging an eventuality. It took me a long time to learn this. I had one teacher I loved so much that she gave notice three times, and three times I talked her into staying. When she finally left, she just walked out in the middle of the day. It was my fault for talking her into staying and hers for thinking she could do this job full-time while going to school. Now when people say they're leaving I say okay, as long as they haven't already committed to us through a certain date.

Student Teachers. We have dealt with a lot of student teachers over the years. Some have been wonderful and some have been horrible.

The horrible ones haven't been horrible because they couldn't teach or were inexperienced. The problem was they had no concept of responsibility. They made excuses for themselves, were late, called in sick on Fridays every other week, and didn't follow through on assignments. What we saw from their supervisors in response to their behavior was coddling, covering for them, blaming themselves, blaming us, and so forth. If I had one wish for colleges and universities who train teachers, it would be that they had a required course around job responsibility which talks about the impact on the children and program when teachers are irresponsible. We understand that student teachers are teachers being trained, but the focus should be training in teaching, not training in manners. And if the schools don't want to waste an entire course on responsibility, they should at least have a code of ethics by which they expect their students to behave.

We have clear expectations for teachers and student teachers alike, and as much as we can really benefit from good student teachers, it is a disaster in our program to have an irresponsible one. Our time and energy is precious, and to have to spend it on someone who adds stress to the program is ridiculous. A lot of these problems could be alleviated by the colleges themselves being responsible and setting clear standards of professionalism for their students. We are very careful about taking student teachers and have actually stopped using one local college because of their lack of responsibility in training their teachers.

Therapists. Although therapists are discussed in detail in Chapter Eight, there are specific issues that as the administrator I have to address on an ongoing basis. Supervising therapists is a difficult task because they come from a very different point of view than the rest of the staff.

First of all, because they are only at the program part time, it is as difficult for myself and the staff as I suspect it is for the therapists to communicate, keep on track, follow through and share knowledge and information. Often it comes down to "I told you that." "No you didn't." And I may have told them and they forgot, or I may have told the other three therapists and forgotten to tell this one.

In addition, their training definitely comes from a medical model that never considered inclusion. Their attitude toward children generally comes from the special educational model of looking at what a child can't do. Given all of this, therapeutic inclusion is in the embryonic stages even as inclusion itself is just being born.

You will hear all the time, "Well, our therapies are done in the classroom." Often no therapy is done at all in that situation. It's one more way for school systems to save money. Consultations to the classroom teacher are another new preferred choice — often this isn't done either. Both of these issues aside, a willing therapist can generally help with creative ideas and help the teachers to understand the child's issues and how to deal with them within the program. We ask our therapists to have their client invite a typical friend to be included in therapy sessions or small group work.

But what is impossible to change (and I have been trying for years to do this) is the attitude of looking at the child as flawed and not whole, what he can't do instead of what he can. I consider this a very negative position for anyone working in our program to be coming from, and yet there is such a shortage of available therapists that often I have no choice if I want the children to get services.

Of course, this attitude can act like a cancer on the positive attitude of the staff towards hope for the children. I have been told time and time again that I'm too positive, that I believe in the children too much, that children I believe can and will do more will never do anything. This has got to change. Therapists have to start looking at what the child is doing and go from there with a positive outlook and enthusiasm. Small gains have to be encouraged and fostered. Parents need to be informed of every positive step a child takes and encouraged to praise the child at home for things they accomplish at school, and also to try these things at home.

Individually appropriate should be the method used, not *developmentally appropriate*. If you have a child who has no means of communicating because no one has found a way to teach him to communicate, then I say whatever works. If that child is ten and the only thing he's ever consistently responded to is Barney, then I say forget age-appropriate — this child is for some reason interested in Barney. Use it. You can't teach the child anything if you can't get the child's attention. Once you can get the child to respond consistently and purposefully, then move on.

I have had to deal with one therapist who is so negative about the children that the kids are written off before they're given a chance. The staff and I have learned to work around this person. The therapy is helping the child, so we ignore the therapist's negative attitude and push forward. If I don't agree with the therapist around service needs, I get an outside opinion.

What has been the one saving grace around this situation is that this therapist has had to come to me and say, "Well, I never would have believed it, but look what so-and-so is doing." And I just smile and say, "I told you so." Sometimes I have to put up with negative things to get what I need for a child. And the rest of the therapeutic staff counterbalance this therapist's negative attitude with enthusiasm and positive attitudes.

Nonbelievers. Which brings me to the issue of dealing with nonbelievers. Parents who are nonbelievers in their child are very frustrating to deal with, but it's understandable. On the one hand, any parent would love to be able to have their child do more. On the other hand, it's difficult for the parents to allow themselves to have hope; they've obviously been hurt so many times that to begin to believe again is almost more painful than accepting that their child will never do anything. Trying to convince parents to believe in their child is very draining and, with some parents, useless.

But then there are parents like Lauren's mom, who was told the worst. Her child would not only never do anything, but she would die an early death. Well, Lauren's mom decided to say "No, that's not happening," and she has been strong and loving and supportive, and together we have gotten Lauren to do things that she was never supposed to do, like be alive today, never mind talk, laugh at friends, use a computer.

I can't judge or blame either kind of parent. I can only keep moving forward for their children and hope that I'll get through for the sake of the child.

Nonbelievers in the professional fields of therapies, medicine, and education, I have absolutely no tolerance for. Even on my staff, I find it very difficult to accept someone being negative about a child. And as we stated in Chapters 2 and 3, sometimes children need to be matched with teachers or therapists who are more tolerant of them and their behaviors than the teacher who may be acting judgmental towards the child. Often this is the other piece of advocating for children which I have to do.

An inclusive program has many components, and sometimes the pieces don't all fit perfectly together. But all together we do get the job done.

CHAPTER FIVE

Curriculum and Materials: Playdough is Playdough

Of greatest concern to a new program considering inclusion is how a teacher manages to give special education services to the children with special needs while giving "regular" education to the rest of the group. In an integrated school program there really is no such thing as regular education and special education. In every area of educational activities, projects and lessons are appropriate for all children. What is sometimes needed is modification of an activity.

For example, playdough really is just playdough whether it is used by a child with fine motor problems or another child without fine motor problems. When a group of children use playdough, several learning experiences are going on. The children are creating, manipulating, and receiving sensory input, and they are in a social interaction. For the child with fine motor problems, the sensory input and the squeezing, pushing and pulling of the playdough are excellent for strengthening weak muscles. Modifications can be made by adding instruments such as pegs, toothpicks and knives for more involved fine motor work or even clothespins to squeeze and pick up pieces of clay.

What is important to realize is that *the modifications are also good for the children without fine motor problems because they also need to strengthen their grasp for writing skills.* A supposedly remedial activity becomes an inclusive activity!

Even a child who can't push the playdough herself can benefit from having a teacher or friend press her hands into the dough. It gives the child sensory input. It even helps with just teaching pressing, which may be used later with switches or other communication devices. And it makes her belong as part of the group. This is probably the most important aspect, since the sense of belonging is what all the children need and value. An open-ended activity such as playdough allows the non-verbal child to be treated by the other children as a friend and important member of the group. Children can learn to communicate with their non-verbal peers as easily as the teacher can. It is also a great opportunity to have the other children work with their motorically challenged friend by helping her to create.

In the next section we discuss some overriding issues to help you frame the contexts within which curriculum elements should be delivered.

Creativity

Throughout this book there is a lot of discussion about creativity and individualized education. Lack of creativity in education often means missed opportunities to educate. Let me illustrate this point using a recent escapade of a pair of eight year olds, one of whom was Benjamin.

In our school we have a Critter Corner with a variety of insects and animals. Once a week a new critter is added, and the children study about it and make observations in their observation journals. Recently, several tadpoles and frogs were added to the Critter Corner. One day Benjamin and his friend noticed one of the frogs had died. They didn't inform the teacher, but instead took the frog from the tank and placed it in a lunch box to take home to do an "autopsy" on. At snack time the frog was discovered, much to the disappointment of the two children, and they got in a bit of trouble for it.

When I learned what had happened, I and another teacher came up with a learning experience for the two children. We didn't want to really punish them because it was curiosity which gave them the idea to perform the "autopsy." So the next day I called the two together and let them know that animals die generally because they are sick. If they're sick, they can carry disease. Disease can make people sick, and a frog that died from disease definitely does not belong in a lunch box. I also informed them that doctors and surgeons study animals for years, dissecting healthy frogs and so on.

We assigned them a project of researching all the diseases that dead animals carry and what those diseases can do to healthy humans. As an autopsy team they had to write a paper and present it to the class. They dragged their feet at first (and quickly learned about plagiarism), but eventually were heard arguing over whether to write about only animals you can get diseases from when they are dead, or all animals you can get a disease from. These two kids learned a lot! It just may have made them more curious, as opposed to squashing their initiative and creativity.

This is what creative, individual education is about: going with those opportunities that the kids themselves present to you, and noticing when they are presented. A set curriculum is helpful and nice, but never be so married to it that you don't let other education experiences occur, especially when the opportunities are presented by the students.

We feel that children should experience as much as possible about the real world. But we also feel that basic skills need to be stressed. Trying to combine these two principles has been a lot easier for our program because we are an all-day year-round program. But programs which are nine-month and fewer hours can also combine the two.

As you will see by reviewing our curriculum, we have an ambitious agenda. Having a vision and helping others see it are often two different issues. Which brings me to an issue of great importance: reviewing our actions.

Evaluating Our Program

A staff *must* review its goals and the reality of its achievements. We look at what has and hasn't worked and set necessary changes in motion, in the program as a whole and with particular children. I cannot stress enough that inclusion in education comes from within the staff and the administrator(s). It attains a life of its own that needs to be nurtured in an ongoing process of commitment to this goal. It needs to be continually renewed and reiterated as a basic tenet of the school program. New staff, children and parents bring new issues and must come to understand the implications of this philosophy for what happens in the program and with each child.

On a daily basis, teaching colleagues should be observing inclusive procedures and educational techniques. These observations need to be shared among the teacher group to decide whether the practice achieved its intended outcomes, and if not, what changes could occur. Individual staff conferences and meetings, even if they are only two minutes long, need to happen on an ongoing basis to maintain communication in the teaching staff and to share experiences and impressions, sometimes *at that moment!* I have observed very useful short conferences structured around a coffee break where all teachers and staff gather in one room for 10-15 minutes, where no one sits necessarily but everyone shares the experiences of that morning with individual children or some program elements. The students will be having a morning snack or playtime under the supervision of some individual staff members, or perhaps volunteer parents or student teachers.

These conferencing techniques by the staff, and those in more traditional formats, enable us to help everyone gain a common sense of purpose toward particular students' needs and the learning opportunities they pose *that* day! Administrators and staff need to consider the best methods and techniques to share information. It needs to be an ongoing process, and sometimes needs to be spontaneous, immediate sharing around significant events.

Updating the programs for each child has to happen on a continual basis. We use quarterly reviews to more carefully evaluate how a given child has progressed, especially in the areas of concern, but also in areas we would like to see him reach out for. These reviews are not just for the children with special needs but for all the children enrolled. Annual reviews allow us to more comprehensively review each child's progress and project the child's program for the coming year. All specialists involved with the child participate, as do parents and the teaching staff.

Negative Interactions Between Children

An absolutely major issue in our school is that every child act positively toward his or her schoolmates. Even with our best efforts, there have been times that certain typical children have not acted appropriately to their schoolmates with special needs. This needs to be dealt with immediately and in a way that really sends the message home to the typical child.

We had a child in our program who was very large for his age and could walk but not talk. To communicate with his peers he would yell sounds and pull on their clothes to get their attention. This was very disconcerting to two little girls who were into Barbie dolls, dresses and were a bit snobby to most of their friends in general. After this child with special needs decided he wanted them as friends, disaster struck. Comments like "We don't like so-and-so," or "We don't like to play with him," could be heard.

In our school this kind of behavior isn't tolerated under any circumstances, regardless of the children involved. In this particular case the staff was very concerned. We talked to the children and their parents, but I really felt it wasn't enough; these kids needed to understand more. Now kids will be kids, and little girls around six seem to catch that disease of being prissy and exclusionary to one another. And in all fairness no one really likes to be yelled at and pulled on.

I waited until a day that the child with special needs wasn't in school and I gathered the class in my office. I told them that this child is trying to tell them things when he yells and pulls on them. And I made each child come up to me. I whispered a statement in their ear such as "I like your dress. It's really pretty," or "Congratulations, Stephanie, on your new baby brother." I had the child I whispered to go and say the whispered statement to whatever child I mentioned in the statement, but they couldn't use any words because they had to make believe they couldn't speak. One by one I saw these children go over, try to communicate with their friends, and not be able to. They experienced the complete frustration that so many non-verbal children go through. So, I said, now you know how your friend feels and why he pulls on you or yells sounds at you.

The results of this exercise were astounding. Not only did the children stop the negative behavior towards their friend with special needs, but the two little girls actively started helping their friend and finding ways to communicate with him.

This story raises a very important point. *No matter how determined a team is to have a quality inclusive program, it doesn't just happen. Quality inclusion is an ongoing process of evaluation, change and facilitation; problems such as these will continuously crop up over the course of time and need to be dealt with effectively.* The best way to teach is through hands-on activities, and the best way for these children to learn what they needed to learn was by experiencing it. You can tell the children how others feel, but to have them feel it can make significant changes quickly.

VARIETY IN THE CURRICULUM

We feel that variety in the curriculum is necessary to grasp and hold the attention of children. Boredom is a cancer to education. We also feel there are many ways to learn basic concepts and skills which are crucial to more in-depth learning. Attached is a description of our language arts program and an explanation of specific activities which take place on a weekly basis.

In general, inclusion in classroom activities needs to focus on:

1) How the child feels.
2) How to change things so that this child can be a real part—
   and I stress *real part* — of the activity.

It takes a caring and sensitive teacher. If you are sensitive to that child's feelings, you will find a way or you'll decide the activity isn't worth doing.

With these introductory comments as context, we present the elements of the program available to all children at the Kids Are People School. We present them to show the broad vision for all the children, the broad definition of learning opportunities, and the variety of the opportunities for learning. *Getting away from the boredom of work sheets, work books and seat-bound activities is a critical and elementary principle.* As you can see, we expect children to be actively learning and involved with classmates, to record and make their learning products themselves, and to critically evaluate the quality of what they produce.

We seek ways for the child who cannot verbalize or write to also become actively involved with stimulating learning materials and to produce work that reflects what they are learning, thinking, feeling and wanting. How to achieve this goal for each of these students is *the* critical problem for the staff. Enhancing each child's communication is seen as a critical effort to enabling his full participation in the school program (see Chapter 8).

In our program, all children partake of all areas of the curriculum, and we suggest methods for modifications to enable them to achieve that goal. The reader should notice that small and few modifications are required to include children with special needs into classroom activities, but an eternal vigilance is needed so that each child is included, not left out, however inadvertently!

Language Arts Program

The curriculum below was created by us for children and teachers to use together to monitor language arts accomplishments. It was designed after I read a wonderful book called *Student-Centered Language Arts, K-12*, written by James Moffett and Betty Jane Wagner (1991). This creative and inventive book describes what the best kind of teaching, in my opinion, is all about. I strongly recommend it! I searched for a very long time before I found a book which came close to discussing teaching language arts in the center-based, child-directed classroom with the kind of open-ended style we feel is necessary to foster creative inclusion.

In order for children to best learn reading and writing, they need to be immersed in language. The five areas of focus are writing, reading, listening, speaking and performing. Children perform at their own rate, choice and interest. They record their progress (with assistance if needed), and the teacher counsels and guides them in their areas of choice so that all five activities are performed in the following ten areas of educational material. Their work is reviewed with them on a monthly basis.

- Word Play – riddles, puns, tongue twisters, poetry
- Labels and Captions – graphs, maps, etc.
- Actual Dialogue – discussions and transcript
- Invented Dialogue – script, improvisation
- Letters and Memoranda
- Invented Stories – fiction, fables, tales, poetry
- True Stories – autobiography, biography, journal, memoirs

- Information – generalized facts
- Ideas – generalized thoughts and abstract statements
- Directions – how to make, how to do different activities.

All children each have:

- A journal for writing
- A book for recording observations in science, math, physics, etc.
- Portfolios of language arts work including tape, audiovisual, and written materials.
- Portfolios of art work.
- Word boxes.
- Student tracking cards for self-assessment of a wide variety of language arts choices.
- Letter boxes of several self-made alphabets for spelling, printing and writing.

Children in the course of the year participate in:

- interviewing individual people
- surveying people — asking people questions about issues of concern in their current unit.
- observing and recording
- researching
- apprenticing (older children only)
- peer teaching and learning/consulting to others
- writing reviews
- performing rock radio/films/drama
- debating/public speaking
- recording on tape readings of published works and created works
- working in teams, whole groups and individually to problem-solve, discuss, create
- writing books, reports, etc.
- learning writing skills

If children have special needs, the above activities are adjusted and modified to fit their abilities and to incorporate their best learning style.

A critical thinking game room is part of the curriculum. Included in this room are ancient games, spelling games, and modern-day strategy games. Children learn the following things from playing games:

- appropriate social interaction with others

- discussing directions
- following others' appropriate behaviors
- working out disagreements
- attending, concentration and memory recall
- using strategies to accomplish their individual or group goals
- using vocabulary
- reading and following directions
- classifying
- sequencing
- logical deduction
- factual information: science, math, geography, etc.

The language arts area should have a listening area. This is another great place for inclusion for a number of reasons. It is an easy activity for children who are non-verbal, non-motoric, or without hand use to participate in, and they can enjoy a tape of stories or music without a lot of effort. Do make sure the child is paired with at least one verbal child who reports to the teacher when the headphones have slipped off his ears or the tape has run out, so that the child with special needs isn't sitting there listening to nothing. This happens a lot.

It is also worth the time and effort to let the non-verbal child pick the story or music she wants to listen to. Whether it involves having the child raise her head, eye gaze or use a computer to communicate, it is very important to have children with special needs participate in choice making. *Just because a child can't talk doesn't mean she doesn't have preferences. Always assume children know more, understand more, and can do more than they are showing you.* Then you will never make a bad decision around how you treat a child, and quality inclusion will result.

As we discuss in the chapter on evaluations, it has been the habit of educators, therapists, and specialists to look at what a child can't do. *To be the best teacher for a child, you have to look at what she might do.*

Tables in the language arts area should be of varying heights so that children can sit on the floor, kneel or be in their wheelchairs.

Multicultural Activities

Children believe, until they are taught differently, that their world is everyone's world. Multicultural curriculum opens up a wildly exciting adventure for children. And there is such diversity with so many cultures that a teacher could create varied multicultural activities every day of the year and never run out of new topics. Most people know and understand how to teach multicultural education and its importance. We use these curricular elements extensively as experiences for the students and as subject matters for the students to work on the activities we have described in the *language arts* area. These are areas of learning that excite each child because they revel in the new and different ways that other cultures offer them to look at everyday activities. Or, costumes from earlier periods in the U.S. allow them to fantasy and develop dramatic materials, again from the perspective of learning an "exotic" perspective.

For example, for the coming year we have built a Japanese Tea House that will serve as a theme for all the children's activities during the coming year. In past years, we have had teepees which the children designed and painted with Native American symbols. The teepees housed peace pipes, books, pictures, posters, games, and dolls from various Native American tribes.

Every year we have a Santa's Workshop filled with art materials for the children to just go in and create whatever they want with no interference from teachers. This includes being able to use as much glue and sparkles as the children feel they need.

Recently we created a Drama Prop room where groups of students go and create stories and plays by picking a theme. One by one each child gets up and adds a character by choosing props and dressing up as the character. The plays/stories are then printed out by the children on the computer, artwork is added, and the resulting books are bound and added to the library by the school.

These kind of hands-on areas child-involving activities that require active constructive learning that is shared with the other members of the group in a cooperative effort. They add creativity and excitement to learning because they are very open-ended: each child can make a unique contribution to the group effort that draws from *her* interests. The open-ended nature of the activity also allows for all levels of participation by children of all abilities.

Our focus in this section, however, is on a multicultural education around special needs. It is very important that all programs, inclusive or not, spend time educating children about the lifestyles of people with special needs; but it is particularly important for a program which is inclusive. Beyond the curiosity factor about braces, wheelchairs, feeding tubes, etc., typical children need to understand the struggles of people with special needs. It automatically sets the stage for children to want to help their friends, and it develops deep commitment and compassion.

The best way to teach multicultural education about people with special needs is to have the children experience it. Careful attention needs to be given to designing the curriculum. For the program we developed, see Appendix 4. We created kits so that the material is at our fingertips, but the raw materials are available in any inclusive setting. There are formal kits commercially available for this if you don't wish to make your own; for information on one such kit, see Appendix 4.

Another very effective way to teach about special needs is to enlist the help of the children with special needs, in a sensitive fashion, to talk about how they feel. This can be done with non-verbal children if they have any method of communicating such as raising their hand to answer questions. It helps the whole program if the typical children can experience how their friends with special needs feel.

Manipulatives/Mathematics Teaching

Manipulatives are small pieces of materials — puzzles, Legos, teddy bear counters, dominoes, etc. — used to teach shape, size, color, one to one correspondence, addition, subtraction, multiplication and division. Cuisenaire rods, for example, are used to teach children number relations concepts. Children love manipulatives and can spend hours sorting and re-sorting.

However, manipulatives can be very inaccessible for children with severe motor problems. For example, setting a pile of manipulatives in front of Lauren is useless because of her hypotonia. It is almost impossible for her to pick one up. The effort is not only physically exhausting but frustrating for her: after all the work of attempting to pick it up and finally getting it, she usually drops it because she doesn't have the strength to sustain a grasp.

A principle of inclusion in general: activities such as these should never just be placed in front of a child incapable of using them. But if you observe carefully, too many times this is exactly what is done with children who can't walk or talk. They are set up with an activity, then deserted while the teacher works on controlling the more mobile and verbal children.

This is not to say that children with little ability to grasp manipulatives shouldn't use them. Quite the contrary. These children often need exactly this kind of work to strengthen grasp, to encourage choosing and reaching, to help teach switch work when necessary, and to improve overall fine motor skills. But it is important that these types of activities be directly facilitated by a staff member or a very tolerant peer who has been taught what to do.

Interaction with manipulatives is a very important activity for children with a variety of special needs such as processing problems, motor problems, and learning problems, and the teacher should make sure to take the time necessary to make the activity maximally beneficial.

In addition, our math programs incorporate our belief that children learn from doing. There are various components to our program, but a major piece is the use of Every Day Mathematics, an excellent math program which teaches concepts through hands-on activities (see Appendix 4 for information on this resource).

As you will see in our discussion of evaluations in Chapter Seven, we feel it is important to do individualized education for all children, and evaluation of children's progress needs to be specific and helpful. The following pages contain examples of our math evaluation forms. During each quarterly evaluation, these forms are used by placing the appropriate mark next to each skill: a *check mark* for a skill that has been achieved, *check-minus* for a skill that is still being worked on, or a *minus sign* for a skill that has not yet been accomplished. As you can see, these forms, once completed, allow a teacher to see at a glance what a child can do and what areas he or she needs to focus on. These ratings sheets are also intended to set forth what "core" accomplishments or facts a child should master in each area such as mathematics.

By March of our first year as an elementary school, we had to develop an eleventh- and twelfth-grade math evaluation form for Benjamin. This is the kind of individualized attention we feel all children deserve.

MATHEMATICS EVALUATION CHECKLISTS

EVALUATION KEY

✓ accomplished

✓— working on

— not yet accomplished

KINDERGARTEN MATHEMATICS (MINIMUM ACHIEVEMENTS)	SEPT	JAN	MAY
NUMERATION			
1 to 1 correspondence using sticks, blocks, etc.			
Counting #'s beyond 100			
Reading and writing #'s beyond 100			
Giving the # that comes before or after a specific #			

KINDERGARTEN MATHEMATICS (CONTINUED)	SEPT	JAN	MAY
Counting backwards			
Skip count by 2's to 40			
Skip count by 5's to 50			
Skip count by 10's to 100			
Use calculators beyond 100			
Number stories			
MEASUREMENTS			
Measuring the length, width, height of blocks etc. with ruler or tape measure			
Measuring distances using rulers			
Finding weight using scales and pan balance: > <, lighter, heavier, etc.			
Introduction to clock time			
Reading and writing time			
Introduction to area and volume using manipulatives			
GEOMETRY			
Shapes and their properties: circle			
triangle			
square			
rectangle			
trapezoid			
rhombus			
hexagon			
pentagon			
Using templates to make geometric patterns			
Introduction to graphs			
SIMPLE ADDITION			
SIMPLE SUBTRACTION			

FIRST GRADE MATHEMATICS (MINIMUM ACHIEVEMENTS)	SEPT	JAN	MAY
NUMERATION AND COUNTING			
Rote count beyond 100: by 1's			
by 2's			
by 5's			
by 10's			
Tally count: write # corresp, to # of tally marks & vice versa			
Knows # before or after a given # beyond 100			
Reading and writing #'s beyond 100			
Read and write 2-digit #'s			
Read and write 3-digit #'s			
PLACE VALUES			
Show a given fraction by folding paper and coloring the given part(s)			
Uses vocabulary to express mathematical ideas such as =, <, >			
OPERATIONS/RELATIONS			
Simple addition			
Simple subtraction			
Simple multiplication			
# stories using addition and subtraction			
GEOMETRY			
Polygons and their properties; triangle			
square			
rectangle			
pentagon			
hexagon			
Circles			
Three-dimensional solids using blocks, boxes and cans			
Understand faces, bases and vertices			

FIRST GRADE MATHEMATICS (CONTINUED)	SEPT	JAN	MAY
MEASUREMENTS			
Finding length, width, height			
Temperature reading			
Measuring height and weight			
Telling clock time			
Understanding: area			
perimeter			
volume			

SECOND GRADE MATHEMATICS (MINIMUM ACHIEVEMENTS)	SEPT	JAN	MAY
NUMERATION AND COUNTING			
Reading and writing 5-digit numbers			
Rote count beyond 1000 by: twos			
fives			
tens			
PLACE VALUE			
Ones			
Tens			
Hundreds			
Thousands			
Hundred Thousands			
Zero or a place holder			
NEGATIVE NUMBERS			
FRACTIONS			
Comparing fractions			
Equivalent fractions			
DECIMAL NUMBERS			
Expressing total amount as dollars and cents			
Odd and even numbers			
Number patterns and sequence			
OPERATIONS AND RELATIONS			
Master addition and subtraction			
Multiplication			
Division			
Comparing Fractions			
Problem solving using: Addition			
Subtraction			
Multiplication			
Division			

SECOND GRADE MATHEMATICS (CONTINUED)	SEPT	JAN	MAY
GEOMETRY			
Shapes and solids: triangle			
rectangle			
trapezoid			
rhombus			
square			
cylinders			
rectangular prisms			
Understands area and perimeter			
Can draw polygons			
Faces, bases, vertices			
MEASURES			
Understands: centimeters			
inches			
feet			
yards			
Converting inches to feet			
Understands: area			
capacity			
weight			
time			
temperature			
area and perimeter of polygons			
volume of solids			

THIRD GRADE MATHEMATICS (MINIMUM ACHIEVEMENTS)	SEPT	JAN	MAY
NUMERATION: Read and write whole numbers through 1,000,000			
PLACE VALUE; Ones			
Tens			
Hundreds			
Thousands			
Tenths			
Hundredths			
Thousandths			
Read and write decimal numbers			
FRACTIONS			
Find a fraction of a given number			
Write a given # as fraction or decimal			
INTEGERS			
Express change using + or -			
Understands meaning of %			
OPERATIONS AND RELATIONS			
Multiplication of whole numbers			
Simple division			
Addition of 4-digit numbers			
Subtraction of 4-digit numbers			
Problem solving involving: Addition			
Subtraction			
Multiplication			
Division			
Ordering decimal numbers			
Understanding the square of a number			
DATA COLLECTION AND ANALYSIS			
Collecting and ordering data			
Preparing: Tables			
Graphs			
Charts			

THIRD GRADE MATHEMATICS (CONTINUED)	SEPT	JAN	MAY
Interpreting graphs			
Understanding: mode			
median			
mean			
GEOMETRY			
Identifying polygons			
Understands perimeter			
Circles: Understands: Diameter			
Center			
Circumference			
Pi			
Triangles: Understands: Equilateral			
Isosceles			
Right triangle			
Three-Dimensional Figures: Understands similarities and differences of: prisms			
pyramids			
cylinders			
cones			
spheres			
Understanding: segments			
rays			
lines			
angles			
MEASUREMENT: Understands: Length			
Area			
Capacity			
Weight			
Time			
Volume expressed in cubic units			
Conversion of metric units of linear measure to another unit			
PATTERNS, RULES AND FUNCTIONS			
Observes patterns and relationships			
Can state the rule in a given pattern			

Science Activities

Through my consulting work, I have found that a large majority of classroom teachers do very little science education and actually admit to being afraid of teaching science because "I don't know how to teach it." Science is one of the best subjects to teach because children love it. They love experiencing new smells, tastes, textures. They love to know how things work and why things happen. The main reason a lot of teachers and parents hate these kinds of questions is that they don't know the answers and have to give an answer like "I don't know. Just because."

What parents and teachers often fail to realize is that in education, if a child is asking a question, you're already halfway there. They've asked the question because they are interested. If you have a child's interest, you have it made. The stage is already set with science because the children are so curious. Most subjects can be taught through science: reading, writing and math can be taught with a strictly science curriculum.

It is quite easy to develop a science curriculum if you are at a loss as to how to teach science. Just ask the children what they want to learn about. Make a list. Get books, read about the topic, and set up some kind of hands-on experiment(s). There are hundreds of books on science experiments for children — it really couldn't be easier. For some books we recommend, see Appendix 4.

And what is especially nice about science experiments is that everyone can get to do something, so it's really a group effort. Even the most physically challenged child can help pour a substance to help with the experiment. Inclusion in science is so easy. All the teacher needs to do is make sure each child gets to do something. And each child gets to experience the results of the experiment.

Computer Education

All schools need their computers to be accessible to students with special needs. This means that wheelchairs, chairs and walkers can get up to the computer table and that the child can get into a position which allows her to use the computer independently whenever possible. In addition, the computer itself needs to be accessible.

At this time, the best computers we have found for accessibility are Macintosh computers because they are designed with accessibility in mind. Several adaptive devices can be purchased which we consider a necessity if a program has non-verbal children who will most likely remain non-verbal. With these devices, the computer becomes a method of communication for the child. Please refer to Chapter 8 for an extensive discussion on adaptive devices for communication and their use.

The computer area should have a variety of educational software covering all subjects including reading, writing, art, science, math, history, geography, and social studies.

The computer is a very exciting tool to most children, mainly because they can control it to do what they want and can work independently. It is also one of the easiest tools to foster inclusion. All children want to use the computers, and all children like to be experts. They love to help their friends with switches or use the mouse together, hand over hand. When you put two kids at a computer, you can sit back and watch the magic happen, as long as a teacher monitors that the children are taking turns.

Good pairing of the children is very important. It is at the computer that I have seen some of the best work of our young integration specialists. These six, seven, and eight year olds can get more out of their peers with special needs than the staff or myself. This is the key to inclusion and to cooperative education. It's how it should be and it's what works best.

Group Time

Whenever the class gathers as a unit it is absolutely essential that all the children be at the same level, physically. The teacher needs to decide whether he wants the children in a circle in chairs, sitting on the floor, or standing. Once that is decided, the teacher needs to take the time to set up the child with special needs who needs special equipment to put her at the same level as her peers. For example, if the child can't sit on the floor without support, then she can be put in a corner chair which is designed for just this purpose. If the group is sitting in a circle, an adaptive chair would be used, and if the group is standing, the child might use her walker or wheelchair or be assisted by an adult.

No matter what, it is *very* important for an adult to take the 3 to 5 minutes it takes to change the equipment so the child is included. Teachers in a hurry often neglect this, which is wrong! Having the typical children sitting on the floor and the child with special needs up in a chair automatically excludes the child from eye contact and physical contact with peers. The child isn't as included as he/she can be. If you are a teacher, you should never be in such a hurry that a child is excluded.

Another important component of inclusion at a group time activity is having a helpful friend sitting next to the child to assist with hand movements during songs, hand raising during question and answer time, and holding objects during sharing time. If this isn't possible, or if the teacher feels it places too much responsibility on the typical child, then an adult should be sitting next to the child with special needs to assist in these activities.

It is critical that the child with special needs be enabled to participate. If the child has behavior problems, she should sit next to the teacher so that a touch on the arm can redirect the child. If the child has attention or processing problems, the teacher must use leading questions to help the child find answers. And the teacher should call the child's name, requesting he look at the speaker throughout the circle time. If the child is non-verbal, the teacher needs to directly ask questions of the child following with instructions for how the child is to answer the question. For example, if the child can raise his hand to answer yes/no questions, then the teacher would ask the question and say, "If the answer is yes, raise your hand by the time I count to five [or whatever amount of time is necessary]." If the child can hit a switch, then use that method. Whatever way the child is able to communicate should be used.

The teacher must realize that he has a responsibility to be the voice of the non-verbal child. The child can't yell, "Me, me! Call on me!" like her peers. The child can't reach up and wildly wave her hand in front of the teacher's face. At all times the teacher has to try and remember to think about how these children feel. Only with our help can their soul's desire be expressed.

Art Activities

All children, no matter how cognitively or motorically delayed, love art. Bright and contrasting colors gain immediate attention from young children. Gluing, painting, markers, crayons and so forth are all wonderful fine motor activities for young children.

Some young children are very sensitive to touching finger paints, glue, sand, and water. These children may have sensory integration problems, and these activities are very good for them but should be introduced gradually, with patience and sensitivity to the child's discomfort with these media.

There are inexpensive materials which can be bought to help young children without motor control hold crayons, markers, paint brushes, etc. Very simple devices can be created with cloth and Velcro by the teacher and/or occupational therapist. Or the child can just be assisted by his teacher or friend.

Easels are wonderful for painting, coloring, markers and printing. This activity demands that the child hold her wrist in a fixed position. This automatically works on strengthening her grasp for fine motor skills. For this reason, art activities should be set up at the easel rather than the table whenever possible. Again, these activities are good for all children for the same exact reasons. They teach creativity, color, fine motor, social, and writing skills.

Cutting is also an excellent fine motor activity. Special scissors can be bought which require very little hand pressure to cut paper. We prefer these for children and really feel that those little red and green scissors of years past, which are still used with young children, are horrible. They set up children to fail. Only the most talented scissor user can succeed with them — and these children, of course, are not the children who need cutting as a therapeutic activity.

Gross Motor Areas

There are several companies now making handicapped-accessible climbing structures and playground equipment. For existing structures, it is important to make them accessible by adding stairs or some other method of access that can let all children enjoy a climber. Some companies have even designed transfer stations so that children in wheelchairs can be transferred from their wheelchairs to the climber.

If, due to the nature of the structure or financial restraints, changes can't be made to the climber, the staff of the program need to make sure that all children are given a turn on the climber whenever it is being used, even if it means the staff have to carry the child onto it. Whenever this happens, every effort should be made to have the child help himself as much as possible.

Whenever dealing with children with special needs in an inclusive program, the team must think Independence/Inclusion, Independence/Inclusion all day every day, and then the child will generally get what he needs in the least restrictive environment. Just because something isn't easy to do doesn't mean the extra time and energy shouldn't be taken to make it happen — *it should be, all the time.*

Dance and Music Time

Music time is an easy activity to include children with special needs in. Listening to and discussing music holds no barriers. Students with hearing impairments can feel the vibrations of the music and use rhythmic instruments themselves. Use of instruments can easily be assisted by teacher or friend. It's one activity really enjoyed by everyone.

It is more difficult to include children in dance activities if the teacher is not sensitive to each child's mobility status. For example, having everyone hold hands and dance in a circle automatically excludes the child who can't stand independently. It is *not* acceptable to have that child on the floor in the middle of the group alone during each dance class. More appropriately:

- Do away with hand-holding and have the children dance in place so that children with walkers can participate.
- Have the children face each other's backs for dancing in a circle so that children in wheelchairs can participate.
- Have an adult hold the child up so the child can participate.
- Have everyone dance on their knees or sitting down so that children who can't stand can participate equally.

The child is excluded if she is not at the same level as at least half the class. If she is on the floor and everyone is standing, she is not included. Inclusive dance takes creativity, which a good dance teacher should already have, and sensitivity to these matters.

Other Activities

The following activities also belong in the array of activities that students can work with as part of their learning activities. While many of these are associated with preschool and kindergarten programs, we have found them to be useful and important in the elementary program.

Water play is probably one of the all-time favorite activities of young children — someone is actually giving them permission to get messy without reprimand. What is great about water is it gives excellent sensory input, teaches measuring, cause and effect, conservation, and fine motor skills, and is a very social situation in the classroom.

The only adaptations needed for a child who has special needs are supervision and accessibility. For example, one day the class was rotating around free-play activities, one of which was the water table. The teacher asked who wanted to do water table, and Marcus' eyes lit up, but he said nothing because he saw the water table was high. At the time he had casts on both legs and couldn't stand, and he figured he couldn't have a turn.

Two things were going on here: Marcus did not want to ask for help, and the teacher had to find a way that Marcus could reach the water table sitting while in a safe position. First, the teacher had to remind Marcus that he always needs to let us know what he wants or needs. Second, a way had to be found that Marcus could participate in the activity. The water table was moved next to the wall, and a tall stool put Marcus just to the right height so he could participate freely with his friends.

For some children it is necessary to have the teacher or a friend directly involved at the water table for safety reasons. Splashing water might cause a child with severe cerebral palsy to easily startle, tighten his muscle tone and have a very difficult time relaxing, which should be one of the positive effects of water play for this child. In order for the teacher to free herself to be with this child and four or five of his friends at the water table, a very controlled environment must be maintained during the play of the rest of the group. Picking children who play well together to use dress-up or blocks, or an area where fantasy play can go on with little supervision from the teacher, is crucial. It would be better to have the child with behavior problems right there at the water table in arm's reach of the teacher.

Interestingly, we have found that children with behavior problems are usually the favorites of the non-mobile, non-verbal children. They tend to touch and move and talk with the children who are non-verbal and non-motoric significantly more, and it's a positive interaction for both children.

Sand play is like water play in that it offers a variety of learning experiences. It does not need as much supervision because sand, unlike water, can be easily brushed off (except from eyes). It is an excellent activity for all children for social interaction, creativity, sensory input, measurement, and fine motor work. If you don't already have a sand or water table in your classroom, low on-the-floor tables are more accessible for all children. A corner seat, which helps children with motoric delays sit on the floor, might be a good investment and is quite inexpensive. Otherwise, a tall chair or stool with a method of securing the child from falling will work just as easily for a regular sand or water table. Inexpensive Velcro straps are a must for any program with children who need to be kept secure in a seat to prevent falling.

Dress-up/Housekeeping/Dramatic play is the easiest area to make accessible to young children with special needs, but it can also be the most difficult. A dress-up area needs enough room so a non-mobile child or a child with a wheelchair, crutches, or a walker can have enough space to be in dress-up. Physical accessibility generally isn't a problem. Having the child who is non-verbal or with attention problems be a real part of dramatic play is the problem. This is where true staff commitment to inclusion can be seen.

The children without special needs at Kids Are People School have been taught to include even their non-verbal friends in play. They give them roles such as daddy, mommy, the princess, etc., and then ask them questions knowing their method of communication. Their friend might raise a hand, eye gaze or smile to answer yes to a question such as "Do you want to dress up as a pirate?" or "Do you want to make dinner?" And then the child brings the toys needed to play.

Obviously, for this to really work takes direction, explanation, and sensitivity from both the staff and the children. Ongoing daily training by the staff of the children to be accepting, caring, and understanding of one another must be an integral part of the center philosophy for true integration to take place. This is especially true in an activity such as dramatic play where it is up to the children to include each other and take the extra time and energy sometimes needed.

Accessibility: How Do I Get Around in Here?

I can't imagine a worse feeling than to be locked into a body which won't work. Add to that not being able to tell someone what you need, and the entire feeling is claustrophobic. At least that's how I imagine some of the children in our care must feel. What could make this situation worse is if the people working with these children did not make the activities and opportunities of the program accessible to them so they could participate freely.

The last chapter discussed how to adapt the curriculum so it was accessible to them and they could participate freely. Perhaps more important is that these persons can move freely into and around the classroom. Even if one follows the federal standards for making buildings, bathrooms, phone areas, etc. accessible, a program can set up its classroom environment so that it is inaccessible to the children.

THE CLASSROOM ENVIRONMENT

Currently, traditional classrooms are set up with rows of desks. The large number of students per class and the small size of the rooms leave little access for a wheelchair. Often children in wheelchairs who cannot move the chair themselves are parked in the same place all day in their chair and moved at the whim of the adult. Most elementary school classrooms with their desks in the middle of the room make accessibility difficult to nonexistent. Early childhood classrooms are generally better because the learning areas are set up around the periphery of the classroom so there is more space to maneuver a wheelchair up to the areas.

If we can assume that classrooms will change for optimal inclusion potential in the ways we discussed in Chapter 2, we still have the issue of making learning centers accessible throughout the classroom. First, the learning centers should be set up around the perimeter of the room so there is a large open space for children to get independently from area to area. Once a child gets to that area, the next question is, are the facilities in that area accessible to each child, e.g., by wheelchair?

All door entrances need to be 36 inches wide for wheelchair access. For example, we are studying Japan at the elementary school this fall. We just completed building a Japanese-style house. The main issue for us in designing it was that it be accessible to all the children. The doorways have no doorjambs and are 36 inches wide. The space between the house and the next area is 36 inches wide so that children in wheelchairs can go down the corridor between the areas. Kimonos, masks, etc., are at wheelchair level so that children can get them themselves. This should be a key consideration whenever designing a new area.

If there is some reason the staff feels that the materials in an area should require the teacher's help for any child, then all the children should need help to get the material. For example, we have just created a drama/prop room. Many of the clothes and accessories are at child level for all the children to reach. However, some full (adult) length ball gowns and jackets are hung in a closet because they would be ruined if they were hung at child level. All the children will need to have the teacher assist them to use these clothes. Pictures of the clothes will be on a board so that children who are non-verbal can eye-gaze or touch the picture of what they want to wear. The make-up table we purchased was chosen because it was high enough, wide enough, and open underneath so a wheelchair could fit under it. The dressing rooms are wide open spaces with long mirrors so that wheelchairs can get in and children of all heights can see themselves.

Accessible to Peers

A principle we have enunciated frequently is that *every child must be at the same level as every other child at an activity*. The child who needs equipment to stand or sit must be included. If everyone is on the floor, don't leave the child in her chair. She isn't accessible to her peers.

Children tend to get wheelchairs because they get too heavy for the adults in their environment to carry. The attitude once a child is in a wheelchair is that that's where she now stays — it has good positioning and so forth. At Kids are People, we do not feel this way. At our school the children are seldom in their wheelchairs. First, wheelchairs are made big so that a child can grow into them because repeated replacement would be too costly. Consequently, they are too large for most preschool and elementary school equipment. They don't fit up to tables, computer areas, or listening centers. If these areas and equipment are adjusted to fit the wheelchairs the furniture becomes too big for the typical children. Most staff's response to this issue is to leave children in their wheelchairs not only because they don't fit anywhere, but also because the children are often heavy and/or a hassle to move.

For true accessibility for all students, each program needs to have a variety of appropriate chairs, walkers and prone standers for all areas, so that the children with special needs are not kept away from their friends. In wheelchairs, not only are they sitting high above their peers, but often they can't get in and up to the table because the seat and arms of the wheelchair are too high.

We find one main value to wheelchairs. That is getting to and from places. It is the only thing they are used for in our school. But children in wheelchairs are walked and/or stand several times each day to keep bones from getting brittle and to keep muscles stretched. We don't really like prone standers because they exclude the child from the group more than most equipment. We have just completed a design for, and are in the process of building, a standing table that is inclusionary.

Surveying the Scene

As important as it is to set up an accessible classroom, it's equally important to keep it that way. Doorways need to be kept unblocked, and open spaces which lead to each area need to be kept open. This kind of surveying of the scene needs to be ongoing by the school staff.

Teachers need to plan ahead. If for some reason something needs to be moved to allow access, this should be done ahead of time, not once the child gets up to the space and needs it moved. It makes the child feel dependent and helpless, like she is more work than the other students.

ACCESS TO THE WORLD

For the most part, the program staff have a great deal of control over accessibility within the classroom. Whenever designing a new center, think about the children you know and what they need, and it's very easy to design the space to be accessible. But how accessible is the rest of the world? Not very good but getting somewhat better.

Public Transportation

Our biggest gripe relates to our subway stop. A major component of our program is field trips in and about the city of Boston. The doors of our school open right onto a public subway stop — but the station isn't handicapped-accessible and won't be until the year 2000. If the subway were accessible, we could go with a minimum of hassle, without having to carry the children in wheelchairs on and off buses (which is embarrassing for some of them), and quickly. The world would really open up to us.

We can walk, but for many of our trips the distances are too far. Or we can take a bus; many buses are handicapped-accessible, but the children still need to be carried on and off the bus. While we don't physically mind doing this, it would be better if the children could do things for themselves. I therefore consider these buses only quasi-accessible. Also, the routes are inconsistent and don't go where we need to get to, or we have to change buses several times.

When I called to complain about this, several bus company employees told me to use The Ride, which is a wheelchair van available for people with wheelchairs. When I called The Ride, they said they could not accomodate the typical children. I explained our concept of inclusion — that if we put the children with wheelchairs all together on The Ride and the typical children on the subway we would be working against everything we were teaching the children: we'd be segregating them. While they understood, they still would not bend. There are accessible cabs, I was told — but we could not afford to bring the entire school somewhere in accessible cabs. So the system outside does not support our transportation needs as we see them.

Historical Landmarks

At Kids Are People School we believe that children learn best from experiential education. Part of our history studies is to end a topic with a field trip to a historical monument or site. Well, back in the 1700s, people were small, doorways were small, staircases were narrow and steep, and wheelchairs were nonexistent. Needless to say, historical landmarks are a difficult access issue. It's important to let the people who are doing the tour know that you have children in wheelchairs and that you intend for them to be accommodated. If you hear "Well, the first floor is [accessible] but the second floor isn't," then you need to have the person you are arranging the tour with agree that extra time will be given to your group to get the children up to the second floor and that people will be available to help. For the most part people are wonderfully accommodating.

Parks and Beaches

But everywhere we go, we must always deal with the issues around accessibility. For example, every Wednesday during the summer we go to a state park for the day, swimming and picnicking. The restrooms are so un-handicapped-accessible it is a crime. The wheelchairs can't even get into the stalls, so the children who can manage their own toileting can't. There are no bars for them to hold onto around the toilets. They need to be lifted out of their chairs outside the stall, while trying to get them into the stall which doesn't have enough room for two adults. You can't get past the door of the stall to turn around with the child, so you have to back into the stall. It's crazy. But what about adults who are used to being independent? It's a state park; it should be fixed.

There's a beautiful state park near where I live. It's along the ocean with quarries and woods. It's one of my favorite places. And there are beaches which are wonderful for long strolls, peaceful and relaxing. But people in wheelchairs can't enjoy these treasures of the world — there are no ramps along the beach for a wheelchair stroll.

Field Trips

It is very important when going on a field trip that all the children be included one way or another. For example, if you go to a place such as the Children's Museum, the children in wheelchairs want to try out things as much as the typical children. No matter how much of a hassle this may seem to you, get them out of their chairs and into the individual exhibits. If all the children are dancing in front of a screen that displays their shadows dancing, get the child in the wheelchair out and dancing. If the typical children are going to get a chance to scale the wall imitating rock climbing, get the child in the wheelchair out and help him do it. Don't ever let it be too much work.

As I discussed earlier, Marcus would not ask to do things. He'd wait hoping we would think of him. Kids often do this, and it's our job as people who care about these children to think about how they feel. Sometimes something may seem scary to a child. If the child has any method of communicating with you, you should ask him if he wants to do the activity. If he's a little cautious, reassure him that you will help and you won't let him get hurt. If he can't communicate, tell him what you are going to do and watch for any signs that he is unhappy or uncomfortable. If he is, then change the way you're doing it, or stop. Kids have a way of letting you know they don't like something. Don't assume just because they are non-verbal they don't have preferences or can't make choices.

Whenever possible, let the children's friends be the ones to help them. Let them push the wheelchairs. When going swimming, there are foam and plastic floating devices shaped like a boat with cloth body holders which children who would otherwise have to be held by an adult can be placed in. Depending on the child's body control, adjustments might need to be made for additional support. But the beauty of this device is that these children do not have to be attached to an adult's body. Their friends can push them around in the water, and they are independent. Of course, with water, careful adult supervision is necessary at all times for all the children.

Sidewalk Accessibility

Most sidewalks in Boston now have ramps for wheelchairs, but often the ramps are only in one place, causing the teacher to have to push a wheelchair into the road to go around. Access ramps should be in two places, to cross the main roads and the side roads. Why weren't ramps put in both places? Maybe if whoever designed this had to get around in a wheelchair, they'd decide ramps need to be in both places.

Three rules of thumb around accessibility:

1) Whenever possible, set things up so that the child can be as independent as possible, even if it takes more time.
2) Whenever possible, have the child's peers help instead of the adult. This can be children with special needs helping other children with special needs as well as the typical children helping.
3) If a place you go to isn't accessible, do whatever it takes to include all children. Use creativity, and if the children with special needs can't be included, don't bring *any* of the children there. Then complain loud and clear about it not being accessible. These days you never know — you might be the cause of a place becoming accessible.

CHAPTER SEVEN

Evaluation: To Label or Not To Label?

So you have this child who is not within the typical developmental milestones. What do you do? After talking to parents, you generally set up an evaluation. Most of the time, if the child is three or over, a full evaluation is performed by a team of experts from the public school system. The evaluations generally include medical, psychological, speech and language, fine motor, gross motor, and social assessments. The purpose of these assessments is to put together an individual educational plan, or IEP.

If the child is under three and there have been no previous genetic or congenital concerns, the parents, pediatrician or child care providers are generally the first people to notice problems. Often the child is referred for evaluations around specific issues, e.g., not yet walking at 17 months old. Whether it's a global evaluation or a specific concern being looked at, the results are the same: reports talking about weaknesses and, hopefully, strengths are written.

There are several things to consider when using a report to help a child make positive changes in specific areas of delay.

How accurate is the report?

1. On that particular testing day, were the circumstances surrounding the testing optimal, or could they have distorted the results? These are important issues to consider when looking at an evaluation, since these factors can depress the child's level of functioning.

- Is the child overly shy or cautious around strangers? The evaluator is generally a person who is a stranger to the child.
- Evaluation is often done in a strange, maybe scary place — a school, clinic or hospital. Does the child get disoriented or intimidated in unfamiliar surroundings? Many children with Down Syndrome, Attention Deficit Disorder, or processing problems test poorly in unfamiliar surroundings.

- The child must be healthy and well rested to do his best in a testing situation. If the child is not, the report may not accurately reflect the child's ability. Did the child sleep well the night before? Had the child been healthy for the past couple of weeks? Had he eaten breakfast?
- Testing should be done in the morning whenever possible. Under no circumstances should a child spend an entire day going from one evaluation to another — that's totally unfair and unproductive, except for the clinicians.
- The environment must be appropriate, child-friendly, and free from distractions. We have seen children tested in environments that we as adults couldn't concentrate in. One time a child with global cognitive delays was sat on a table in a school hallway and evaluated. No wonder the psychologist thought this three year old child was functioning at a six month old level.
- Was the evaluator well rested, not rushed, and a person who should evaluate children — warm, caring, able to be funny and silly if necessary to elicit responses?
- Did the evaluator do her homework? Was it obvious she had the basic background information on the child? Had she interviewed the parents, teachers and other professionals who had key knowledge of this child? Had she read recent reports before evaluating the child? We have received reports from neurologists, psychologists and behavioral management specialists which have been totally off the mark because they never bothered to get any information from us or other sources, and often, we were the only program the child had attended for years.

2. Does the report give an overall true picture of the child?

- In reading the report, does this sound like the child you know?
- Does the report discuss strengths you know the child has?

3. Does the report include specific classroom recommendations that:

- Are realistic to implement? Can the recommendations be carried out by the existing staff with the available equipment in the available space?
- Address specific areas of concern? Does the report address the questions originally asked which brought this child to the evaluation in the first place? For example, we have sent children for speech evaluations and gotten back an entire report discussing only the difficulty the evaluator

had setting limits with the child.
- Incorporate the child's strengths to help improve his weaknesses? For example, if the child has poor attention and difficulty focusing on tasks, does the report incorporate activities the child enjoys doing which can be adapted creatively to address academic areas?
- Are safe to implement for this child? Were the child's overall abilities considered? For example, a report might recommend that a child catch himself 80% of the time when a loss of balance is elicited. For a child with low muscle tone or brittle bones, this may not be a general skill you want practiced in the course of the child's day. Specific safety instructions need to be dispensed with the recommendation. What may seem obvious to some, we know from experience, is not to other staff or programs.

Parental Response

It is important to help the parents deal with reports from evaluators. We have had parents say that they "live from report to report." Since this is the case, consider the following.

Be objective when reading the report. If you, as the professional who knows this child, disagree with elements of the report, express your disagreement, but be able to specifically support your position. Give the evaluators the benefit of the doubt. Call and talk with them about the parts you disagree with. The report may not have been clear or you may have misinterpreted it.

If you feel the report is unfair because of the conditions under which the testing was done, something surrounding the testing day, or if the evaluator is really off the mark, recommend to the parents that they seek another opinion. Most likely this evaluator saw no more than an hour of this child's abilities. Also, the evaluator is human — you don't know that he/she didn't have a fight with his/her spouse that morning, a sick child at home, a recent death in the family, or whatever. In addition, some evaluators are just not good and shouldn't be doing this work.

If the report has good recommendations, support them to the parents and recommend they be implemented immediately. Make sure all staff working with the child read the report and implement the changes in the child's program in the same way. This is especially important around positioning issues and learning methods to be used.

If the report is accurate in your opinion but the parents have trouble dealing with it, or have been denying what their child really is capable of doing at this time, use the report as a way to:

- Set realistic expectations. Let them know that you "generally" agree with the report, try to state some strengths you see not mentioned in the report, and specifically discuss what can be done in each area of weakness to help make positive gains.
- Find out what specifically about the report the parents do not feel is accurate. They may be right. The report may not cover positive changes the child has made. If you agree, indicate to the parents that they are right and that you will add those accomplishments to the child's file. Then do it.
- Motivate the parents to get more involved. For example, if a child with very low muscle tone could benefit from extra strengthening on the weekends, let the parents know this is something they can do to help make changes.

Give parents power. Some may feel helpless; others may feel more powerful, but may need their energy channeled to focus constructively on the child. Often how their child is doing feels like a direct statement of how they are doing as parents. But don't make parents *feel* they have to do "therapy" or "work" with their child — their child needs them to be parents first. The exception is when you're dealing with a medical necessity, such as a child who has to be stretched to prevent surgery. Then it is imperative to impress upon the parents that they must follow through on the home program.

Of course this must be done without criticizing or judging the parents. It's easy to say a parent should be doing this or that because we love their child. But we do not walk in these parents' shoes. Often they are looking down the road 20 years and feeling stuck with a child who will always be dependent on them for all their needs. This is a very difficult thing for anyone to face the future with. So be supportive and try not to judge them.

Be honest. If changes really have not occurred, state why. For example:

A 3 year old we worked with had a severe seizure disorder which was controlled by medication. She came to us not walking or talking, not making eye contact or following directions, and with no self-help skills. In the course of the year in which she was with us, she made gains in all of these areas. One day after several months of progress she came in with more delays than when she had entered the program. After several attempts at eliciting some response from her and getting none, we talked to the mom and had her referred to the neurologist. The little girl had had a severe stroke in her sleep.

We had to responsibly be honest with the mom and let her know that there really was no guarantee that her daughter would regain the small gains she had made, nor that another stroke wouldn't happen again even if she did make progress.

Obviously, this is an extreme example, but honesty is the best policy.

When the Child Doesn't Match the Diagnosis

What happens if you have a child referred to you and after a few weeks of classroom observation you're seeing a completely different child from the reports? Let's take Afanwi for example.

Kids Are People was asked to accept Afanwi for three months until he turned three, at which time the evaluation team was going to place him in a residential year-round program. The reason we were asked to take him was because we were one of a few programs at that time which accepted children under three with special needs into a five day per week full day program with typical children. And more importantly, the state was not responsible for Afanwi until he was three.

Before Afanwi was accepted to Kids Are People, I went to a team meeting at an area hospital where Afanwi had had a full evaluation. I was told that he could not feed himself or chew, so he had to be fed and his food had to be ground up. He had no affect, i.e., he did not change the expression on his face in response to others or circumstances in his environment. People did not interest him; he made no eye contact, had no speech and had bizarre ritualistic self-stimulation patterns. His only "normal" skill was in motor, and he was considered extremely agile and hyperactive. His mom was told "he's like a bird, there is nothing there."

On my first meeting with Afanwi, he ran all over the school. At one point he threw a book. I picked up the book, handed it to him and said "I'm sorry, we don't throw books. It hurts the books and you could hurt someone." He looked me straight in the eye and threw the book at me. That was the first inkling that maybe he wasn't so "birdlike" after all.

Over the next two months, we observed several other incidents which did not fit the Afanwi presented at the team meeting. We happened to take the school to the circus and we gave the children popcorn. Afanwi took the popcorn from his friend and started chewing it. A few days later we had a birthday party for a child in Afanwi's class. Afanwi picked up the spoon and started feeding himself cake and ice cream. A few days after that I observed Afanwi whispering to another child in the class. I called the child over and said, "Did Afanwi just say something to you?" He said, "Yes, he said 'play with me.'" At this point no adult in Afanwi's life had heard him talk, and for several months he did not talk with us or make eye contact, so we always had him work with very verbal children and "caught" him in several conversations.

Right after he first spoke, I called up the neurologist who had headed the evaluation team and told her what was going on. Luckily for Afanwi, she was very honest with me. She told me that the team had been divided right down the middle. Some people suspected Afanwi was capable of more, but since there was no way to prove it and his mother reported the same behavior at home, they felt they must go with the more serious recommendations.

I asked that Afanwi be allowed to stay at Kids Are People. She agreed, as did the mother, although at this time the school systems never placed children in private regular education programs, especially when they had these kinds of issues. Afanwi stayed at Kids Are People for three years with no funding — it was the best money we ever spent. He was given speech and language therapy five days per week, mainly to get him to have to talk with an adult, although he had significant speech and language delays once he did start speaking. Occupational therapy was given to Afanwi for sensory integration issues two times per week.

When it came time for Afanwi to go to first grade, we went to a mediation to get him placed out of his district in a program which allowed him to be integrated. At the time, the public school system in his town did not integrate children with special needs except at recess, gym, etc. We could not risk Afanwi being placed in a segregated classroom with children with special needs who would provide negative models, where he might slip back into his own little world.

Over the course of the next year I made several trips to his new school specifically around discipline problems. The connection was crucial in keeping Afanwi on track behaviorally.

In the end Afanwi's diagnosis was attention deficit disorder. He was found to be highly intelligent. His math and reading skills were well above grade level. He currently attends a regular educational classroom without any outside services. His only area of delay appears to be in social skills.

I can't help but think about what might have happened to Afanwi if he had gone to the originally recommended placement. And while this may seem extreme, it is a perfect example of why evaluations are *always* to be taken for what they are — a few people's opinions of where a child is now and what he may be capable of. Afanwi's is not the only story of this kind at Kids Are People School, and if it could happen several times in our experiences, think how often it happens in the general population.

An Evaluation is Just an Evaluation

As the above example illustrates, not only can evaluations be misleading, detrimental and completely wrong, but an evaluation is really just an evaluation. Even when they're accurate, what's their purpose? Many times they are helpful in indicating small changes in classroom design or curriculum which can make big differences for children. For example:

> Esther needs to be given extra time to answer questions. She gets nervous and just gives any answer trying to please the teacher and evaluators. Esther takes a little longer to process the question and then organize the answer to verbalize it correctly. This is written in all of our evaluations so that whenever Esther is tested, if she should go to a new program, she will be given the extra time necessary to make her feel secure enough to get the "right" answer — which she can do 95% of the time.

Our biggest gripe about evaluations for children with special needs is that evaluations are designed by someone somewhere testing what are "normal" skills for the general population. When our children with special needs are tested on these skills, the result is the most prejudiced, unjust, cruel thing that can be done.

For example, there is a little boy I know who can't talk or move. He is very intelligent, yet he would score very low on an IQ test — profoundly mentally retarded — which he isn't! Half the test is verbal skills, the other half is performance skills. He can't do either. The IQ test, and every other test designed to test skills, assumes that the individual has verbal skills and performance skills (generally, use of hands), among other things.

How do I know this child is intelligent? There are three things I go by to judge intelligence in children who are non-verbal and/or non-motoric.

1) Is there intelligence in the eyes — are they making eye contact or observing their surroundings? (of course this is not a criterion for a child who is blind)
2) Do they have a sense of humor?
3) Are they manipulative?

Understanding humor and attempting to manipulate others to get what you want are two rather involved intellectual processes. If a child can do these things, there is much more to that child than he presents by our usual evaluation standard. Afanwi is an excellent example: he had manipulated an entire team of specialists and all other adults in his environment into believing he was incapable of anything. What a wonderful little world he created having everyone doing everything for him.

Another child the IQ test is unfair to is Esther. A large portion of the test is timed. Esther definitely needs extra time. I don't know how many times I've read in her evaluations "she got the answer right eventually but she didn't receive credit because the time was up." How unfair!

Now some people reading this will say yes, it's unfair, but in the real world we have to work within a specific time frame. In the future in taking tests she'll have to complete them on time. But this is just how the *world* is unfair to people with special needs. I have found Esther to be one of the most creative children I have ever worked with. She can make up beautiful, in-depth stories from her imagination, far surpassing peers who are her own age or older and who are strong in all academic skills. So if Esther wants to be a writer, should the timed SAT's keep her from getting into college; should *any* tests keep her from her goals? Should the fact that she will most likely always need a computer to produce written work, due to the severe weaknesses in her hands, prevent her from attending any classes she chooses to take? In other words, should the results of an unfair IQ test, or the necessity of specialized equipment, prevent Esther from striving for goals and becoming the best she can be?

Another example of an unfair test is the Peabody Picture Vocabulary Test. It is routinely used to evaluate children with speech delays — to give them a *score*, a *result*. I have looked at some of those pictures, heard children's answers, and thought they were right only to have the evaluators say that's not the answer "they" were looking for. Some of the pictures are so unclear that I had in my mind the same answer as the child gave and I can't figure out what was wrong.

This test, like the IQ test, is very long. A lot of children start falling apart due to fatigue and lack of concentration rather than that they don't know the answers. For a child with low muscle tone such as Esther, having to sit for so long depresses her ability to perform well.

The most beneficial service the medical community could give to children with special needs is to stop worrying about scores and put together a developmental sequence evaluation which doesn't look at scores or ages, but instead looks at the child's strengths — what he or she can do, any missed development sequences, and recommendations for retrieval of skipped skills. Does it really matter that a child is 2 months behind her normal peers? Isn't it more important to say Ricky needs to focus next on high kneeling and protective responses motorically, or Jane needs to work on letter sounds? After all, when do we stop comparing? You don't see in reports "Joey is an 18 year old functioning at a 16 year old level," because it doesn't make sense for the student, and it doesn't help the school staff structure an appropriate program for him. No more does it make sense to say a 4 year old is functioning at a 20 month old level. In both instances it may tend to reduce the staff's willingness to challenge these students since they "can't" achieve at "normal" levels.

The bottom line is that people make a lot of money from testing and developing tests, but most of these evaluations and testings do not have a positive impact on changing a child's life. The results do tend to negatively impact these children, adding stress, discouragement, and panic to parents' lives.

Factors to Consider when Evaluating Children

1. Has anything happened recently in this child's life to change his or her typical behavior?

- A move.
- Death of someone close or important to the child.
- Hospitalization or serious illness of the child or someone close to the child.
- Problems between parents or a separation or divorce of parents.
- Loss of a pet.
- Problems with any siblings or close friend.
- Witnessing a random violent act.

2. Is there any reason that the behaviors observed in the evaluation aren't typical of the child?

- The child didn't sleep well the night before the screening.
- The child didn't eat.
- The child is getting sick.
- The child is just getting over being sick.
- The child had an argument with someone prior to the screening.
- The child is very shy and slow to warm up.

There may be others factors to add. You may want to consider a brief pre-screening survey. Or at least try to get information on these factors from the parents on the day of the testing.

Observations Which Can Be Transient

- Child will not interact with others and tries to cling to parent.
- Child is all over the room touching everything in sight.
- Child will not follow teacher directions.
- Child is aggressive with others.
- Child does not appear to hear you consistently.
- Child will not talk or attempt communication.
- Child does not attempt activities.
- Child cannot remained focused on task and is fidgety.
- Child is whiny and demanding.

Observations Which May Not Be Transient

Motor Problems
- Is the child's gait awkward and clumsy?
- Does the child's upper body seem weak? Shoulders slumped?
- Does the child appear to lead with his/her upper body?
- Does one side of his/her body appear to be significantly weaker than the other side?
- Does the child slightly drag his/her arms or legs (one, one of each, both of one)?
- Is there any evidence of weakness in the facial muscles: overly wet lips, slight drooling, slurring of words, open mouth, tongue slightly hanging out?
- Does the child have weakness in hands: weak grasp, immature pencil hold, slight pressure when forming letters or drawing, looseness at wrist?

Sensory Integration Problems

- Does the child seem hypersensitive to touch? Withdraws from hugs, pats etc?
- Does the child avoid water play, sand play, finger painting or any other medium which involves wetness textures, differences in temperatures?
- Is the child hypersensitive to changes in lighting, loud noises, changes in movement, wind, changes in environment (in extreme cases the child may get upset going for walks, going in elevators, etc.)?
- Does the child have self-stimulation behaviors which appear to calm him/her down? Finger flicking, bouncing, rocking, humming, and so forth?
- Does the child seem slow to respond, confused, unfocused, in his/her own world?

Speech and Language Problems

- Child cannot or chooses not to talk and parent reports that child doesn't speak. This can indicate one of several possible problems, and augmentative communication may be necessary.
- Child speaks, but cannot be understood. This indicates a possible articulation or expressive language problem.
- Child looks confused, afraid or deliberately ignores direct questions asked of him/her. This indicates a possible receptive language delay or processing problem.
- Child's answers to questions have little to do with the question asked. This is probably a concern only if it happens several times.
- Child speaks in disjointed, choppy phrases. This is probably a concern only if this is continual; remember, these children could be very nervous at this new situation in an unfamiliar, perhaps scary place. It is important to ask parents if these are typical ways the child communicates.
- Child pulls peers, adults, etc. by the hand, or points to what he/she wants or needs without speaking.

Behavioral/Emotional Problems

- Child is deliberately destructive to classroom objects.
- Child is deliberately dangerous to himself or others.
- Child is extremely overactive and parent reports that this is typical behavior for their child.
- Child displays bizarre, ritualistic behaviors.
- Child is unable to follow one-part directions and parent reports that this is typical behavior.

- Child does not attend to one of three different activities after three attempts for more than a few minutes.
- Child's conversation is disjointed, disassociated, irrelevant and/or inappropriate.
- Child appears unaware of his/her environment and parent reports that this is typical behavior.

There are other behaviors you may want to add to these lists, but this is a good beginning.

EDUCATION AFTER EVALUATIONS

Medical and psychological reports provide a helpful overall picture of a child, his relevant history and medical and neurological status with implications for his probable course. For example, if there is a lesion in the speech center of the brain and the child is non-verbal, augmentative communication is the most likely direction to go. Knowing this can save valuable time for the child in program planning and implementation.

Clear and concise educational evaluations which point out specific areas of weakness with common sense recommendations of methods for teaching can also be useful.

Conversely, making a vague or incorrect diagnosis because the specialist doesn't know what's wrong is irresponsible, useless and potentially counterproductive to the child. Currently, the favorite diagnoses being handed out for children with emotional/behavioral problems and delays in other areas are:

Autism;
Pervasive Onset Disorder;
Pervasive Developmental Delay;
Attention Deficit Disorder; and my favorite,
Pervasive Developmental Delay with Autistic-like tendencies.

For all of the above cases and several other diagnoses not mentioned, the treatment from our perspective is the same: a slow, steady developmental focus on academic skills, appropriate social skills and behavioral changes, and a developmental approach to motor, speech, and language skills.

If a child cannot walk or talk and is intellectually intact, you should work on the developmental sequences of motor skills, but it is equally imperative to find a method of communication for that child. It is important to unlock that child from his body and find a way to let him make his needs, wants, desires, and thoughts about the world known to the people in his world. Finding a way for a child to communicate is the greatest gift a program can give. For more information on augmentative communication, please refer to Chapter 8.

There is no mystery here. All persons involved in education who work with children with special needs — parents, teachers, and specialists — must know and understand the fully "normal" developmental sequence in all areas of development. To be able to look at a child, see a motor weakness, and understand how that can impact the other developmental areas of a child's functioning is critical. Colleges and universities need to focus the education of new teachers on an understanding of basic developmental skills.

To construct a more useful evaluation tool for educators, we must develop a uniform, informal evaluation method which focuses on developmental sequences rather than comparing the child to his "normal" peers. It shouldn't look for a score, but should focus the examiner on the child's strengths. This type of test would result in a common sense understanding of what the child has accomplished and of how stable his accomplishments are in each developmental area. By trying to help the child work on the next steps in each developmental sequence for him, one could determine how easily, and with what aids, supports or adaptations, it may be possible to move him along this sequence in each area. This information would suggest practical educational approaches and specific manageable adaptations to his work in school and to his home to help him learn, move, communicate.

The Individual Education Plan

Individual Education Plans (IEPs) are designed for each child with special needs to describe the specific goals and objectives he or she should pursue. We certainly believe in individualized education — but the IEP system in practice does not live up to this ideal.

- The IEP planning team often excludes the people who will implement the plan: the child's own teachers.
- For private schools, the IEP is often created by the public school who is paying for the private placement. The people creating the IEP do not even know the child, which is absolutely ridiculous.
- The receiving teacher receives the IEP well after the child appears.
- In an inclusive context (where the teacher may not be extensively trained in special needs education), does the receiving teacher understand it? Can he or she implement it without some sustained staff support?
- Many times, the IEP isn't even looked at all year long until the next year's IEP needs to be created.

- To make an individual plan which will last a year is ludicrous. It once again speaks to how we don't see children as individuals. Some children will reach all the goals and objectives in the first quarter of the year, making that year's IEP obsolete after only three months. Other children will work on the same goals and objectives year after year.

Part of the reason for the uselessness of the IEP is that it is incredibly cumbersome and unrealistic. And more than one school system that I know computerized their goals and objectives so that the child has to be fit into the existing lexicon of goals and objectives created by a group of adults. So much for *individual* education plans.

Rethinking the IEP

It would be so much better if quarterly assessments were done showing where the child is in each area of development and what the child should be working on *now*! A checklist type of format based on developmental sequences in the different areas of development (such as gross motor, fine motor, sensory, daily living, reading, writing, math, speech and language skills), with sections for comments and a beginning statement describing the child, would be much more sensible, appropriate and easy to use; it should be easy to fill out so that it is not too time-consuming to do more than once per year.

Appendix 3 contains an example of a Daily Living Skills Checklist which can easily be used by everyone involved with the child. Like the math evaluation forms featured in Chapter 5, it is used by placing the appropriate mark next to each skill: check mark for an achieved skill, check-minus for a skill being worked on, minus for a skill not yet accomplished. Specific simplified checklists on this model could be combined from each area of performance to make an educational plan.

A narrative report should be done for children who are very low functioning, because their educational course in an inclusive setting needs more detailed recommendations, and careful attention paid to implementing them, in order to assure inclusive involvement.

But no matter what, educational plans should be created by the people in the school who are teaching the child. The reports should not be for an entire year. They should be simple to understand and refer to. They should be written in a fashion which parents, specialists, teachers and aides can all understand and work with.

CHAPTER EIGHT

Specialists: How Do They Fit In?

Children with special needs come to programs in need of special help in the areas of gross and fine motor, speech and language, perceptual and sensory integration, and general developmental skills.

Out come the physical therapist, the occupational therapist, the speech and language therapist, and a variety of specialists to deal with these special needs. Historically, these therapies have been administered on a one-half-hour session, twice a week, on an individual basis, and generally in a medical setting. Unfortunately this type of intervention does not work, or at least is not of optimal benefit to young children's growth and development.

If a child will eventually gain independence from a therapist working to strengthen his muscles twice a week for one-half hour, how much faster and easier will a child gain skills if his parents and teachers have the knowledge to assist the child with performing the exercises throughout his day, every day, all day? If a child will begin to produce sounds through repetition with his speech therapists, how much sooner will he produce sounds if his peers, parents and teachers encourage him consistently on a daily basis?

MAXIMIZING BENEFITS

The key to optimal development is integrated instruction across the elements of the curriculum. For students who require specialist services, their progress is increased when this work is supported in the classroom and also at home. We have found four important ingredients to maximize developmental gains for children with special needs.

Imitation of Typical Children

We feel the single most important factor in the rapid, remarkable gains of the children at Kids Are People School is the imitation of the typical behavior of their friends. Hundreds of pages have been written on the fact that young children learn by imitation and modeling. This fact has never been verified as clearly as by the young children with special needs in our program.

The desire to move, to talk, to belong, is so great that often the child and his friends do more therapy than the therapist. Therefore, it makes sense to put a child who is developmentally delayed in a program with children who are not. The imitation of what is "normal" fosters normal development. For example, put a child with serious behavior problems and autistic-like qualities with children who are developing typically, and imitation, peer pressure, and consistent expectations will change that child's behavior a lot quicker than putting that same child in a class in which all the children exhibit abnormal behaviors and the child has no positive role models to imitate. In fact, in the segregated situations, peer pressure may worsen the problems: the child may pick up through imitation more bizarre, unique, and inappropriate behaviors than he could have thought up on his own.

> This was certainly true of Afanwi. He came to us with a diagnosis of Pervasive Onset Disorder and autism. He was scheduled to be with us only for three months until he turned three and then could be placed in a non-integrated program for children with autism. It was the direct imitation of his friends at Kids Are People School that allowed us to get a peek into Afanwi and led us to keep him in our program. Today Afanwi is in a regular elementary school program. He is diagnosed with Attention Deficit Disorder. He is a highly intelligent child with some behavioral problems, and serious processing and sensory integration issues. He has grown to become a successful fourth grader.

Given what we know of Afanwi, if he had in fact been placed in the program for autistic children, he could now be another lost child with serious emotional problems and bizarre ritualistic behavior such as licking his teacher's shoes, which was his favorite pastime seven years ago.

Individual or Small Group Therapy

One-on-one or small group therapy is extremely important to children with special needs. The expertise, skill, and medical knowledge the therapist brings to the program cannot be substituted, and is very important to the children's development and success. At Kids Are People School, we have identified certain specific situations that can maximize the therapeutic benefits the children receive.

- The traditional therapeutic sessions of one half hour are too short for a young child. Most people would think that more than that would be too tiring. In fact, 45 minutes to one hour works much better, because getting the child to attend and perform at the level needed could take ten minutes at the beginning and end of the session. This really leaves only ten solid minutes of therapy. With the longer session, behavioral and transitional issues, etc., can be dealt with and there is still a good solid chunk of time for real work.
- Some children, especially those with severe physical involvement or serious attentional problems, may need individual therapy. To not segregate or overly identify the children with special needs, the activity room usually has more than one child in the room at a time.
- Children can pick a friend to go to therapy with them. The friend does not have to have special needs. This works great because the children without special needs do not feel left out; the child with special needs feels less stigmatized and more normal; and the therapy is de-mystified for the other child. Most of all, therapeutic activities are great for all children, whether it be tossing bean bags, bouncing on therapy balls or sequencing picture cards. Whenever possible, therapy done within the classroom, with a friend, is optimal.

Integration of Therapy into the Classroom

In a well-organized, well-run program, children receive a variety of experiences in all areas of development. All children learn how to use their bodies and minds skillfully. Children with special needs often require extra help to move, communicate and learn.

Since it is appropriate for a program to focus on helping children increase their skill motorically, verbally, socially, and academically, all program activities are beneficial for all children whether they have special needs or not.

Ideally, the skills learned and practiced during a therapy session, whether one-on-one or small group, should be carried over into the classroom. While this may seem to be a difficult task, it can be done quite easily with very little or no modification to existing activities found in ordinary classrooms. This process can become an everyday event when teachers know what skills the child is working on that are ready for partial or full support in the classroom. They can work with the specialist in advance, identifying activities that will support the skill. They are then prepared when the specialist tells them the child is ready for more extensive work on the skill — in class and at home.

Fine Motor Activities. The pediatric occupational therapist specializes in helping young children with special needs to learn muscular control and coordination, self-help skills (dressing, eating, etc.) and helps them with sensory integration issues for better control over their environment.

> The occupational therapist working with Esther teaches her buttoning skills. Carryover in the classroom would be to encourage Esther to dress and undress the dolls in the dress-up area. No special planning or material is needed, yet Esther is continuing to practice a necessary skill.

For a child who is severely involved, things can be more complicated. With the help of the therapist, a teacher can easily learn the best methods of encouraging such skills as independent eating. Learning the best way to position a child can make things easier on both the child and the teacher. For example, a five year old child with severe cerebral palsy with tonic neck reflexes still intact will be able to feed himself much more easily with his head slightly turned in the right direction. It does not take a great deal of time or energy for a teacher to learn these kinds of things; a onetime demonstration by the parent or therapist is usually enough.

Some other classroom materials and activities which can be used by all the children on an ongoing basis and which are great for fine motor work are: stringing large beads, sewing cards, clothespins, musical instruments, tracing shapes, painting, clapping to music, wind up toys, zippers, snaps, laces, pegs, Colorforms, playing checkers, cards, tiddlywinks, playdough, scissors, Legos, etc.

If a teacher is given a basic understanding of the needs of the children in his or her group, the everyday curriculum and materials can be turned into a therapeutic experience for the children with very little effort.

Gross Motor Activities. The pediatric physical therapist works with children to help them learn large muscle control, to strengthen muscles and reduce joint stiffness, normalize tone and generally learn gross motor skills such as crawling, standing, walking, balance and coordination. While the therapist works on specific skills within the therapy session, activities in the classroom can help the child practice the skills learned in the therapeutic session. Safety is always an issue to consider when working with children, but most playground activities can be modified for the child with special needs to make daily gross motor activities fun and beneficial. For example, marching, dancing, kicking, throwing or catching a ball, climbing, swinging, and hopping are all part of the day in most early childhood programs and are also excellent therapeutic gross motor activities.

While it may not be obvious, activities as routine as a long walk or climbing up and down stairs are excellent therapeutic activities for children such as Marcus, Sean, Esther, and Danielle.

Speech and Language Activities. The pediatric speech therapist works with children to encourage communication skills. The focus is on expressive and receptive speech and language skills, oral motor skills, auditory processing and memory skills, and articulation. In some cases when a child is seriously language deficient, alternative means of communication are taught.

All early childhood and primary grade programs should foster a language-rich environment. Singing, reading stories, children creating their own stories, are all part of a daily curriculum. These activities, along with specific teacher-directed activities, will automatically cause carryover from therapy.

A specific practice such as having a child continually use words to express his needs and desires is very helpful in therapy and in the classroom. Having consistent expectations and placing demands on a child who can talk, but is manipulative and tries not to talk, will force the child to realize she has to start speaking to others in order to get what she wants. The adults working as a team can change the child's non-verbal behavior if home, therapy, and classroom expectations are firm and consistent.

> An excellent example is Afanwi, who refused to speak to the adults in his environment. Working with his mother, his therapist and his teachers, and expecting Afanwi to use words and then sentences to express himself, has resulted in Afanwi, who once was labelled as autistic, becoming a very verbal child who is reading above grade level.

High, Realistic Expectations of the Children

Over and over again we have found that professionals and parents are afraid of expecting too much from young children with special needs. Adults working with children who are challenged or developmentally delayed may fear that the child does not understand or cannot achieve. Expecting the child to respond to appropriate demands may be considered cruel and can prevent adults from setting realistic expectations and appropriate limits for children who have special needs.

At Kids Are People School we try to be realistic. We feel if we do not demand certain behaviors from the children they will not try. This attitude is helpful for the children. We cannot assume ahead of time that a child cannot progress. We have seen children with all kinds of diagnoses and delays make gains. We expect them to try. We expect them to work and practice skills. We are consistent in expecting these efforts from the child.

ADDRESSING COMMUNICATION ISSUES

Communication beyond all else is the most crucial component of education. It is the most important gift we, as educators, can give to children.

In the spectrum of special needs, if a child can talk, the educator's job is much easier because there is a developmental sequence to most teaching. For example, children learn letter names, sounds, blends, sight words, read small phrases, then short sentences.

For children with no means of communication, the world is a difficult place. They can't tell you that they need their basic needs met. Something as simple as wanting a drink of water is out of their reach. Finding a way to help these children communicate is very important but is also time-consuming and can be expensive. In my opinion, it is well worth the time and money. The choice of method and/or equipment depends on the specific child and his/her special needs. Although each child is different, the children can be placed in general categories for communication intervention.

Children with Emotional/Behavioral Problems who Refuse To Talk.
Several times over the last 14 years I've had children referred who "just won't talk." Reports from parents are that all areas of development were within developmental milestones, but for some reason the child is three or four and isn't talking. Digging deeper into the history, the child babbled at the correct time, made word approximations, may have even had single words, but then stopped talking. For the majority of these children, the reason they didn't talk was because they didn't have to. On most occasions, when asked "Does the child pull you to get what she wants or point to things?", the parents say, "Yes, all the time." When asked "What do you do?", the answer is, "I give it to her."

Children can go on for years not talking if this is the situation in their environment. It has been the rare circumstance that the child doesn't start talking within a couple of months once he is in school or once parents change their response patterns at home. We have had some children who, when they did start to talk, talked in full articulated sentences. Children do not talk if they aren't encouraged to and if they don't need to. Wishing they will isn't enough. I've seen parents who go over and over letter identification, flash cards, etc., etc., trying to help with their child's development. I say, throw the flash cards away and *be a parent*. Read to them, and ask them questions to get responses.

Not all children who do not talk because of behavioral or emotional reasons are going to start talking because a change in their interactions with parents, teachers and other adults forces them to, but many will. People working with these children have to be consistent in their approaches and demands, as do the child's parents, grandparents, siblings, and babysitters. Change will come with time.

What about children who don't just start talking, who fight every step of the way? Or children who had speech and stopped talking? In our experience, play therapy, along with consistent demands from the people in the child's environment, are two ingredients which can help. A behavior modification program may be indicated. Introducing some signing to help make communicating safe, and using computer programs, can get the pressure off the child and help him slip back into using language. Positive reinforcement of any language used is very important. One word from this child is equal to an entire conversation by another and should be praised by peers, teachers and family. Generally, in our school, hugs and kisses are dispersed, because often the child is in the need of this kind of attention, too.

Sometimes children stop talking due to some severe crisis in the child's life. Often, the loss of language can be due to depression or even fear. Psychotherapy is crucial for this child. Unfortunately, if the behavior is directly related to actions or situations caused by parents, it's more difficult to get the parents to agree to psychotherapy for their child, partly because the parents are expected to participate in the therapy. If, for example, depression is due to the death of a relative, parents are often willing to go along with therapy. Whatever the cause, it is important to be sensitive to the family — firmly encouraging therapy for the child without placing blame. Most parents love their children enough that they are willing to get their child involved in therapy to help make changes.

Probably the most frustrating situation is the child who comes to us not speaking and who, with hard consistent work, does start talking at school but not at home. I'm not one to blame parents because I know parenting is very difficult. But it is very hard when parents do *not* follow through consistently at home — when they're sick, tired or just sick and tired — and they won't believe their child is talking at school! Progress is very slow in this situation. Often there are setbacks. It is crucial to enlist the parents' commitment; otherwise, for the child, it is the same old situation at home. This lack of home support for change is often seen in other areas, especially self-help skills such as eating and toileting. It is a fact of life. There just are some parents who do not follow through and who get in their child's way. We try every method of encouraging these parents and then are very direct if encouragement doesn't work. Ninety-five percent of the time, the parents have seen enough positive changes in the child's behavior that they won't pull their children from the program.

Children with Severe Delays in Language Production. These are children who have no language, or have some language but are far below age-appropriate speech and language production, yet have the physical capacity to talk. For example, a child who leaves off the beginning and/or ending consonant sounds of words, which leaves his expressive language unintelligible to others, is a child with a severe delay in language production. The child may be constantly attempting to communicate and getting very little satisfaction because others do not understand him. There are two concerns. First, how do you help the child to express himself more clearly, and secondly, how do you make sure his self-esteem doesn't get damaged, resulting in his being less willing to attempt language use? This most often leads to the child being frustrated and often to behavior problems.

Many times a child's delay in language production is made worse by weak facial muscles, processing problems, or attention problems. Processing problems are one of the main causes of expressive and receptive speech and language delays. It is often one of the more difficult areas of communication delay to work with because it's difficult to know what is and isn't understood by the child.

Children with Language, Reading or Writing Disorders. There are a variety of language, reading and writing disorders children can present, such as aphasia, dyspraxia, dyslexia, etc. It is not the intent of this book to discuss these in detail; there are several good books on the subject. However, we do want to impress upon the reader that it often takes special programs, equipment, and creativity to teach children with severe communication disorders or no method of communication.

For children who have processing problems, reading or writing delays and articulation problems, the best methods are often the most boring — presenting the whole and then breaking it into parts; practicing the same material, or at least the same skill, over and over in repetition. It is painstaking and takes a lot of extra time, but it is critical and needs to be done. It should not *just* be the job of the reading specialist or speech therapist. It should be part of everyday life with peers and teachers, and it should be made as much fun as possible. Peers can be helpful as models, and the right peer — nominated by the target child — can probably gain more involvement and better output than a teacher or parent. But the latter should not be left out.

For children who stutter or have articulation problems, it is important that all adults, especially parents, speak correctly. Time and time again I hear parents talk back to their children repeating the incorrect pronunciation of words — thinking it's cute. Children need to hear it correctly; otherwise adults are giving the message that the child said the word correctly after all.

In general, stuttering should be ignored. Children who stutter should be encouraged to talk and given *whatever* time it takes for them to say what's on their minds. Peers should not be allowed to make fun of or imitate stuttering.

Children Incapable Of Talking Due To Physical Challenges. Probably the thing I knew the least about, and have learned the most about, has been communication methods for children who will never talk. Communication is the key to humanism. For the person unable to communicate, they and the world are locked away. It is a lot easier for people to turn their backs on someone with no communication, because they can allow themselves to assume the person without communication can't understand; therefore, they don't have to try for that individual.

And then there are children who stop talking due to medical reasons, such as brain damage from an accident. The circumstances and treatments differ from child to child, but augmentative communication methods can replace the child's spoken language if it is not possible for the child to regain language skills, or while the child is working on regaining skills.

We consider several issues when trying to determine when to give up on speech and language and move to augmentative communication. A good speech and language evaluation by someone skilled in augmentative communication methods is the best place to start. I have found them extremely helpful, and these specialists are really very special people in the field.

The methods chosen to help the child communicate depend on a number of factors.

Potential cognitive ability of the child will often determine the recommendations for augmentative communication. If a child is intact cognitively, as evidenced by consistent responses to others and situations, then a more sophisticated method of communication may be recommended which can be expanded as the child learns how to use it. Some computerized methods can go from simple training to hit a switch through writing and reading on a variety of subject areas of study. A child who displays very little evidence of ability to follow directions and attend to task, or awareness of meaningfulness in his world, would start with a much simpler task such as picking between two pictures to make a choice.

Physical limitations play a big part in what methods of communication are taught to a child. For example, it is useless to use sign language with a child who has severe cerebral palsy or significant hypotonia, because they are physically incapable of signing.

In addition, a child's range of motion (how far can the child stretch out his hand to touch a picture, switch, etc.?) and his accuracy (how consistently can a child with a weak tonic neck reflex still intact due to cerebral palsy, get his body in position to hit a switch?) play an important part in determining what method or methods to use.

Financial restraints. Sophisticated augmentative communication methods are very expensive. Until a child can prove on simpler tasks that a method might work, recommendations are often held up on more expensive equipment. Even if a recommendation is made, it can be six months to a year before the child gets what's needed because the case needs to be proved to the child's insurance company. If it's covered, there is a lot of red tape and a long wait. Things are even worse if you are looking for equipment through Medicaid. Think how long a year is to wait in the life of that child!

Often communication and hearing are not considered medical necessities. For example, many companies will not pay for speech and language therapy or hearing aids.

If money weren't an issue, many more children would have computerized augmentative communication systems attached to their wheelchairs. The cost of systems such as Dynavox (a small computer for augmentative communication which can be attached to a wheelchair) needs to come down and be subsidized. What good is it for 10 children to share one at school where "sometimes," when it's their turn to use it, they can communicate? What about communicating outside of school?

Potential For Follow-Through With Adults In The Child's Life. There really is no sense in recommending a method to parents which they can't or won't use because it is too involved, confining or confusing. This must be considered when making a choice of augmentative communication methods. A system of communication which can't easily be accessed by peers, family and teachers doesn't make sense and can just add to the frustration the child is already experiencing, with not being able to communicate simple wants and needs.

Methods of Augmenting Communication

Assistive technology comes in many forms, and more are being developed on an ongoing basis. Most of what is available is very expensive, and it seems to be hit or miss as to whether a method or piece of equipment will be successful with a child. It is imperative that an in-depth augmentative communication evaluation be done to help determine the best method for communication and to try and avoid purchasing expensive equipment that won't help. The beauty of a good augmentative communication evaluation for children who are physically challenged and non-verbal is that an occupational therapist and speech therapist will work together to determine the best seating, the best position and even the best part of the body the child should use to activate switches for maximum access.

As with all highly specialized techniques or therapies, the program administrators must locate high-quality resources and personnel in their community — often in the larger area where teaching hospitals are available.

For children who are non-verbal, it is imperative that someone take the time to teach them a method of communication that is accessible to all members of their environment, in school and in their world. Whether that be eye gazing, hand raising, hand hitting, a Dynavox, or whatever, children who are non-verbal need to have a way to let people know what they think, feel, want and need. This method needs to be taught to parents, relatives, friends, siblings and classmates, and needs to be used consistently. For more information on the resources mentioned in this section, please refer to Appendix 4.

There are several methods and pieces of equipment we have used with various children which have helped them to communicate.

Eye gazing. This technique is generally used with children who most likely will never talk nor have the ability to accurately control a part of their body for switch work. The technique involves exactly what it says: the child looks at something purposefully. For example, children can answer questions by gazing purposefully at the answer.

One piece of equipment used with this technique is an eye gazing board. It is made of clear plastic with a section cut out in the middle for the person eliciting the answer (teacher, peer, parent) to show their face through. Different letters, words, etc., can be on different sections of the board. The person asking the question watches the person with special needs to see where he eye gazes. This determines the answer to the question.

This is a good method to use one-on-one, and to help train the child to use this technique with more sophisticated computerized equipment. The weakness in the method is if a child can't communicate clearly and people are guessing that the answer "offered" is the one intended. Another problem with this method is that it's not effective with a child who has strong uncontrollable reflexes, since it is difficult for the child to be accurate.

Others in the child's environment need to be trained to communicate with him or her. Since the eye gazing board is bulky, it may not be as accessible a form of communication as one may want. It does work well for many people, though.

Switches. Switches are small machines of different shapes and sizes which have large buttons for people with special needs to hit. Their purpose is to help children control their environment, communicate, learn, and demonstrate what they know. There are several kinds of switches of different types and sizes. The beauty of switches is that a child does not have to have good fine motor skills to hit the switch and access a variety of equipment including radios, tape recorders, computers, toys, etc. If a child can consistently and purposefully hit a switch with a part of his body, then several different pieces of equipment can be used to open the world up to the child to communicate and be educated.

Latch switch. A latch switch (a large oblong sensitive switch) can be hooked up to an adapted tape recorder. Tapes are then created around areas of interest for the child. The child can hit the switch to turn the tape recorder off, allowing the child to answer questions, make choices, or express needs. For example, one tape could be a list of choices of friends to work with. The tape says, "I want to play with Lisa," pauses 5 to 10 seconds (depending on how long it takes the child to reach and hit the switch), "I want to play with Jerry," pauses 5 to 10 seconds, and so on. The child hits the switch when he hears the name he wants. The teacher may want to play the tape through twice, once for the child to hear all of the choices and once to allow the child to make the choice.

Tapes can also be made of the materials his peers are reading and discussing so that he can listen and learn. Tapes of lesson materials, assignments, etc., can be used by children who read poorly to acquaint them with the discussion materials. Again, this is bulky, and it does take time to make the response tapes and keep them updated, but it is much more accurate to gain the student's choices.

We have found this method very successful.

Jelly Bean Switch/Big Red Switch can be installed in a child's wheelchair at the site that it is easiest for the child to consistently and purposefully hit. It can be used with computers in the classroom and/or attached to the child's chair. We like this switch because it is large, bright and easy for the child to use.

Touch Talker. This piece of equipment consists of an electronic board divided into 8 or 32 sections. We did not find it helpful for the child we originally got it for. The shape of it is quite large and awkward, and any child with tonic or punitive reflexes still dominating voluntary movement has a difficult time accurately hitting the specific area on the box. Children without adequate fine motor control can't possibly use the 32-section board. In addition, we found it very difficult to program, the voice quality was poor and difficult to hear, and it was very time-consuming. It has been retired to the speech therapy program to use with less physically challenged children as a method of eliciting more accurate language production and so forth. It's an expensive tool for this, and we would recommend a two-month trial period for the child and the touch talker before purchasing it. Its shape is of some concern, because it doesn't sit easily on a child's lap, and its height when placed on a table makes it hard for children who are physically challenged to get their hand up and over it or to have good eye contact with the top to make choices. I do feel it would be a good tool for children who are non-verbal with no physical challenges, if the voice quality could be improved.

Dynavox is a very expensive (over $4,000.00) piece of equipment which resembles a laptop computer. Its shape is very compact and accessible, and its method of linking symbols to create sentences is extraordinary. It's a wonderful communication device once it is programmed for a specific child's use. The main thing that makes it inaccessible is the cost. Insurance will not pay for it, and most families can't afford it. A school program could purchase one, but it would have to be shared among several children, which doesn't give an individual child the access to it when he or she needs or wants to communicate. If it can be purchased for a child, it is well worth the money. Maybe if Sentient Systems Technology, Inc., sells enough of them, they might lower the price so more children can have one.

Computer Hardware and Accessories

The computer is a valuable tool for helping children who are non-verbal to develop a method of communication. We have found the best computer for augmentative communication to be the Macintosh. The designers spent a lot of time creating ways for physically challenged and non-verbal children to access the computer. And while there may be other computer companies which have done this, Macintosh is the one which thought about children who are non-verbal and physically challenged.

Below is a discussion of pieces of equipment and programs which can be used with the Macintosh to successfully use the computer to teach children who are non-verbal and severely physically challenged.

Kenex This piece of equipment (about $800.00) is crucial to access the computer with switches. It is hooked up to the computer, and the jellybean switch is hooked up to it. Now children who couldn't possibly purposefully hit a key on the keyboard or use a mouse due to lack of physical control can hit the switch and make the computer work.

What is crucial about this for the education of globally challenged children is that it is one way to prove to parents, outside agencies and medical personnel that a child has cognitive capabilities — that he does understand simple directions or conversations. The most heartbreaking part of my job has been to know that a child understands and to have everyone around him treat him as incapable.

Touch window. The touch window (about $300.00) fits over the screen of the computer monitor and allows a child who can't maneuver a mouse to touch the screen to make the computer work. This is particularly helpful with children from whom you are trying to elicit any level of response. It is great for cause and effect with children who have shown little evidence of purposeful communication to this point. It is also good for children who do not have fine motor control and need to use a headpiece with a swatting type of motion.

Turbo Track Ball. The trackball (about $160.00) is like a mouse, only it's a large ball cradled in a stand which is rolled to make the cursor on the computer move. It's great for all young children, but especially for children with weakness in their hands or children for whom a typical mouse is too difficult to maneuver.

Keyboard letters These are very large adhesive letters and numbers (about $20.00) which fit over the individual existing keyboard symbols to help children find the symbols more easily. They come in black background with white letters or white background with black letters. They are actually helpful to children and adults and are worth it for anyone using a computer.

Computer Software

Everyone knows there is a huge amount of software available for computers today. In the next section we discuss programs which we have used and found to be particularly helpful. They have helped children who are non-verbal and physically challenged, children who have severe language delays, and children with severe attention problems and/or reading delays. There are other wonderful programs available, but these are some of our favorites.

Boardmaker is a program which allows teachers or therapists to create programs for children who are physically challenged and non-verbal. Boards of eight "buttons" can be created to represent whatever you want the child to be able to communicate to you about. We have created boards around needs, favorite books, science lessons, computer choices, etc. Attached are examples of boards we have made.

A main board (Example 1) is created. This covers all the main areas of choice you think you'll need at the present time with a child. What the computer does with the Kenex is scan each choice, pausing while it names that choice. For example, on the main choice board, when it gets to Areas, the computer says "I want to go to an area." If that is what the child wants to do, he hits the switch, and the Area Choice Board (Example 2) will appear on the screen. The computer then scans the Area Choices, which are customized to the areas in their school. If the child wants to go to the Listening Area (Example 3) or the Library Area (Example 4), he will hit the switch when the computer highlights that area and says "I want to go to the Library Area." The screen will then display the choices in the library area. These should be designed with the child's preferences in mind and do need to be changed periodically. When the computer highlights the book the child wants and says, for example, "Go Dog Go," the child hits the switch and the computer says, "I want to read *Go Dog Go*." All of this takes only a couple of minutes. It is critical that all choices be easily available and that the child be immediately brought to the library area and given or read *Go Dog Go*.

This is a wonderful individualized piece of technology. It can be designed in color. I highly recommend it. It can be used with a variety of children with special needs but is specifically beneficial to children who are non-verbal and physically challenged. Boardmaker requires two other software programs to work: Aldus Superpaint and Speaking Dynamically. With these three programs, you can use already created images, as with all the buttons in Area Choice (Example 2), or you can draw your own, as with Put Me In The Zoo (Example 4).

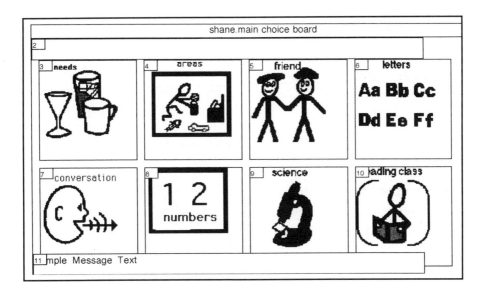

Example 1: The Main Choice Board

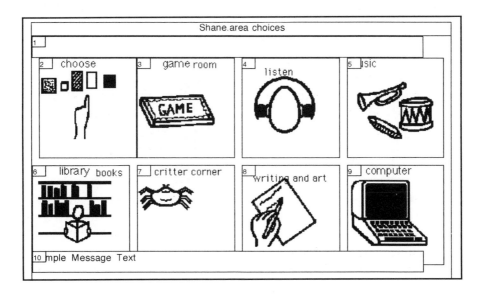

Example 2: The Area Choice Board

The images on these boards were either adapted or taken directly from the Boardmaker/Speaking Dynamically software (see Appendix 4). Actual size of these boards is 4.5"x8".

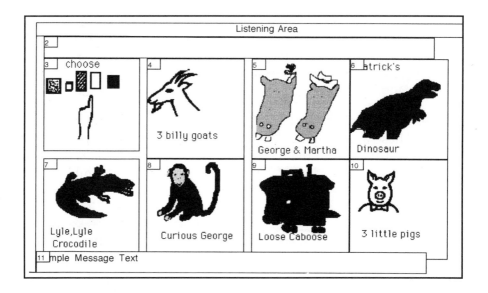

Example 3: The Listening Area Choice Board

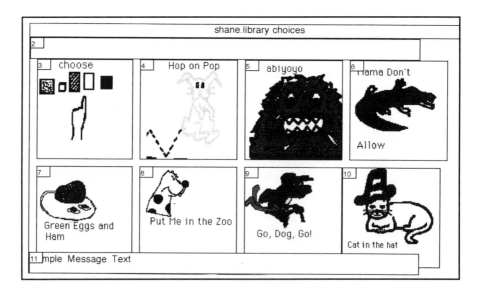

Example 4: The Library Area Choice Board

Some of the images on these boards were either adapted or taken directly from the Boardmaker/Speaking Dynamically software (see Appendix 4). Others were hand-drawn by the author. Actual board size is 4.5"x8".

There are two flaws with this program: it takes a great deal of time to learn how to design the boards, and it takes a great deal of time to create the boards. But all of this time is very well spent, and most boards, once created, can be used for a long time and with several children. The cost of the program is about $1,000.00.

Living Books. Another program we really love is the Living Books series. These are computer disks of existing storybooks; you need a CD-ROM drive to use them. Two that we have are *Grandma and Me* and *Arthur's Teacher's Trouble*. The children love them. Children can click on their choice of English, Spanish or Japanese. What's wonderful about them is that after the computer reads the text, the child can click on the picture and the picture comes to life. For example, on page one of *Grandma and Me*, if the child clicks on the flower, a bee will come out, buzz around, and land on the character's head. If you click on the mailbox, it will open, water will pour out, and a frog will jump out. This kind of interactive program grabs the attention of even the child with the most serious attention deficit. In addition, it can be used with the touch window or the Kenex and Big Red or jellybean switch. It's great for language stimulation and reading. Each book costs about $50.00.

Magic Reading Library by Tom Synder Productions. Titles include *Hilary and the Beast, Flodd, The Bad Guy, Jack and the Beanstalk,* and *Hansel and Gretel*. These programs are fantastic. First, the children have the choice of having the computer read them the story or recording the story themselves. They can read the text already created by the program or make up a story of their own which will be programmed into the story and can be played back as a whole or piece by piece. The beauty of this design is the help it gives to teachers in teaching reading, creativity, articulation training and voice tone. It's an incredible tool, can be used in numerous ways, and allows creativity on the part of the teacher or therapists. It really encourages cooperation, sharing and turntaking between the children, increases the desire to read, and is wonderful for shy children who find it difficult to talk in front of a group. This series is by far our favorite because of what it has done for our kids socially and academically. I find no flaws in it. The Macintosh needs a microphone to access this program. Costs: microphones about $12.00; individual computer programs $59.95 for one, $99.95 for two, $249.95 for all five.

In addition, Tom Synder Productions is in the forefront of designing cooperative educational materials for computers and videodiscs. Most of these materials are exceptional, at least all that we have used, including *The Great Solar System Rescue* and *The Great Ocean*

Rescue. These are strongly recommended.

KidsPixs, The Play Room and **The Tree House** are three quality programs to help children who have severe attention problems and children with language delays. All three are excellent for use for language stimulation activities.

Millie Math House is a great program for getting children to attend. It teaches basic math skills and is great for language stimulation.

Communication Books and Boards

Communication books are used by children who are severely language delayed or non-verbal. They are created by the teacher from Picture Communication Symbols. Sets of communication symbols in two sizes and books to hold them can be purchased from Mayer Johnson. Teachers, therapists, or parents cut and paste pictures to put in the boxes around communication for individual children. Attached is a sample (Examples 5 and 6).

On one side of the book would be the child's name and the word "I" plus a picture of a verb or two. The opposite page (Example 6) has pictures of nouns. The child can tell the teacher, parent or peer what he or she needs by pointing at pictures. For example, Katie wants to play in the sandbox, so she points at her *name*, *want*, and *sandbox*.

Communication books come in various sizes, even small enough to hang on a belt loop. They are very helpful. People often fear that children who speaks a little, or may at some point speak, will not because they become dependent on the non-verbal communication of using the communication book. This is not the case. If anything, the use of the communication book relieves the pressure these children feel when they have language issues and people are trying to get them to talk.

Communication boards are used around the school for children who are non-verbal, deaf or hearing-impaired to help them make choices or communicate needs. For example, pictures of different areas of the room should be taken and placed on a board so a child who needs to can point to a free choice area. A board can be made for listening tapes, books, needs (food, toileting, etc.) and so forth.

Sign Language

As difficult as it is to learn, it is important that the majority of the staff know some sign language for children who are non-verbal or language-delayed. It is critical, if there are children who are deaf or hard of hearing, that their teachers be fluent in American Sign Lan-

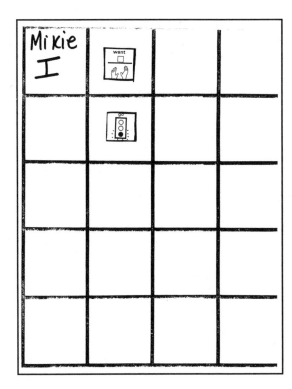

Example 5: The Communication Board, Page 1.

Actual size 8.5"x11"

Example 6: The Communication Board, Page 2.

Actual size 8.5"x11"

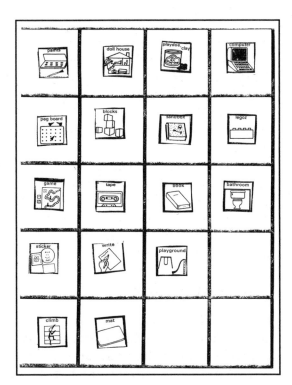

guage (ASL). Also, it is important for the child to have as role models deaf peers and adults in the environment who know and use the language with him.

In addition, the environment needs to be made accessible for the child who is deaf or hard of hearing. Communication boards, as they are described above, need to be in the various areas around the room to facilitate communication. Fire alarms need to flash a light to let children and adults who can't hear know it is going off. Door buzzers buzzing, phones ringing and doors knocking need to be identified to the nonhearing person by devices designed to flash lights.

Telecommunication Devices for the Deaf (TDD's), used to type messages through the phone for telephone conversations, need to be available for parents, staff and children who are deaf or hard of hearing to make phone calls to and from the school.

Televisions need to be closed-captioned, or a decoder (device used to print out on the screen what is being said in the TV program) needs to be purchased to make programs accessible. Videotapes which are either closed-captioned or in sign language need to be purchased for the classroom.

Alphabet and number sign language charts should be in all the rooms. Cubbies and objects in the room should be labeled with the printed word and the sign word.

Hearing peers should be taught sign language to communicate with their nonhearing peers. All peers and teachers should be given a sign name and taught one another's sign names. Teachers who are speaking should remember to sign all the time so they are not excluding the child who is deaf or hard of hearing. They should just sign when they are communicating with the deaf or hard-of-hearing child individually.

Dramatic play areas should have old hearing aids, TDD's, etc., for role play for all the children.

FM systems which amplify what the teacher is saying (the teacher wears a microphone, and the children who are hearing-impaired wear receivers) should be available to the program for use in the classroom.

Teachers who are deaf need peers who are deaf or peers who can sign fluently. If this is not available, then the school needs to invest in an interpreter for when the teacher is working with children or having meetings with other staff and/or parents.

SENSORIMOTOR DEVELOPMENT

Movement, like communication, is an individual experience that leads to independence, social interaction, and inclusion in the human family. Young children explore and learn through movement. They grasp and discard objects, express pleasure and anxiety through movement toward and away from various stimuli, and generally spend every waking minute practicing skills which quickly evolve into increasing control over themselves and their environment. A child's motor skills impact directly on self-care, cognitive maturation, communication, social interactions, and perhaps most importantly, self-esteem.

By the time a typical child is three years old, we expect she will independently explore her world. By this age most children are ready to meet their world running — literally, and they seek playmates who are prepared to spend the day jumping, climbing, pulling, and pushing. For many children with special needs these activities are difficult if not impossible without lots of help, supervision, and encouragement.

Gross motor skills include locomotion, or how a child moves from one place to another, and the ability to maintain an upright posture. *Fine motor skills*, the ability to manipulate small objects and use the hands to perform "pen and paper" activities, are closely linked with eye-hand coordination. Gross and fine motor development are closely interrelated. Together they are often referred to as sensorimotor skills. Sensorimotor development is a complex process which hinges on the interaction of a number of internal and external factors. Internal factors include muscle strength and flexibility, processing and use of a number of sensory systems, personality, and the genetic predisposition for movement skills. External factors include all the environmental variables which may either encourage or discourage skill development.

The maturation of sensorimotor skills depends on a self-perpetuating system of sensory input, processing, interpretation, and sensorimotor adaptation. The internal and external sensory feedback a young child receives as a result of active, independent movement encourages and shapes increasingly difficult and complex activities. This feedback, along with growing control, strength, and flexibility of muscles is essential to the ongoing development of every child's gross and fine motor skills. If something is wrong with any of these systems, feedback is distorted and sensorimotor skills can be distorted or delayed.

A child with a history of sensorimotor delay or dysfunction is often at a disadvantage as she moves through her day.

> Esther, who at age 8 walks and runs independently, has difficulty with motor planning due to a combination of weak muscles and problems with sensory processing. The simple instruction "Everyone go and get a piece of paper

and some markers, bring them back to the table and sit down" begins a difficult and confusing process for her. She must carefully think through every part of the task, and in the end may become too disoriented to complete it without help. When she was a toddler Esther was at another end of the sensorimotor special needs spectrum. Severe muscle weakness, particularly in the trunk and legs, meant that at age 3 she was just beginning to learn to walk with a walker. Though Esther at age eight can figure out how to get the paper and marker and come back to the work area, and walks independently, she will take much longer than the other children to get there. Esther at age three could not do this task at all.

Some Background and Principles

Sensorimotor development occurs for all children as they practice both gross and fine motor skills, moving from the simple reflexive motions of a newborn to increasingly refined and challenging activities. Typical children move through a specific sequence of sensorimotor activities during the first year of life. The steps overlap, and the age and intensity at which each stage occurs varies for each child. Every movement experience contributes to a child's future maturity and independence, laying the foundation for increasingly complex skills. All children generally follow the same developmental path to sensorimotor independence; children with special needs simply require some help along the way, and may progress at different rates from their classmates.

Movement is an integrated function of the neuromuscular-skeletal system, processes of the tactile, visual and auditory, proprioceptive, kinesthetic, and vestibular sensory systems, and movement experiences. Evaluation and intervention are based on consideration of specific elements of each of these systems, and how they intersect to create the building blocks of mature motor behavior.

The first and most basic element of sensorimotor activity is the neuromuscular-skeletal system. This includes "reflexes and reactions which develop according to specific functions, muscles and muscle groups which develop specific patterns of mobility and stability, and bone and joint structures which grow to support neuromuscular functions" (Gilfoyle, Grady & Moore, 1981).

Reflexes and reactions are automatic, stereotypical movement responses to different sensory stimuli. They evolve from the very simple movements of a newborn child to complex movements we all use to maintain our balance throughout our lives. Typically, children move through a clear sequential pattern of automatic actions, using increasing muscle control and strength to develop an ever more complex and secure repertoire of sensorimotor skills. For most children, early, primitive reflex responses become integrated into more advanced and controlled movements. By the time a typical toddler is three years old, postural reflexes allow her to have secure balance in running, jumping, and climbing. For many children with special needs, this integrating and maturing process is delayed, or a child is actually 'held up' at an immature level of reflex behavior. These delays or holdups interact with other neuromuscular problems, such as muscle weakness or tightness, or imbalance of muscle strength around a joint, to disrupt a child's motor development.

Muscle tone and strength can be imagined as on a continuum of weak to strong, and from very taut to very loose. We all have our own individual place on this continuum, and other factors like coordination, experience, and enjoyment of physical activity interact to determine who becomes an Olympic athlete and who prefers the couch, or a nice seat in an athletic stadium. Children with special needs are also on this continuum, but often must cope with the far side of either end. Lauren, whose muscles throughout her body are very weak due to hypotonia, has to make extraordinary efforts to move independently. She needs braces to support joints and keep her body properly aligned, and supportive seating and a walker to do the work strong muscles would ordinarily do. Extremes and uncontrollable fluctuations in muscle tone are common in children with cerebral palsy, spina bifida, and in many children with a variety of central nervous system disorders.

Hypertonicity refers to muscle tone which is very tight, and is often associated with uncontrollable, primitive reflex patterns of movement which are normally seen in very young infants. When these reflex movement patterns are still observable in toddlers and older children, they help prevent or interfere with the acquisition of more complex, independent movement skills. If a child with significant hypertonia and associated delay in reflex development is not encouraged to move and stretch tight muscles, those muscles can get tighter as the child grows, particularly around joints such as the shoulders, hips, or knees, leading to increasing stiffness and weakness. A child who is not encouraged to move, working against the tightening and loss of strength, enters into what could be called a 'negative spiral', with increasing loss of control of the muscle activity and difficulty with independent movement outside these primitive reflex patterns.

Hypotonicity refers to muscles which have very low tone and are quite weak. In extreme situations the low muscle tone and poor strength can prevent a child from developing even the most basic ability to hold her body upright against the forces of gravity.

> At fifteen months, Esther was clearly aware and interested in her environment, but she could barely hold her head up when lying on her stomach, and needed full support to sit. Hypotonic oral muscles affected speech and language articulation. A therapy program that emphasized muscle strengthening and encouraged Esther to develop more advanced automatic balance reactions contributed to her current status an independent eight year old. Her desire to play with her classmates and the encouragement she received from them, her family, and teachers surely tipped the scales toward success and full inclusion in school and community.

Physical and occupational therapists assess bone and joint structures to make sure that *range of motion*, the movement flexibility of a joint, is within normal limits. Hypertonicity and hypotonicity can both result in a reduced range of motion. In hypertonicity the problem is tight muscles and an imbalance of movement around joints, with muscles on one side pulling too hard, and muscles on the other side of the joint getting weaker. Hypotonicity can cause a decrease in active, independent movement, sometimes resulting in muscles getting stiff just because they are not being exercised enough. In both cases, movement, particularly functional activity within the home and classroom, is the key to helping children reach their maximum potential strength and sensorimotor independence. Joints are also checked for structural soundness to make sure that imbalances in muscle tone or strength have not pulled a joint out of alignment, or to determine if a joint might give better support with some form of bracing.

During the first year of life typical children progress through a sequence of purposeful motor postures and activities that lead to walking. This *developmental sequence* is a basic progression of observable skills that is constant for all children. The steps of this progression frequently overlap, and the age and intensity for each stage vary for individual children. But all the activities contribute to a child's developmental maturity, and lay the foundation for more complex and challenging skills.

There are many variations of the gross and fine motor developmental sequence, but all the scales are tied to chronological milestones that have been determined according to observations of thousands of typical children. Younger children are assessed against this framework to determine where they are in relation to expected motor milestones. For each stage therapists include several subcategories of postures and movements. The following were taken from Capute and Accardo (1991).

GROSS MOTOR MILESTONES

Milestone	Mean Age of Attainment (Months)
Roll (stomach to back)	3.6
Roll (back to stomach)	4.8
Sit (supported)	5.3
Sit (unsupported)	6.3
Creep (locomotion on stomach)	6.7
Come to sit	7.5
Crawl (on hands and knees)	7.8
Pull to stand	8.1
Cruise	8.8
Walk	11.7
Walk backward	14.3
Run	14.8

Developmental milestones for fine motor skills are more complex and lengthy. They are often divided into two categories: visual-motor (eye-hand coordination), and graphomotor, or observable pen and paper skills. Graphomotor milestones for ages 1 through 12 years can be briefly summarized as follows:

GRAPHOMOTOR MILESTONES

Drawing Skill	Mean Age
Marks with a pencil	12 months
Imitates scribble	15 months
Scribbles spontaneously	18 months
Makes vertical/horizontal strokes	26 months
Imitates circle	30 months
Copies circle	36 months
Draws circle on command; draws cross	40 months
Draws square	4 years
Draws triangle	5 years
Draws horizontal diamond and Union Jack	6 years
Draws vertical diamond	7 years
Draws Greek cross	8 years
Draws cylinder	9 years
Draws transparent cube	10 years
Draws solid cube	12 years

A typical child is expected to perform in this area by age one, and these skills are often judged to offer insight into potential cognitive ability. Children who have neuromuscular problems such as hypotonia or hypertonia are at an obvious disadvantage when judged in this arena. We have cautioned against the very serious problem of children with motor deficits being misjudged on potential cognitive and social-adaptive skills because they cannot express themselves through regular sensorimotor activity.

Physical therapists tend to concentrate on gross motor development, with emphasis on general muscle strength, postural control, and locomotion. Occupational therapists are more concerned with fine motor and eye-hand coordination, and with the integration of sensory processes which are necessary to the development of more skilled, functional activities. The training and activities of occupational and physical therapists overlap, however, in many areas, and this is particularly true for assessing and working with young children in inclusive classrooms.

As a child is encouraged to move through these progressions, it is often possible to uncover specific neuromotor strengths and weaknesses which are considered in planning a therapeutic program.

As children get older and are able to perform more challenging activities, therapists expand the scope of their assessments and programs to include both 'foundation building' activities such as those within the developmental sequence and later, more skilled, age-appropriate activities. In addition, therapists are concerned with the quality of a child's physical activity. A quality assessment checklist might include independence, timing, speed, coordination, rhythm, and endurance. A child's emotional response to motor activities can tell much of his experience and self-confidence. Feeling good about movement, as with any area of development, is the key to success.

Children who have problems with sensorimotor development can generally be identified as belonging to one of three groups.

Children with a specific diagnosis of physical challenge. A relatively small proportion of children have conditions which are identified at or shortly after birth. These include Down Syndrome, cerebral palsy, spina bifida, congenital amputation, or severe toxic exposure such as Fetal Alcohol Syndrome, to name a few. Many of these children will have significant motor problems.

For example, children with cerebral palsy and their families must cope with a potentially wide range of problems across the developmental spectrum. Danielle had very mild muscle weakness on one side of her body, resulting in poor balance when walking and delays in fine motor skills. She had above average cognitive and speech and language ability. Another child with cerebral palsy can be totally affected, with pervasive muscle weakness or tightness causing imbalances in muscle tone that pull many joints out of alignment. This child can be completely aware of everything that is going on around him, but be unable to move or speak without significant and constant assistance. Both of these children need specific interventions to strengthen muscles, improve balance, and encourage them to move towards maximum independence.

Over the years the most common and in some ways plaintive question I have gotten from parents whose children have significant motor disability is "Will she/he ever walk by him/herself?". A typical child starts walking at anywhere from 10 to 18 months. Marcus learned to walk with the help of braces and crutches at 18 months. I have taught children of 5 and 6 years to do the same. All of these children do well in inclusive settings where adjustments for their individual needs enable full participation in all activities. Encouragement and motivation from their friends often facilitates the process and is the key element in their success.

For a small group of children, independent walking is not a realistic goal. A wheelchair (motorized or manual) enables a child who otherwise would always have to wait for others to move from place to place to develop a sense of independence and self control. In many cases the combined use of crutches and wheelchair are a holistic approach to a child's need for independence and continued exercise and building of muscle strength and joint stability. For a child in this situation to be truly included, the classroom and building must be completely accessible, including all the activity areas. Movable desks, computers, and art areas designed to accommodate wheelchairs tell a child that the classroom belongs to him as much as it does to his classmates. A child who must spend the day either in the front, back, or side of the room will feel very much a 'fifth wheel'. Inclusion must be physical, social, and academic. An individual, balanced, and practical approach with *all* the child's developmental needs in mind is usually the most successful.

Children with developmental delays. A second and much larger group of children are developmentally delayed or demonstrate atypical patterns of development with no clear cause or diagnosis. These children often present parents and teachers with a confusing array of strengths and problems. At Kids Are People we have three year olds who walk independently but still cannot – or will not – run, jump or kick a ball. We have special sensorimotor groups for children age 5 to 8 years who cannot follow simple three-step motor directions without substantial assistance and repetition. The sensorimotor delay is usually only a piece of the developmental picture, and clear causes for the delays are not available for many of these children, although some are diagnosed as having minimal brain damage (MBD) or learning disabilities.

This group constitutes by far the largest and most puzzling segment of young children with sensorimotor delay or dysfunction. A typical child reaches maturity by moving through naturally ordered and progressively more complex activities.

Many young children with sensorimotor developmental delays appear to function just like their more typical peers. Because the range of developmental maturity is so wide in early childhood, parents and teachers may not even have concerns until a child is falling behind in fine motor and more complex adaptive skills. For all children in this category, a systematic sensorimotor evaluation can reveal fundamental weaknesses that may be undermining a child's capacity to progress. The areas that should be considered are:

1. neuromuscular and skeletal status, including the presence of immature reflexes which may have a subtle effect on voluntary movement, postural reflexes, muscle tone and strength, range of motion of joints, and bony structures and possible deformities,
2. gross motor skills, including balance, coordination, strength, and endurance,
3. fine motor skills, including eye-hand coordination and manipulative activities,
4. motor planning, and
5. sensory integration and perceptual motor skills.

The sensorimotor problems of these children are often the easiest to overlook. They usually walk, often run, and perform self-help tasks with their peers. However, subtle problems such as low muscle tone, poor sensory integration and motor planning skills, and immature reflex behavior, particularly in postural-balance activity, can have negative and sometimes devastating effects on the quality and even safety of sensorimotor activity. The saddest outcome is the child who simply gives up on movement, refusing to participate and compete with classmates, frustrated and hurt that activities which are supposed to be fun are painful and scary.

Children at risk due to environmental or biological factors. A third group of children are at risk for developmental delay due to biological or environmental factors which increase the possibility of problems. Sensorimotor development is completely dependent on a continuous cycle of action, practice, and adjustment of movements to all kinds of sensory feedback. When the environmental feedback is negative, or even violent, some children become fearful, slowly digging deeper and deeper into themselves, and into a world in which movement is not the joyful source of challenge and reward that nature intended.

For others, a positive, supportive environment is not sufficient to encourage a child to participate fully in sensorimotor activities. Children may be biologically at risk due to a history of maternal nutritional or metabolic deficiencies, premature birth, low birth weight, or complications during or immediately after birth (Meisels and Wasik, 1990) Though there may be no clear, identifiable cause, some children simply withdraw from motor challenges, cutting themselves off from an important source of social interaction and inclusion in the games and fantasies of childhood. Abrupt or other significant changes can also cause children to withdraw from movement.

> At three years, Sean, who was happily running, climbing, and playing with his classmates, received a new prosthesis. Due to a new design and poor fit, Sean experienced increasing difficulty walking, and was easily pushed off balance while playing. Slowly his self-confidence eroded and eventually disappeared. He avoided the gross motor activities which had been his greatest source of joy, and became a very unhappy child. Time and several adjustments corrected the problems with the prosthesis. It took much longer for Sean to regain his confidence and join his friends with the old sense of adventure and pleasure.

For these children, a carefully mapped program of sensorimotor intervention provides a safe, controlled place in which they can develop and practice skills. When a child is comfortable with movement and eager to participate in the constant motion that defines the world of young children, self-confidence grows, often spreading to other areas of development where the challenges are even greater, and the rewards less immediate and obvious.

Understanding the Child's Needs: Screening and Evaluation

Concern about a child's progress is usually first voiced by parents, day care providers, or teachers. A parent may notice that her nine month old really isn't very sturdy when sitting, or isn't sitting at all. Parental intuition about the quality of their child's development is very strong, and based on constant observation, attention to detail, and comparison with the developmental course of their older children or children of the same age in the extended family or neighbor-hood.

Teachers at Kids Are People observe and interact with a child five days a week. They have the benefit of formal training in developmental expectations for each age. In addition, during their careers, teachers observe and compare the development of hundreds of children, becoming experts in discerning the difference between the usual ups and downs of childhood behaviors and long term developmental problems which may be a red flag for concerns which merit more specialized attention. After several weeks or months of observation, a teacher or parent becomes convinced that "something is just not quite right" about a child's sensorimotor development. They have just completed the initial phase of the assessment process. They may decide, with the child's parents and school administrators, to consult a physical or occupational therapist — or both if they are available — for an evaluation.

The goal of both physical and occupational therapy is to enhance a child's ability to participate in all activities at home and at school, to be as independent as possible, and to prevent future problems which could interfere with that independence. There is a universal shortage of both physical and occupational therapists experienced with working within school settings; many programs which need both physical and occupational therapy must settle for one or the other. Others make do with consultant services, which may consist of brief weekly or monthly visits by the therapist. The questions administrators ask are "Whose services should I seek if either budget or availability limits me to one or the other?" and "Many occupational and physical therapists seem to offer similar information and services — where is the difference?"

The basic training for pediatric physical and occupational therapists overlaps in many areas — neuromuscular and developmental evaluation and treatment planning, functional perspective, and long-range considerations for prevention of sensorimotor problems. In general, the two professions diverge at the point of higher-level skill attainment. Physical therapists emphasize gross motor control, postural control, and walking. Occupational therapists tend to concentrate more on perceptual motor, fine motor, and activities of daily living skills: dressing, feeding, and toileting. However, the child who cannot sit and hold her head up independently cannot dress herself, and the ability to walk without the perceptual ability to plan where you are going can be dangerous. Ideally, the two therapists complement one another and work together with teachers and parents to create a total developmental program.

The answer to the dilemma is, therefore, that the choice, if one must be made, really depends on the individual therapist, his or her perspective and training, and a clear message from school staff as to what they see as the needs of the child and the program.

It is also necessary to say that although the training and focus of therapists differs significantly from teachers and parents, it is every therapist's obligation, and the legal and ethical right of teachers and parents, to have both written and oral reports done in language that everyone understands. Technical terms which can only be deciphered by physicians or other therapists will not help the team understand a child's needs, and often render a therapist's information useless in the real world of home and school.

Regardless of the cause of delay or dysfunction, physical and occupational therapists follow a fairly consistent path in evaluating sensorimotor behavior. The age, nature, and needs of each child shape the scope and direction of the evaluation and recommendations for intervention. Assessments and programs are based on principles of neuromotor control and development and the understanding that all aspects of growth and development are interrelated and sequential.

Therapists view each child through the lens of this hierarchical structure, trying to determine strengths and seeking to identify specific neuromuscular problems which are getting in the way of a child's progress.

> Danielle was progressing nicely in all areas at age 2, but she avoided using her weaker right hand, resulting in a general slowdown of progress in both fine and gross motor activities requiring use of both hands. Increased attention by her mother, teachers, and therapists to strengthening her right hand and arm and encouraging its use in everyday activities quickly led to rapid remediation of this problem.

Following initial interviews with parents and teachers, and hopefully an observation of the child in a setting familiar to him, the therapist starts assessing the specific systems that support sensorimotor development. A review of all sensory systems is essential. For example, chronic visual problems affect a child's ability to meet motor challenges. If her view of the world is fuzzy, or her perception of distances between herself and objects is distorted for any reason, feedback will be distorted, leading to increased caution, if not actual fear of free movement. Many children with motor delays or dysfunction cope with distortions of feedback from movement due to dysfunctions of proprioceptive, kinesthetic, and vestibular systems. Problems in these areas can affect a child's ability to gauge distances between himself and others, creating situations where uncontrollable bumps into classmates in line for lunch are perceived as negative behaviors, or attempts at simple eye-hand coordination activities become an exercise in failure and frustration. These problems are not easy to detect, and are difficult and sometimes impossible to correct, but when teachers and parents are aware of the possible source of some behaviors, they are viewed and handled differently and in a more positive light.

The specific elements of any sensorimotor evaluation are determined by the child's age, predetermined diagnosis if one exists, and the specific functional needs that may have led to a referral in the first place. In most situations, however, there are certain elements of sensorimotor behavior that are always considered. A complete evaluation is organized around careful assessment of each of these elements, followed by an attempt to fit findings into a total developmental picture. The purpose of sensorimotor evaluation is to detect problems and needs related to daily functional activities; treatment promotes progress to the next developmental level and prevention of problems which could cause trouble later, such as joint deformities or tightening due to muscle tone imbalance.

Like teachers, therapists use a large variety of formal and informal evaluation tools, including specific developmental charts, tests such as the Peabody Test of Motor Proficiency, and informal qualitative observation. A typical evaluation includes a review of pertinent historical information, medical history, current medications, and special observations from teachers and parents. The assessment might begin with a description of the child's behavior with the therapist, special considerations such as whether or not a child is verbal and able to understand directions, and the circumstances of the evaluation, location, who was present, and whether the timing was supportive of the child's best behavior and effort. One of the benefits of having therapists on your staff is their familiarity with the children, eliminating the "stranger" effect on the dynamic between the child and the examiner.

The next major step is an analysis of the specific neuromuscular elements which affect sensorimotor behavior. This section can vary, but should always include the following:

1. *Neuromuscular status,* including muscle tone and strength, level and quality of reflex or automatic movement, range of motion (movement flexibility) at all the joints.
2. *Orthopedic considerations,* including specific problems with joint structure and stability, possible imbalances in leg lengths which could affect walking and running, and pos-

tural control and screening for scoliosis (curvature of the spine). The therapist should also check braces and mobility aids such as walkers and wheelchairs.

3. *Developmental level*, an assessment of a child's basic movement skills within the context of the gross and fine motor developmental sequence described in this chapter.

4. *Perceptual motor skills*: spatial relationships, body image, laterality and crossing midline, form discrimination, tactile sensation, eye-hand coordination, and balance — all of which are necessary foundations for more complex advanced fine and gross motor skills.

5. *Skilled fine and gross motor activities* which depend on the integration and healthy development of all of the above and are needed to progress to the highly complex fine motor and cognitive skills which are the work of every elementary school student.

The next step could be any or all of the following:

1. Meeting with parents and teachers to explain findings and discuss activities, specific needs and future referrals.

2. Referral to an orthopedist and/or neurologist. Kids Are People School often refers children to these specialists to screen children for more complex and/or specific concerns.

3. Individual, regular therapy sessions to remediate a very specific problem, carried out either in a private space within the classroom or a separate room, depending on which works best for the child; and with or without a buddy who may or may not also need therapy.

4. Small group sensorimotor activities which address common developmental needs, including group interaction and developing self-confidence in a safe, non-competitive environment.

5. Adjustment of typical fine and gross motor classroom activities to ensure not only inclusion of a child with special needs, but some activities which will specifically address some of those needs while the child is moving through a typical day.

Referral to an orthopedist or neurologist. Many children come to teachers, programs, and physical and occupational therapists following evaluations by various specialists — sometimes a whole team of them! In many more situations, however, where there are vague concerns around a child's development or specific motor or other behaviors, a visit to a pediatric orthopedist or neurologist may lead to clarification of a particular issue and recommendations which can support a child's sensorimotor program.

> At age seven Esther was walking independently, but her balance was poor, and at times a dangerous problem, due to ankles which were very weak and poorly aligned. She was, in effect, almost walking on the outer sides of her feet. Her parents were concerned, and an orthopedist supported the opinion of both the school director and physical therapist that short leg braces would give Esther the support – and security – she needed. The braces were ordered; it took several months for her to adjust. Within a few more months Esther climbed stairs with more confidence, walked forward and backwards on a 4-inch balance beam, and attempted standing on one foot with no help from surrounding tables or people.

Individual, regular therapy to remediate specific neuromotor problems. One of the most controversial issues in implementing an inclusive education model is the perception that children with special needs will receive less individual attention, and particularly less one-on-one therapy, in fully integrated settings. Our experience is that at some point many children need and benefit from individual, intense regular therapy. When a specific need is addressed in therapy, during the school day, and at home, remediation can be speeded along, allowing a child to progress onto other activities. For example, a four year old child who is very hypotonic with poor head and trunk control, may be still be coping with primitive reflexes which inhibit full voluntary control of arm and leg movement. The poor head control and primitive control of arm movement by these reflexes hinders the child's efforts to participate in typical daily activities. For several months a therapist works intensely – and individually – with the child to strengthen muscles, encourage him to hold his head upright, sit securely and independently, and gain independent control of head, arm, and trunk movement. During this same time teachers and parents encourage positions and activities which support the goals of therapy while including the child in the daily routines of life. The therapy may be hard work, and sometimes not much fun, but even the youngest children seem to understand that this work is an essential part of their life, and hard work can be rewarding when the goal is clear and positive.

Small group sensorimotor activities. At Kids Are People, regular small group activities for children needing sensorimotor support are a very rewarding and effective form of delivering therapeutic services. The groups are small, five to six children with two adults, and are somewhat homogeneous for age and therapeutic need. The goals of these groups are multifaceted, and include the enhancement of muscle strength and flexibility, gross motor and eye-hand coordination, motor planning, and visual, auditory, verbal, and motor memory. In addition, emphasis is placed on group interaction skills such as appreciation of the efforts and skills of peers, waiting turns, and experiencing motor activity as pleasant and rewarding.

We attribute the success of these groups to several elements:

- From a purely practical standpoint, this is an efficient use of therapeutic and student time. In a program where there is a cross-section of children with similar sensorimotor and behavioral needs, this is a rational way of getting services to a maximum number of children with minimal disruption to regular school time.

- This appears to be a needed "let down" time away from often more demanding and frustrating classroom activities. Even though demands are made, it is usually more fun to play 'hokey pokey', roll like a snake through the grass, and try to balance on a large ball than it is to do math. Success comes more easily – though hard work is involved – and there is a certain camaraderie that comes from the children seeing others in the group struggling with similar tasks. The staff and children share the rewards of small steps forward, and often children who do not have special needs beg to join the fun. For once 'special' does not mean less.

- We have found these small groups to be an effective route to remediating an array of developmental disabilities. Activities can be designed, and changed, to fit the specific physical, social, and behavioral needs of the children. The group process is a large part of the therapeutic benefit. The children cheer and egg each other on; often a child will attempt something new and difficult because the rest of the group, all of whom are challenged in some way, are willing to take some chances. There is no way to quantify the impact of this support system, but the progression of skills the children demonstrate over time, the joy with which they come to the groups, and the hurt that occurs if participation must be denied for some reason, all indicate that this is a successful route to therapeutic intervention for groups of children with special needs.

Inclusion of therapeutic activities in the classroom and home.
Just as a child cannot be potty trained only at home or in an educational setting, sensorimotor activity is a constant in every child's life. Individual and group therapy gives a child the big boost he or she may need, but muscles are hypertonic or hypotonic all the time, and even though crawling through a make-believe jungle is fun and therapeutic, the real goal is the strength and security to move easily through life's daily tasks. Though specific goals and activities vary for each individual child, there are three general areas for therapists, parents, and teachers to consider when creating a truly inclusive, therapeutic environment for a child with special sensorimotor needs.

1. If a child has special equipment such as leg or arm braces, a walker, standing table, special seating, or prosthetic device, everyone involved with the child – parents, teachers, teacher assistants, school directors, and classmates – needs to understand the purpose of the equipment, and how it will be used in both home and school. A child in braces must always be watched for skin breakdown caused by pressure or poor fit. A walker does not work for a child if it sits in the corner of the classroom waiting for 'therapy'. The most valuable therapy comes from the child using the walker to get to the bathroom, or to art.

> Marcus learned to walk with braces and crutches at 18 months of age because he was encouraged to see walking as a means of getting where he wanted to go both at home and in school. His friends understood what he needed to do, and they quickly became part of the process by bringing the crutches to him as needed, and waiting for him to arrive at activities when the trip took longer for him than the others.

2. For many children, small but specific activities which are integrated into regular routines can have significant therapeutic impact.

> Danielle's right side is weaker than her left. Fluctuating muscle tone in her early years led to increasing tightness, or hypertonicity, in the flexion, or bending muscles, of her right hand and arm. She held her right arm in a somewhat self-protective 'flexed posture' which if left unchallenged, would have led to increasing muscle tightness and weakness, and decreasing use of her right hand and arm. In addition, this downward spiral of use and function resulted in delayed bilateral and midline hand activities which are an essential foundation for later perceptual

and cognitive skills.

Besides individual therapy, we engaged her mother and teachers in an intense effort to relax the tight muscles, and stimulate and strengthen muscles in both right and left hands and arms during all her regular activities. Within a few months Danielle was using both hands with almost equal strength and coordination, participating with joy and confidence in the routines of home and school.

3. It is often possible, particularly in early childhood programs, to engage all the children in activities which are therapeutic for those with special needs. For example, a common problem for young children with physical delays or disabilities is weakness of the muscles of the trunk, shoulders, and hips. This weakness creates delays and instability in walking and balance in general. One way to address this issue is to encourage a child to kneel for substantial amounts of time during the day. This position, with hips extended, or a straight postural line from shoulders to knees, strengthens the muscles of the trunk, hips, and lower back. When a child can hold this posture for longer periods of time, balance and stability in standing and walking is enhanced.

At Kids Are People the children are often encouraged to use this position at the sand or water table, both of which have been lowered to accommodate this activity. All the children benefit from this 'therapeutic' posture, and the children with special needs are just part of the regular action. For the child with very weak hips and poor balance and endurance, 30 minutes at the water table becomes 30 minutes of physical therapy.

Planning and Sequencing Sensorimotor Activities

The importance of childhood motor activities and general exercise is recognized by educators and parents. Movement is an essential part of any educational plan. For typical children it offers an added dimension, enhancing growth and development. For children with special needs, a carefully planned motor program can help remediate specific neuromuscular and other problems, be used as a mechanism for inclusion in group activities, and develop self confidence and pride as children meet new and difficult challenges. Including children with special needs in motor activities is a two-way street. Any child, regardless of the severity of his physical limitations, can be included — with a little imagination and some adjustments — in regular movement activities. Alternatively, a sensorimotor curriculum which is planned with systematic attention to some basic rules of sensorimotor development can lead to a program which really addresses the needs of all the children and helps those with special needs build a repertoire of foundation skills and strengths.

There are many books, tapes, etc. which offer specific ideas for motor games and activities for children. Below are some principles and suggestions to guide you in planning motor curriculum which will be particularly supportive when including children with special needs.

General Planning Guidelines

1. A carefully planned sensorimotor curriculum is an important part of any developmental program. Though free time for independent play is vital, particularly with younger children, this should not be seen as the "motor" part of your program.
2. Planned motor activities are often an enjoyable, stress-free time for inclusive participation of the whole class.
3. Activities should be age appropriate. A 12 year old does not want to play "Ring Around the Rosy," but an entire class of 5 year olds can easily be enticed into games which feature rolling, crawling, and high kneeling, all of which may be therapeutic — and easy — for a child who cannot walk due to a physical disability.
4. As much as possible, start children at their current level of ability. Getting lost during a complex game, or never once getting a ball in a basket, leads to frustration and often refusal to participate.
5. For many children with special needs, activities must be broken down into very simple steps, with a slow weekly buildup to more complex movements. Constant repetition of old skills reinforces a child's sense of mastery and gives confidence to try new activities.
6. Structure activities to meet developmentally sequenced skills. This includes fine and gross motor, and perceptual motor skills.
7. If a child is receiving physical, occupational, or speech therapy, ask for recommendations for meeting specific needs in any or all areas. For example, many children who have difficulty with motor planning have problems sequencing in general. Having the child repeat directions for sequenced motor tasks is very helpful and contributes to the integration of auditory, verbal, and motor skills.

General Sequencing Guidelines. Sensorimotor development oc-

curs when a child can experience and practice gross and fine motor activities in some structured sequence. Assuming muscle strength and tone, reflex development, sensory reception and processing, and inborn coordination is within normal, functional limits, a child pretty much moves through the process with minimal support and guidance. If there are any problems in any of these areas, the child can be confused or stopped altogether from moving on. Planning a motor program with the following developmental sequence in mind can give the teachers and children a blueprint for the orderly arrangement of sensorimotor activities.

1. Rolling strengthens trunk muscles, including muscles needed for shifting the body to maintain balance and the rotation needed for smooth, coordinated walking. Rolling is also helpful in creating awareness of the two sides of the body, precursor to the perceptual motor sense of laterality and bilaterality.

2. Crawling strengthens the neck (for stable head control), trunk, shoulders, and hips. It also provides a foundation for the bilateral, asymmetrical movements of the arms and legs which are needed for walking.

3. Sitting while being gently pushed off balance strengthens the trunk muscles and a child's balance and postural control. Though helpful in strengthening balance and control in walking, many children with special needs have subtle weakness in sitting balance, sometimes contributing to the inability to sit still or stay in any one position for very long.

4. High kneeling, both staying still and "walking", contributes to strengthening trunk and particularly hip muscles. This position can be used while young children are at water and sand tables, or for circle games where several children have poor standing or walking skills.

5. Walking can be used as a therapeutic activity where a variety of challenges, movement patterns, and integration of sensory and motor skills is the goal. The only limit to how you use this activity is your own imagination. Examples include instructing children to walk forward, backward, side to side, slow, fast, with arms in various positions, following a path set down on the floor with tape in the shape of circles, squares, numbers, letters, etc.

6. Jumping, hopping, galloping, and skipping can be introduced as children reach each level of skill. Lots of support and straightforward recognition of an individual child's

physical limitations become very important as children grow and perhaps fall behind their classmates in some activities.

7. Strengthening and relaxation activities including pulling, hanging, pushing, and lifting can all be done with support and in a variety of positions. A child who cannot stand independently can, with assistance, 'hang' from suspended rings or a bar; tug of war can be played with the whole team sitting or kneeling; and everyone can lie down and 'stretch' arms and legs as far as possible.

These suggestions provide just a few examples of how motor activities can be designed around structured developmental needs of all children, while at the same time including and adjusting to some of the specific therapeutic needs of individual children.

Children with a wide range of sensorimotor delay and disability can be included in regular school programs. Specific therapeutic needs fluctuate in type and intensity with the age of the child, and the degree and type of disability. Some children just need a periodic boost which can be delivered during regular school and home activities. Others require intense, long-term attention which can encompass individual therapy, specialized small group activities, and adjustments and activities which are included in the school day.

The real issue is recognition of the fact that sensorimotor competence is a crucial piece of the foundation that leads to the development of independent, happy, and growing children. There are many ways an educational program can address the special needs of children for whom movement is a difficult and challenging business.

CHAPTER NINE

Parents, Children and Staff Speak: Telling Their Own Story

THE PARENTS SPEAK

Parenting young children in today's society is a demanding and complex job. When a child has special needs which place extra demands of time, attention, and cost on the family, parenting simply becomes even more complex. It is our belief that one of the major roles of educational programs should be to support family efforts to raise their young children and to support them in school.

Parents of children with special needs deal with all of the above, and must contend with a wide variety of extra demands which also impact on the family. Most parents experience emotional turmoil from time to time. For parents of children with special needs, the emotional impact of the child's problems on the parents and the family can be intense and chronic in nature.

We have asked the parents of Marcus, Lauren, Sean, Esther, and Benjamin to write about their children, telling us about their feelings and experiences.

Marcus, as told by his father.

Marcus was born with myelomeningocele (a form of spina bifida) and is hemiparetic from the knees down with a ventricular-pulmonary shunt. There was no family history or warning to indicate Marcus' condition. We did not realize there was any problem until excess fluid in the brain was detected one day before Marcus' birth. Surgery was performed within a few hours of birth to close the spine, and the shunt was implanted within the first week. Marcus was placed in isolation at Children's Hospital for 18 days before his discharge.

As parents we were instructed how to manipulate and stretch

Marcus' legs by physical therapists while Marcus was still at Children's Hospital. This was successful in that prior to our intensive therapy he was unable to bring down and straighten his legs. From the age of 8 to 15 months Marcus was visited at home by an early intervention therapist to assist in reaching age-appropriate milestones in physical activity. Said program was only marginally useful in that Marcus did not respond enthusiastically in his familiar environment to someone he apparently deemed a stranger, due to the relative infrequency of visits (one per week). There were also changes in personnel in terms of those making the home visits. Also the particular exercises were little different in substance to those we were performing after instruction from therapists at Children's Hospital.

Marcus has made a tremendous impact on us as parents and upon everyone who has ever known him. His care has been, and will remain, very consuming in terms of time and emotional involvement. Everyday activities require a great deal of logistical planning, since transportation and access are difficult. Hygiene issues are paramount in importance and very time-consuming. Due to bowel and bladder incontinence, Marcus requires much supervision. Earlier credeing (emptying bladder through pushing on the abdomen) and current catheterization are time-consuming with an ever-present danger of infection. Bowel management is very difficult, with medication necessary. Furthermore, possibilities of leg fracture or dislocation and shunt malfunction are always present. Visits to myelodysplasia clinics and to other specialists — neurosurgery and neurology, brace straps, etc. — are time-consuming. Every week involves some sort of scheduling dilemma, and it is primarily Mary's devotion to her family and high degree of organization that make everything manageable.

Moreover, Marcus is so cooperative, good-humored and intelligent that he makes his personal care much easier. Marcus fully understands his condition and is very independent and at times very self-diagnostic. Marcus' determination is superb and his response to love and challenges have been very heartening. Marcus really doesn't realize just how amazing he is. He is so loving, hard working, and eager to please that he has overcome many hurdles and keeps doctors, teachers, therapists and family alike constantly amazed. Any detractions brought about by Marcus' condition are compensated for manyfold by the great satisfaction found by all in Marcus' accomplishments; and most importantly by the tremendous love of others Marcus has. His love of other people is so great that it begets love in return which really makes Marcus strive even more to conquer any barriers.

In need of child care for employment reasons, and in need of an integrated program for Marcus' stimulation, Mary called the Federation for Children with Special Needs. She saw several programs and Kids Are People School was the best in terms of its reputation, the generally loving, nurturing environment, and its location. We absolutely have wanted an integrated environment for Marcus from the start. Kids Are People School fits the bill perfectly! Marcus counts as friends children from every economic and ethnic background. Some friends have disabilities, others do not. This environment has been invaluable in Marcus' shaping a positive image of himself and his value in society. He appreciates and understands both the vast differences of and common bond among people better than do most adults.

The impact of Kids Are People School has been nothing short of phenomenal. Marcus has positively thrived in the warm and supportive atmosphere. After only a few short weeks his progress in physical development astounded Mary and me. The quality in physical therapy (and later O.T.) has been extremely professional and there has been excellent continuity as well.

Moreover, the integrating concept began to prove its merits. Within a few weeks of his arrival at Kids Are People School, Marcus began to emulate the physical activities of his "normal" or more fully able peers. From crawling, to walking, to later "dancing," Marcus has participated in a full range of physical, every day activities from the day of his arrival. Through the encouragement of staff and peers as well as therapists he is truly a full participant at Kids Are People School. At Kids Are People School Marcus finds a very stable environment where he can explore his physical, intellectual and social potentialities. This point is critical in that there have been numerous interruptions in his life in the form of operations and recuperation. Kids Are People School is truly a haven and a rock in Marcus' life. Conversely, everyone at Kids Are People School benefits from Marcus as well in that they learn to appreciate and understand differences in others. For the kids it is a very important lesson and one that most adults have never had the opportunity to learn early in life since all the "different" children were segregated years ago.

Kids Are People School's existence is critical to the functioning of our family for what it has done for the development of both Marcus and his younger sister Kendra who also benefits from this supportive, loving atmosphere. Both have and will benefit immeasurably from the "melting pot" atmosphere that fosters love and cooperation.

Mainstreaming is the only way to go, I believe, unless the needs are so great that the child cannot function in a group setting. I have seen other kids with special needs thrive at Kids Are People School as well and it truly is heartening to see the sense of community such a program fosters. It is evident that the parents of Kids Are People School kids benefit as much as do the kids from the program. I believe Kids Are People School is a model for what education programs should be. The public school system needs to be "educated" about the limitless possibilities such programs provide. As parents we do whatever we can do to "spread the word" and will continue to do so.

Lauren, as told by her father.

June 12, 1988 was the day Lauren was born. Marybeth delivered her about six weeks early.

We were living in Plattsburgh, NY, the sticks, and were rushed to a special neonatal unit at the University of Vermont Medical Center. Marybeth had eaten very healthy, she's a nondrinker and nonsmoker, and had also taken aerobics throughout the pregnancy. She was even the subject of a TV news piece on exercising while pregnant.

Lauren's initial problems were related to episodes of apnea and bradycardia. Near as I could figure out, it meant that she stopped breathing for no reason. After a month of commuting two hours each way, part of it on a ferry, we were able to bring Lauren home from Vermont on a monitor.

The monitor would alarm when she stopped breathing — then we would rush to stimulate her and get her breathing again. The monitor was a necessary evil, as it kept her alive but it provided six months of hell fearing that the monitor would alarm at any time of the day and night and had us wondering whether our baby would come out of the episode alive. The monitor and drugs she had to take while on it were just the beginning.

When we moved to West Point, NY, it was closing in on Lauren's first winter. She was off the monitor now, but because of her hypotonia, low muscle tone, she could not fight off colds. Colds led to bronchitis and bronchitis to pneumonia. Not exaggerating, she was at the pediatrician's office three times per week switching from one antibiotic to the next. She also was put on a suction machine which removed infected mucous. It was so prevalent we had to buy one for home just so she could breathe without choking on her mucous.

Her pediatrician could not explain her numerous illnesses, but Marybeth knew that something was not right. Lauren ended up in the hospital shortly thereafter for a week with roseola. About a month later she began coughing blood on Easter and was rushed to Westchester Medical Center for emergency inter-susseption surgery. After two weeks she was allowed out. Honestly — this was the end of our simple problems.

We decided we should see a pediatric neurologist because Mary-beth felt Lauren was not developing like other babies. It was tough to tell, though, because she was our first and we had nothing to compare her to. We saw a specialist at the Helen Hayes Hospital in New York. He told us that she was seriously delayed and his initial diagnosis was Cerebral Palsy. We went from having an inkling something was wrong to getting hit in the head with a baseball bat. Cerebral Palsy? It is strange how as parents you definitely want to know what is wrong with your child when problems arise, yet when it is bad news you wish you had never asked the question. It's the "no news is good news — because it's not bad news" deal.

This information crushed us. What had we done wrong to bring this upon this angel of a child? But we did not believe it was CP. This marked the beginning of two horrible years of testing and evaluation by some of the preeminent pediatric neurologists in the Northeast, taking us from the Columbia Presbyterian and Mt. Sinai Hospitals in New York to Mass General and Children's in Boston to ultimately determine Lauren's condition.

Lauren endured a battery of tests: the EMGNC for nerve conduction studies (which basically jabbed her with needles until she looked like a practice dummy for an acupuncture school), surgery for muscle biopsy, MRI's, CAT scans, EEG's, etc. Simultaneously she began a proactive program of physical and occupational therapy. Marybeth and I were both working full time and not making much money. Every time we turned around there was another hospital bill for this or another doctor bill for that. This put a tremendous stress on our marriage. And what happens when you only have one child is that you focus in on her problems and it just takes your life over. You do not have anything else as a distraction, and being in New York we had no family support — so we moved back to Boston.

With Lauren's situation worsening (she was about 1-1/2), we moved back to Boston for two reasons: (1) so that she could be treated at the Children's Hospital, whose doctors made us feel the most comfortable, and (2) for family support.

By this time Lauren's diagnosis had gone from CP to KooKooBird Wheelander Disease to Rett's Syndrome. Dr. Yessayan at Children's provided us with a comfort level we needed and a diagnosis that we believed in — probably because it was the most optimistic one we had heard. The diagnosis was and still is PDD, Pervasive Developmental Delay, which provides a category but not a strict definition. This point is important, because without a diagnosis insurance companies will not pay for treatment and testing, so that the doctor/patient/parents must strategize on a diagnosis in order to leave the most options open for treatment of the patient.

The diagnosis has allowed Lauren the opportunity to improve, which she has been doing for the past four years. It did not box her into a forced diagnosis and a specific treatment. The primary reason for her improvement and state-of-the-art therapy is the work of two people: Lauren's mom Marybeth, and Katie Blenk, the director of Kids Are People School.

I had taken (and probably always will take) the "one day at a time" outlook with Lauren. I love her immensely today and always, and prefer not to think about tomorrow yet. But Katie and Marybeth took one look at Lauren and predetermined that this child was going to improve: to be able to sit up by herself, eventually stand up with assistance, walk with help, take part in math class, and start to say words. I know I looked at Katie like she was crazy, but inside I believed her.

Moving back to Boston meant a higher cost of living, so Marybeth had to work. Day care for Lauren and her situation was extremely difficult to find and very expensive. After looking at many top-quality schools, Kids Are People School was an easy choice because of Katie and her staff. The first time we met her, she believed in Lauren and made her a personal challenge.

KAPS is not your typical school, and Lauren's typical day is very different. It encompasses physical, speech and occupational therapy to go hand in hand with all the other events that go on daily in school. As one of only a handful of special needs children at the school, Lauren is exposed to positive role models daily and aspires to make strides in that direction.

KAPS supports Lauren, but they also support Marybeth and me. In our early days at KAPS, Marybeth had a physical ailment that hospitalized her for two months. I could not figure out how I could get Lauren back and forth from school daily, pay for it with Marybeth unemployed, take care of Lauren at night, and attend to my wife in the hospital. I decided the only thing I could do was pull Lauren from school and have her grandparents take care of her. Wrong! Katie would not allow it. She told me not to worry, we would work out the money issue. The most important thing was Lauren's development — I had to keep her in school. Wisely, I listened to Katie. Had I taken Lauren out at that point, it would have been my biggest mistake ever. Lauren stayed and things worked out.

Katie and her staff are a special group of people whom I admire, aspire to, and appreciate very much. She's a best friend and a sister rolled into one. Her strong will and dedication persevered many times in our battles with doctors, insurance companies, equipment companies and special needs agencies, just to name a few.

With the high stress raising a special needs child places on your marriage, Katie has become a part-time marriage counselor. Katie, the teachers and the therapists have been special to us. They have all taken Lauren from the infant room where she could barely sit on her own and transcended her into first grade. Lauren loves math class, takes steps with help and is beginning to put words together.

When you see a beautiful little girl go from doing absolutely nothing to saying "daddy" — it truly melts your heart and puts tears in your eyes. To see her stand and take steps raises your spirits and hope. None of this would ever have happened without KAPS and Katie Blenk.

It is tough to explain to people why I would never move Lauren out of KAPS to take a job in another city. Hopefully I just explained why. It is not only what they do for Lauren, it also is because of what they do for Marybeth and me.

I'd like to outline how Lauren's particular situation has affected Marybeth and me:

- Before, we basically took everything for granted — now we appreciate everything, especially the little things.
- It makes for a lot of spontaneous crying — especially for the mother to see her daughter incapable of doing and experiencing the things she has done all her life.
- It makes me cry in my heart every time I go to a wedding knowing that I will never be able to give Lauren away as a bride or dance with my daughter the way the father is with the bride.
- It strained our marriage to the point where we needed professional counseling to keep our lives together.
- We found that her condition was no fault of ours, and after much grieving we finally believed it.
- It has inhibited my career professionally, passing up jobs and opportunities elsewhere to keep Lauren at Kids Are People School and the Children's Hospital — but it is worth it.
- It is a full-time job for Marybeth to feed, dress, bathe and generally take care of a special needs child. This has also wiped out any chance of her ever pursuing a career.
- Because Marybeth could not work, it forced me to take on two jobs to pay the bills. With me not around to help her take care of Lauren or the other kids, it makes her job as homemaker/mother extremely stressful because she never gets a break from it.
- Our life is not "normal" like other people's because you can't get just any babysitter for Lauren. This makes it tough

to get out for dinner or a movie unless you can get a family member to help out. Thank goodness we have supportive families.

- You can't just take the kids to the park like most families. If it is chilly out, Lauren cannot go because she will get deathly sick. This means her younger brother and sister suffer because Lauren can't go. If Lauren stays and the other two go, it splits up Marybeth and me. We never seem to get to stay together.
- You learn to deal with people staring at Lauren, even though you despise it.
- You find out what a strong person you are married to when she's able to deal with this daily stress and still run a household.
- You learn how to put your broken heart back together after you've seen her leave on a special needs bus by herself.
- You learn how to deal with her body quivering and contorting during a seizure, even though you're not sure what to do.
- You learn that life isn't fair — but others have it worse.
- You learn to take life one day at a time and appreciate what you have while you have it.

I don't like to think of what might happen to Lauren in the future. I appreciate her now because no matter how tough it is, when she beams her beautiful smile at me, nothing else matters. Her love is unconditional, and that's why we are all lucky to have her in our life.

Sean, as told by his mother.

January 31st, 1986 I was told I had to have an emergency C-section. The ultrasound I had showed my baby was still breech with the cord wrapped around his neck. My sister Janet, an RN, who is also my best friend and Sean's godmother, was my coach and, thank God, was by my side through everything. When Sean was delivered, I was told there was a problem: he was a fine healthy boy but his right leg was missing below the hip. Sean was brought to me wrapped in a blanket, and I held him and cried. I didn't want to look at his leg that night, so my daughter Trisha and I looked at it together the next day. Trisha, who was 11 at the time, bravely hugged me and said it will be OK. I cried off and on an awful lot the first couple of weeks, but I soon came to realize that I had a beautiful healthy little boy. He is very special, he gets a lot of love and attention, and he has made me a stronger person.

He was seen by an orthopedic surgeon at Children's Hospital

when he was 3 days old, the first of many trips. Sean's first X-ray showed that he had a normal hip joint and could be fit for a prosthesis when he was ready to walk. I had to start taking him for physical therapy when he was a couple of months old to learn exercises to strengthen his right hip. When Sean was 15 months he got his first prosthesis. He learned to walk with a small metal walker. I spent Sean's first 3 years with him every minute; loving him, teaching him, and watching him grow into a fine healthy boy. Sometimes it is tough and frustrating going through all of this as a single mother, but after our many trips to Children's and the many very sick kids I see, I realize how lucky I am.

Before Sean got his prosthesis, when we were waiting for the bus to go to Children's, or when I had him out for a walk in the carriage, I got so I hated when people would stare at him or say "Oh the poor thing," or at the beach when parents would keep their children away from him. Kids in my neighborhood who have grown up with him love him because he is special, but they also play with him and treat him as the normal little boy that he is. Sometimes I wonder, are kids going to pick on Sean or make fun of him? Will he be able to defend himself? Will he hate me or be mad at me for his birth defect? Will he be able to ride a bike or drive a car? I guess we will handle these issues when and if they arrive.

Sean started going to Kids Are People School a year and a half ago. The separation was very tough for both of us at first. Sean had never been away from me. I hoped and prayed that I was doing the right thing. I was a single mother getting off welfare and going to work full-time. I wanted Sean to be in the best school, where he would be loved and educated as well as get the help he needs for his "special needs". Kids Are People School is the best thing that has happened to us. Sometimes I hate driving to Kenmore Square every day, but I wouldn't send Sean anywhere else. He loves his school, his teachers, and his friends. He also sees a physical therapist at school. I wish that all schools could be integrated and as special as Kids Are People School.

Esther, as told by her father.

Something surprising, strange, unexpected was happening. The woman — her name was Katie Blenk and she was the head of the day care center — assured me after about fifteen minutes of talking to me and looking at my daughter, that Esther was welcome to come, that it would not be a problem, that she would fit right in.

How could it be so easy?

Esther, after all, had a lot of problems. Hypotonic (suffering from extremely low muscle tone) since birth, plagued by ear infections, long bouts of flu and digestive troubles, a terrible sleeper, seriously delayed in gross and fine motor coordination, in language development, in everything *except* the ability to fix on an adult's face and make emotional contact (and this skill too only lately emerged) — Esther was clearly a "special needs" child.

How could accepting her into the school be so easy?

Well, Katie Blenk explained, she believed in "mainstreaming" or "integration". Quite simply, she felt that all different types of children belonged together, that they would learn from each other, stimulate each other's growth, and develop a loving capacity for acceptance.

This made sense to me. We weren't then — and we aren't now, seven years later with Esther nearly nine — completely clear on what her problems are and what limits, if any, they will impose on her in the end. Esther's problems are not easy to characterize or categorize. There are no national foundations for hypotonia, the basic thrust of which at times seems to be that Esther simply is not fully *in* her body: not fully grounded on her feet, or aware of her hands, or of any other muscle group. Consequently, everything that takes muscular action – from walking to talking, from reading (eye movement and focusing) to getting dressed – is extraordinarily difficult for her. There never has been a way to decide if her cognitive delays stem just from all the extra effort she has to put out to organize her body, her movement, her balance, her sense of herself in space.

So I was quite happy to find a place for Esther to be taken care of by others — a place where she would not be immediately defined by limits no one could be sure of.

Since her birth she had woken an average of four times a night, sometimes staying up for an hour or more after waking. For the first 9 months she had cried most of the time, needing to be held and walked and soothed. She had chronic diarrhea, then chronic constipation, eye infections, flus and fevers. My wife and I were exhausted, terribly apprehensive about her future. We needed some relief, some rest and respite, for the rest of our lives outside of Esther: for our work, for Esther's older sister, for each other. And Esther, who had had some baby-sitters for limited amounts of time, needed some stimulation and care from other adults — adults who perhaps had slept 7 or 8 hours the night before and who weren't distraught with fear and resentment. Adults who, like Katie, were committed to seeing and cultivating Esther's strengths, rather than writing her off as "disabled" because of her rather obvious weaknesses.

Esther also, to a degree that we could not fathom beforehand, needed the examples of, the stimulation of and the connections with other kids. She was not the kind of child you could just plump down in most play groups. At sixteen months, when we first came to Katie's school, she could not yet crawl, and while she visually interacted with adults she did not talk yet either. She could barely sit up for any length of time, and had few if any interests in toys or games. She was not yet fully aware of her hands, and so the fine motor activities that keep many kids of her age amused for long periods simply did not yet exist.

We needed help. And so did Esther.

And we got it.

Esther went into Kids are People School half-time, around 20 hours a week. (About a year later she made the transition to full-time.)

And two weeks after she arrived she started to crawl. She had seen all the other kids doing it, and I guess it looked like such a good idea, she pushed herself along like they did.

Suppose all the kids in her group had been unable to crawl, in wheelchairs, all burdened with the same "special" difficulties that faced Esther?

What then?

Where would her inspiration have come from? Could it really have come just from adult teachers, therapists, caregivers? Or could it be, as I believe it is, that there is a simple and unrepeatable gift that children can give each other — that connections and imitations and games among children educate in ways that no adult can?

Since those early days Esther has continued to grow, and flourish, and deal with her fate. She walks and talks. Now at 8 she has the beginnings of reading and math skills, knows how to argue with me when she wants more TV, has friendships, and likes swimming and dancing and movies and music. She has made "normal" friends at her school. Not as close as I would like, but there remain ways in which she is socially limited by her physical problems.

And I am confident that she has been pushed to adapt and achieve by relating to a full range of kids, many more competent physically and developmentally than she is, and some considerably more compromised. She has tutored those who need her help, and often been helped and protected and instructed by those more advanced.

And, perhaps most important, she has found a home away from home where she is loved and respected; a place where her disability does not cause her to feel excluded, where "difference" is accepted because with the enormous range of children in the school, *difference is the norm*.

Because of the loving welcome this school extended to her, Esther, while as crazy as the rest of us, is no more so. She has confidence in herself and values her own soul. Her schooling in this setting has not crippled her further, but helped to heal her.

For this I am enormously grateful; and I cannot imagine her in a setting where she is not integrated.

Benjamin, as told by his parents.

Our son Benjamin is now eight years old. He and his brother, Jeremy (4), have both attended Kids Are People School since early infancy. Unlike his gregarious brother, Benjamin is a quiet and shy child who often prefers to play by himself. A self-taught reader at age four, he progressed rapidly through elementary and middle-school mathematics and is now studying algebra and analytic geometry at roughly tenth-grade level. His interests are diverse: nature, computer programming, drawing, languages, inventing machines (on paper or with Legos), music, board games (often of his own design), puzzles, and, above all else, books. Although this short list of his aptitudes and interests is clearly out of the ordinary, he did not always seem precocious to us.

At ten months, Benjamin was not yet crawling, nor was he even trying to crawl. We had no particular worries about his development (one of us was a late walker), but his teachers noticed that his muscle tone was low and recommended physical therapy. Within another month, however, he had decided to crawl, and did so. As with crawling, Benjamin learned to walk seemingly by observation, rather than by trial and stumble. One day, at 13 months, he decided he was ready to give it a try; when we arrived at school that afternoon, his teacher told us that he had taken 46 steps in a row. We began to notice a pattern of punctuated development in Benjamin.

Speech followed a similar pattern: Benjamin's speaking vocabulary progressed within about a week from fewer than ten words to hundreds (we tried keeping a list during the first days of what we afterwards called his "speech explosion," but the task rapidly became unmanageable).

Reading together has always been a large part of our family life. Benjamin was a quiet baby who would sit happily for an hour in our laps as we read to him, long before he could understand what we were reading. Perhaps because of the association between reading and being cuddled, he treated books as gently as we treated him, and often fell asleep holding one. Before age two, he was able to locate any of his (hundred or so) books by looking at their spines on the bookshelf, and he had memorized at least ten of his favorites, which he would "read" to us, turning the pages at approximately the right times. Although we realized that this was unusual, we took it as evidence not of precocity but of Benjamin's simply having responded to our own love of books; if we had spent as many hours playing catch as reading, he would probably have responded as positively to a baseball, but we would not have assumed he was headed for the major leagues.

Benjamin liked to have "reading parties" on his bedroom floor, carefully arranging his stuffed animals in a circle, each with its own party hat and a carefully chosen book ("Curious George" for the monkey, "Ellen's Lion" for the lion, "Winnie-the-Pooh" for his favorite teddy bear, and so on). His attention to detail was remarkable. If, while reading a book for the first time, one of us made a comment, Benjamin would notice its omission on the next reading and repeat it if necessary. Once, shortly after he had turned two, we were reading a picture book. "Look," said the reader. "There's a crib just like yours." "Actually," replied Benjamin, after close examination of the picture, "it's similar."

Until he was nearly four, Benjamin's daily routine included reading while riding to school, with whichever parent was not driving. After Jeremy was born, one of us stayed home with him, and Benjamin lost his reader for a few weeks. Once he was convinced that it really was not possible for the driver to read to him while driving, he decided to learn to read himself, beginning with the books he had already memorized. He quickly progressed to other books, getting help from the driver by spelling out the words he didn't recognize. After two weeks he rarely needed to spell out words, although sometimes he would pause for a while between sentences while studying an unfamiliar word. Once he figured it out from context, the whole sentence would come out, fluently and with expression.

It is stretching the truth only slightly to say that he learns everything this way. He may watch others with rapt attention, or he may appear to pay no attention at all, but somehow he absorbs what he wants to know. He demonstrates what he has learned only when he can do it well. For a child like Benjamin, acquiring purely intellectual skills (such as learning to read or do arithmetic) can seem effortless to those who follow his development, because he gives virtually no evidence that he is even attempting to learn such skills until he has mastered them. In contrast, most tasks that require an integration of mental and physical skills (such as writing) or interaction with others (such as game-playing) can seem to require inordinate effort from Benjamin; the difference is that learning such skills can't be completely internalized. For Benjamin, a large part of the struggle is to risk doing something less than perfect; for our part, we are still learning how to offer encouragement without condescension.

In preschool, Benjamin often played by himself. In part, he may have done this simply because his interests differed from those of many of his friends: even at age three, he often became totally absorbed in activities such as drawing for an hour or more at a time, long after most others his age would have lost interest. When asked if there were anything he disliked about school, he would sometimes admit that noise made him uncomfortable. This may account for his tendency to withdraw from groups of physically active children. He preferred adult company to that of children; he could talk to adults about things he wanted to talk about, but other children didn't have the patience to listen to his long explanations. His inclination to observe others before joining in, together with an awareness of his own differences and a reluctance to expose them to others, may have further contributed to his frequent preference for solitary activities. Nevertheless, he was clearly comfortable and happy among his friends at Kids Are People, and chose to play with them more and more often.

Although his progress reports always indicated that Benjamin's achievements were well beyond those typical of his age group, he had occasional episodes of what his teachers described as "spacing out" (often sitting in a corner staring at something written hanging on a wall); rarely, his teachers would report that he was being stubborn or uncooperative. Katie recognized these episodes as symptoms of boredom and encouraged Benjamin's teachers to give him something more interesting to do. Almost immediately, he would be happy again, and cooperative. On one such occasion, knowing Benjamin's love of drawing, Katie suggested to his teacher that she encourage him to work with a slightly older boy who drew very well. The two of them had a lot of fun together and became very good friends. For the first time, Benjamin had a friend whose talent at something that mattered to Benjamin was superior to his own. They won and valued each other's respect, and drew inspiration from each other.

As the time approached for Benjamin to enter kindergarten, we were faced with a difficult choice. Katie pleaded with us not to send Benjamin to the public school kindergarten, predicting that he would become bored and isolated, and that the school would be unable to respond to these problems appropriately. We had no worries about sending Benjamin to KAP kindergarten: he had always been happy there; it was a familiar and comfortable place for him; he would have a good teacher and be surrounded by his friends. Our worries were centered on the possible consequences of not sending him to the public school kindergarten: that he would then enter first grade the following year, a painfully shy child who would know none of his classmates, while they would have had a year to form friendships among themselves; that in such a setting he might find it even more difficult to adjust to a class almost three times the size of his existing one; that opportunities to place him in classes appropriate to his abilities might be missed in future years. The public elementary school was reputed to be one of the best in the state, and its principal assured us that their teachers were accustomed to teaching bright children, and were skilled in drawing out shy children and encouraging them to play with others. Apart from these considerations, we also strongly supported the ideal of public school as a means of fostering tolerance of and respect for diversity in our multicultural society. (As it happened, the public school was far less representative of American society than is KAP. This irony was not lost on us.) We finally chose the public school, but arranged to bring Benjamin back to KAP for after-school activities.

In September, the public school arranges conferences between parents and teachers as an opportunity for teachers to learn more about their students. We told Benjamin's teacher that he was very bright and very shy; that he had been reading for about a year and a half; and that he had a strong aptitude for and interest in mathematics. We asked her to help us help Benjamin to find a friend in his new class. If she were able to identify some child he seemed to like, we would invite that child to visit. At that time, she said, she was still getting to know all the children.

Unlike KAP, the public school keeps parents at arm's length. To encourage independence among the children, parents are discouraged from bringing their children into the classroom, and parents are specifically asked not to enter the school to pick up their children. (At dismissal time, teachers bring all the children outside and wait until they have all been picked up.) As a result of this policy, we were not able to see Benjamin in the classroom setting. At the end of the day, while his teacher was trying to watch 24 children, we often asked her how Benjamin was doing, and her answer was usually "Fine." Occasionally she mentioned that Benjamin had taken a long time to do something, or to join a group, but we expected that we would hear more if there were any serious problems. Meanwhile, Benjamin himself seemed to like school, though he would say less and less about it as the year progressed; he wouldn't tell us who his friends were, but in the past he had rarely mentioned his friends by name. We asked his teacher again to let us know who might be good for Benjamin to play with, who might challenge him in the way his drawing friend at KAP did. We mentioned that many of Benjamin's friends at KAP had special needs, and asked if there were any child whom Benjamin might help. Benjamin's teacher said that she knew he was shy and was giving him time to make friends by himself.

Benjamin's year of public school kindergarten had started out far worse than we realized, but the near-total lack of communication from his teacher left us unaware of any serious problem until the end of January, at the second parent-teacher conference. As Katie had predicted, Benjamin was isolated and rapidly became bored. His teacher was not only unable to respond to these problems, she did not recognize them and refused to address them when they were identified to her, first by us, then by Katie (who attended two later parent-teacher conferences with us), and finally by the school psychologist, to whom the teacher had referred Benjamin for evaluation. His teacher wanted Benjamin to make his own friends, and flatly rejected the suggestion that he was bored ("How could he be bored with so many different things to do?"). His teacher reported that he wouldn't hear her when she asked him to do something. He would sit in a corner, just reading the signs on the walls. When another child approached him, he would leave whatever he was doing and walk away. Most of the time the other kids just left him alone. When the kids were supposed to sit together near the teacher, Benjamin would hide under the desk. These and other problems his teacher recognized (that he "spaced out" frequently, and was often the last to line up for recess, the last to finish lunch, the last to get his coat, and the last to finish a project), she addressed by allowing the other children to criticize his behavior. (As she reported to us, the others frequently asked her, "Why is Benjamin always last?" Since having to listen to such complaints from his classmates didn't seem to affect him, she needed to have the school psychologist suggest another way of dealing with the problem.) We couldn't believe our ears. How had we not heard of these things earlier? She failed to recognize that being made a scapegoat *was* affecting Benjamin's behavior, but not in the way she intended: instead, Benjamin started having accidents (wetting his pants). At first the accidents were rare, but they had become more frequent in the weeks preceding the conference.

It took six weeks for the psychologist to evaluate Benjamin. By now it was the middle of March. Although Benjamin continued to have frequent accidents at school, he had very few at KAP in the afternoon. He played with the other kids there, and talked with them. He volunteered answers when his teacher at KAP asked questions. His behavior was not exactly the same at KAP as it had been before he started kindergarten, however. He was definitely not as happy as he had been before, but was unwilling to talk about what might be wrong.

At the next meeting at the public school, we asked Katie to come with us, to talk about Benjamin at KAP. The psychologist started the meeting by summarizing her observations of Benjamin in the playground. He was dumping sand at the top of the slide, watching to see what would happen. Two other children came over to see what he was doing. Benjamin walked away. The other kids tried it for a while, then left the slide. Benjamin returned to his experiment. The psychologist's conclusion was "he seemed adrift." For this we had waited six weeks! The teacher just wanted to talk about Benjamin's accidents and nothing else. We wanted to talk about the other issues as well: "spacing out," not playing with others, and hiding under the desk. Katie presented a completely different picture of Benjamin: a child who plays with other children, shares well, is extremely bright and needs challenges, accepts kids with special needs, and helps them when playing with them. She said she thought he was bored at school. The school psychologist had been thinking that Benjamin should be evaluated for emotional problems; reflecting further on her observations of him in light of Katie's comments, she concluded that he simply needed more time to get over his shyness.

We continued talking to the teacher in the following weeks, calling her often to keep up with what was happening. She was becoming fed up with the accidents. Benjamin would space out when he was supposed to be changing into dry clothes, and it would take too long for him to do it. She asked us to come in and change his clothes, in the inexplicable belief that if we did so, his accidents might stop. We pointed out that this might mean that he would be in wet clothes for an hour or more — cruel punishment for involuntary behavior. We suggested trying to find out what was causing the accidents in the first place. We also suggested that we come in to the classroom as a reward rather than punishment — perhaps if he was cooperative for three days, or if he stopped hiding under the desk, we could come in and do a project with his class. His teacher would discuss only the importance of stopping the accidents. Our relationship with her rapidly deteriorated. Perhaps uncharitably, we felt that she dismissed our concerns about Benjamin's boredom and isolation because addressing them would have required action on her part, and that her obsession with the accidents resulted from their effects on her, rather than their effects on Benjamin. We met with the psychologist again, and on her recommendation decided to make a sticker chart for Benjamin. He would get a sticker if he were dry all day. This still wasn't dealing with the cause of the accidents, but at least it was better than making him sit in wet clothes for an hour.

By this time, it was almost Benjamin's birthday. He wanted a party. We asked him whom he wanted to invite, but he couldn't tell us. In trying to get him to name some kids we asked him if he wanted to invite his whole class. He said no, he didn't want to invite them all. We asked if he wanted to invite all except one child. Surprisingly, he said yes. This was a major breakthrough. We asked who the one child was, and he couldn't tell us. We took the class list and went through them one by one, until we came to Sam. Then Benjamin admitted that he was the one. "Why not Sam?" "Because he calls me names." "What kind of names?" "He calls me crazy." Perhaps to most people, being called crazy is no big deal. It obviously was devastating to Benjamin. About a week earlier we had taken a trip to the Boston Children's Museum, where Benjamin spent over an hour at an interactive computer video exhibit about racial prejudice, listening to the stories of children who have been called names, and how they felt. Now we understood why he was so absorbed with the computer at the museum. We tried to say something about Sam, how he probably wanted to be Benjamin's friend, and he replied, "He's not my friend, he tells me so every day."

We told Benjamin's teacher about Sam's name-calling, and how it had affected Benjamin. She expressed surprise, and told us she had never noticed any problems between Benjamin and Sam. A week later, we asked her if she had noticed any problems between them. She asked why; when we repeated that Sam had been calling Benjamin names, she didn't remember having been told about it. When we asked her directly to take action, her answer was that if a child was calling Benjamin names, he should tell her about it himself, and then she would take the two aside and talk to them both about it. We reminded her that Benjamin was shy and would be highly unlikely to approach her on his own initiative, especially given that he was so reluctant to speak with anyone about this problem. Although we asked her to do so several times in the following months, Benjamin's teacher never talked to Benjamin about Sam's name-calling.

In contrast, the day we told Katie about Sam, she was deeply upset that the teacher would let this happen and do nothing about it. She took Benjamin aside and asked him about Sam. He wouldn't talk to her about it. So she took him over to the school's computer and had the computer "talk" to him. Even though he could see that she was typing the words, Benjamin was willing to talk to the computer about it, but not to her. The computer said things like, "I don't like to be called names." Benjamin said he didn't like it, either. They went on playing this game for most of the afternoon. Immediately, Benjamin's accidents at school became less frequent, and eventually stopped. We continued calling the school to talk to the teacher, but she still didn't want to talk about Benjamin's boredom, his shyness, or his being called names; the accidents were her sole concern with respect to Benjamin, and when they stopped, she considered her job done.

Summer started and Benjamin returned to KAP full time. He blossomed. He instantly became more cheerful, both at home and at KAP. He decided to write a play. He made a plot. He made characters for each of the children in his group. He worked with all the kids, making costumes, designing "cars" out of cardboard boxes, making props and scenery. They had a great time. All this from a child who avoided the other kids at public school. At the end of the summer, they put the play on for the other kids. They all had fun.

At Katie's suggestion, Benjamin took an intelligence test during the summer; he loved it! The psychologist who administered the test concluded that Benjamin had very superior intellectual skills and very superior academic skills in reading and arithmetic, that he was very cooperative and attentive, but also shy and withdrawn, feeling anxious and socially isolated. She recommended that he attend a school with similarly gifted children, where he could develop socially.

There is no statutory recognition of the special needs of children such as Benjamin, and the idea that any public funds at all should be spent to accommodate the needs of a group that is perceived as "advantaged" is anathema to many. Nevertheless, the public elementary schools in our city had a program for gifted children until it was eliminated in cost-cutting measures during the late 1980s. The chief school psychologist told us that the materials that had been used for this program could be made available to Benjamin's first grade teacher for his use, and wrote a letter to the principal on our behalf. (Nothing came of it. We never saw any of these materials, even though we specifically asked for them.)

Private schools usually accept new students in January and February for September admissions, so we had little realistic hope of finding a suitable place. After many phone calls, we found we had no choice but to return Benjamin to the public school for first grade. We were determined to work closely with his first grade teacher, to make sure we weren't kept in the dark. We would also start visiting private schools as soon as possible in the fall to plan for the following year.

First grade started. We met with the teacher, and showed her the results of the testing done over the summer. She said she didn't know what to make of Benjamin's scores: he was reading at an eighth grade level, but what did that mean? She was sure he was very smart and that she could keep him interested in school. We sincerely hoped she could, but this year we did not want to wait for January to find out if she were wrong. We started looking for private schools, visiting several. All the schools said they had nothing special for gifted children, but they had many bright children attending. We talked to many other parents who had children in private schools. All said that the curriculum in the private school is slightly more challenging than in the public schools. Few had found significant attempts to provide individualized attention, and even in these cases it was clear that individual initiative, rather than an institutional commitment, was responsible. At one school, for example, the principal used to take four of the kids aside for a special reading group. That principal had left, however, and the new principal didn't do that sort of thing.

We visited a Montessori school near us, recommended by a parent of another gifted child. They had a lot of interesting materials, but it seemed that they put too much emphasis on the materials and not enough on the child. They talked about one child who had made an enormous number roll (to well beyond 10,000; it was displayed in the public library). It showed remarkable persistence, but we could not help wondering what the child could possibly have learned from the experience. We thought: the tool is taking over here, becoming the central focus, when the child should be. Still, this school looked more promising than the others because they mixed ages in one class and they proceeded at each child's pace. Finally, we found a school specifically for "gifted and able learners." The children did not stay with the same group all day, but moved to different groups, depending on what they were working on for each subject. We visited this school, and really liked it; unfortunately, it is far out of the city, and we reluctantly decided against it. Around this time, Katie decided to open an elementary school. It would open the next September, in time for Benjamin to go to second grade. We decided to stick it out with the public school, hope for the best, and wait for the new KAP elementary school.

In the meantime, the public school was doing better. The first grade teacher was trying harder, but she still had 25 children, so she couldn't give Benjamin the attention he needed. We called frequently, and visited often. Once when we went in, the children were sitting around and the teacher was pointing to a word on the blackboard. We saw Benjamin's hand go up, but it was pulled in close to his body, barely visible, as if he either didn't expect to be called on, or didn't want to be. This, however, was still a major improvement over hiding under the table.

The teacher tried to individualize his work. He had his own list of spelling words, for example. He was very proud of this. Trying to capitalize on Benjamin's summer and the play he had worked on, the teacher had Benjamin's reading group read a play and perform it. When we asked Benjamin what part he had and asked if he had picked it, he said no, the other kids picked parts and that was the only part left for him. He was not really part of the group, and was certainly not leading as he had been in the summer. On the other hand, he did take part in the play, which he would not have done at all in kindergarten.

Benjamin frequently didn't finish projects in first grade. We would see the other kids leaving school, each with a paper wind sock or a brightly colored paper turkey feather in hand, and Benjamin had none. It seemed that in art he would see thousands of possibilities, and could not focus on one to work on. In other subjects, lack of challenge was a significant obstacle to completing his work. He had a mathematics workbook that was much too easy. He did a page or two, then became bored and stopped. Since the workbook wasn't completed, he wasn't given anything more challenging to do. He started drawing pictures in the margins of his work, giving himself harder problems.

The school system had just adopted a new approach to teaching mathematics, with the goal of incorporating more mathematics and more challenging mathematics into the rest of the curriculum. Unfortunately for Benjamin, what the school thought of as more challenging mathematics was still material that he had mastered years earlier. Meanwhile, his teacher was trying to become familiar with the new curriculum and had, if anything, less opportunity to provide individualized mathematics for Benjamin than she might have had otherwise.

One part of the new mathematics approach was a game in which the children would pretend to have a machine that followed a mathematical rule. The challenge was to figure out what the rule was. For example: if you put in 2, the machine gives back 4; if you put in 5, the machine gives back 7; if you put in 4, the machine gives back 6. What is the rule? Add 2. The children were asked to make up their own machines. Benjamin's did this: if you put in 8, the machine gives back 2; if you put in 27, it gives back 3; if you put in 1000, it gives back 10. His "machine" was doing cube roots, while his teacher continued to give him problems involving adding 1 or 2. At one point he was given a simple set of addition problems, which he did. He then wrote on the paper "too stinking easy." His teacher circled his words and wrote back, "Uh oh, language." He was telling her, in the clearest way he could, that he needed more challenge. We were disappointed with her reaction, but again, we considered this to be an improvement from the kindergarten year because at least Benjamin was trying to communicate with his teacher.

Near the end of the school year, we arranged a meeting with the principal and the teacher. When asked what we wished to discuss, we said we were thinking of sending Benjamin to a private school the following year, and that we hoped to get an idea of what the public school might be able to do for him if he were to stay there. One day before the meeting, Benjamin was suddenly allowed to spend math time with the fourth graders, doing fractions. He loved it. His teacher told us that he did just fine, and understood everything. This was the kind of thing they could do for him if we left Benjamin in their school. We responded with enthusiasm — but the experiment was never repeated. If extra math was only available when we scheduled a meeting with the teacher and principal, we would have to meet with them every day.

The following September, Benjamin began "second grade" at the new KAP elementary school. What a difference! Classes are small (just 12 kids in each), so that teachers have time to work with each child. Individualized education is the rule, not the exception. Benjamin's teacher keeps us informed daily of what's happening. His progress reports are glowing. He is challenged at school, and proud

of the work he does. In mathematics, he is currently factoring poly-
nomials and plotting linear equations. For homework he gets questions such as this one: "The earth is 93 million miles away from the
sun. Explain what the effect would be on the seasons if it were 103
million miles away."

Benjamin is in a mixed age group, one that includes social peers,
physical peers, and intellectual peers. He and the others in his group
belong together not because they were born within the same twelve-
month period (they weren't), but because they all learn from each
other. Even though he works on different problems, they work on
the same subject. For example, the entire class may be studying the
solar system. He reads his own choice of books and has his own
spelling list, but Benjamin talks to the other kids about his work and
shares his knowledge. When we go to see the class in action, he is
with the other kids. If the teacher asks a question, Benjamin's hand is
way up in the air; he is ready and eager to share his ideas with the
class. When he talks, it is with confidence. He is happy.

He still has a hard time choosing from an open-ended list. In art,
for example, he may look at the project, see endless possibilities, and
have difficulty getting started. His teachers work with him and help
him get started, instead of letting him sit there and do nothing because he is stuck. They give him time to make a decision by himself,
but if he doesn't, they start making suggestions, in a way that will
help him make future decisions by himself.

Shortly after he started second grade at KAP, Benjamin com-
plained to us that every day at lunch someone would start playing
the computer spelling game, and he would be called over to help
spell. He couldn't get away from it. Benjamin wanted to be helpful to
the other children, but he also needed time to work on his own
projects. We talked about it with his teacher, who helped Benjamin
resolve this internal conflict and made sure Benjamin was not always
pulled into the spelling game. Benjamin needed to get out of the
social niche he had found himself stuck in at the end of first grade —
not being able to do his own work because he was spending too
much time helping others, which would eventually result in his being valued by the others for his knowledge only. Benjamin still wants
to help the other kids, and does so frequently. He now knows, however, that when he wants to do his own work, he can. Now the other
kids see him as more than just an encyclopedia; they value his company because he is fun to be with.

Socially, the transformation is incredible. We observed the difference firsthand when the entire school took a trip to a beach to
swim. After a short time in the water, Benjamin went to the shore to
make something in the sand. A few minutes later, one of his class-

mates noticed and joined him. Soon most of his group was around him, and he welcomed them and showed them what he was doing. There is no tendency on his part to retreat from the group at all anymore. The other children actively seek him out. When he returned to KAP recently after a week's vacation, Benjamin stopped in the doorway, looking like the conquering hero returning from his travels. Then the other children noticed him and a great cry went up. Benjamin just basked in the welcome.

When he was in first grade, Benjamin was one of 25 six-year-old middle-class white kids. Each one of these children was unique, but the unmistakable message transmitted when such a group is assembled into one class is that they belong together because of their superficial similarities, and that those who are "different" don't belong. Any child with the self-awareness to realize that he or she is different is likely to feel anxious and isolated in such a setting; this was certainly true for Benjamin. Had Benjamin joined a class of gifted children, as had been recommended to us, he would have felt less like an outsider. We are convinced, however, that sending Benjamin to KAP has accomplished the same goal in a far more satisfactory way. In an environment where differences are obvious and unremarkable, where diversity is valued rather than hidden, Benjamin and his friends celebrate each other's accomplishments. We believe strongly that we can best nurture self-respect, a sense of community, and tolerance of and respect for diversity in our children not by imposing homogeneity on them, but by respecting their differences.

THE CHILDREN SPEAK

Just Once A Week

An interview with Jammie Wellington, age 10

Q. What's it like for you to be in a wheelchair?

A. Some people push me and some people don't.

Q. Do you want people to push you?

A. Yes.

Q. Don't you want to do it yourself?

A. No. I like for Rachael and Jeanie and Michael to be nice and push me. Sometimes they don't get to push me. They have to take turns and sometimes Nicholas gets to push me and sometimes James does.

Q. How do you feel about that you can't walk and need to be in a wheelchair?

A. Because people say I'm handicapped.

Q. What do you think when people say that?

A. It hurts inside my heart when people laugh at me.

Q. How do you feel when you come to this school?

A. Happy.

Q. Why happy?

A. Because I like making new friends like Rachael Lofton, who laughed when I said "Nice ant Rachael!" She laughed because the ant she's drawing is in a tuxedo. Danielle, Gloria, Miguel, Cameron, Esther, Molly — she's not in our class, but she is still in our school. Who else comes to this school?

Q. Do you like everyone here?

A. Yes.

Q. What was your other school like?

A. I forgot Ivonne, Ivonne — it was kind of boring. I went to a day care after school that was fun. We did dance and had snacks and watched movies.

Q. Why did you want to come to this school instead of your old one?

A. I was bored and they put me in this class I didn't really like.

Q. What kind of class?

A. A baby class.

Q. How old are you?

A. I'm ten. I'm too old for a baby class. I shouldn't have been watching Barney all day at my age!

Q. Why did they put you in a baby class?

A. Because I don't like it. It was just little kids except one little boy in a wheelchair. He was mentally retarded. And a girl with a choke in her neck.

Q. A choke?

A. Yeah, a thing — I think it's called a choke. She was kind of like me except she couldn't talk.

Q. How was she like you?

A. She had braided hair like me and she was cute. But I wanted to be with the big kids.

Q. Why wouldn't they let you be with the big kids?

A. Just once a week and only at lunch, I could visit my big friends.

Q. Why do you think you couldn't be with them all the time?

A. Because they wouldn't let me see them all the time. Just once a week. It's not nice for teachers to make a child be with little kids all the time when you're ten years old.

Q. Do you get to visit the big kids at this school?

A. No — but I see Vanessa [a teacher], visit Liz's class.

Q. Why don't you get to visit the big kids in this school?

A. 'Cause, I'm too busy doing my work to "visit".

Q. Are you with the big kids all day here?

A. Of course I'm with the big kids all day here.

The Tale of the Princess and the Troll

Once upon a time there lived a princess. Her name was Grace.

On Friday there was a royal ball. She was invited. Her date was going to pick her up at 7:00. Her date's name was Prince Miguel. The princess took three hours to get ready.

The prince came to pick up at 6:45. When the prince arrived, the princess was shocked because he was a troll. The princess had never met a troll but she knew she did not like them because they were so different. She told him to leave the kingdom and he began to cry. The princess felt bad because she had hurt his feelings.

The princess asked the troll to stay and they talked and laughed and got to know each other. The princess found out that just because the troll was different it did not mean that he was bad. The troll and the princess ended up being best friends and they fell in love and got hitched.

The lesson the princess learned was that just because someone is different does not mean that they are bad or cannot be our friends.

THE END

Rachael Lynn Lofton, age 9

Learning About Other Cultures

We should learn about other cultures because it might be fun to learn about people. You should not care if someone looks different. You should not care if someone is a different religion. We should get to know people and not judge them based on the way they look or the way they speak.

Some people hurt others just because of their race or religion. These people are prejudice. They should study other people's cultures. If prejudice people studied other cultures they would learn a lot and would have more friends.

Jeanie O'Neil, age 10

I Like To Help

It is more fun to be at Kids Are People, because at Kids Are People School every person is at a different level, but they don't get rushed. And in my class not everybody is in the same grade. Almost everybody is in a different grade, as well as at a different level. And at this school they have computers and art classes and a lot more stuff then at my other school. At my other school for a playground it was concrete. But at Kids Are People we have grass. And our other school we could not use the computers, it was fun but I like Kids Are People better.

At my other school there were all the same kinds of kids. They could walk, talk and write. I did not like that, because I like to help people. I could not. There was no one to help. At Kids Are People I have four people I can help. And I love to help. And I have a bunch of friends all over the school. I help them to write, walk and talk, I really love to help. And that is really why I like Kids Are People, because I can help.

Rachael Lofton, age 9

THE STAFF SPEAK

When I think about Kids Are People School, and what it has meant to me, I have to reflect back to when I first realized that I wanted to be a teacher. It was right after college and I had decided to apply to an early intervention program in Philadelphia as an assistant teacher. Part of the interviewing process was spending 45 minutes in the classroom interacting with the children and talking to the teachers. Almost immediately I was struck by the severity of some of the special needs and how helpless a few of the children seemed to be. After leaving the interview I went home and said to my mother, "I just don't know if I can love these kids." The idea of working with special needs kids, of having a child depend on me so openly, and with so much trust and devotion, was paralyzing to me. What if I don't succeed? What if these children don't make any progress? What if I can't handle the responsibility? These questions terrified me and I spent several days pondering whether or not to accept the offer. What I finally concluded was that I was a passionate person and I needed to put myself out to be vulnerable and to take a risk. These kids needed someone who wasn't afraid to be vulnerable. After ten minutes in the classroom on my first day of work, all of my fears and apprehensions melted away. Immediately, I came to the realization that above and beyond anything else these people were children who deserved everything that life should offer a child: a chance to grow, a chance to experience challenges, and a chance to be loved in an environment where they can evolve into their own, unique person. I learned very quickly that a sign of a good teacher is one who creates a world where these things can happen and flourish; and, where the availability of love is unconditional.

This experience was a genesis to the many things I was to learn at Kids Are People school a few years later. Having had this preliminary exposure to special needs, I know what kind of determination and commitment it takes to be successful in such an environment. But Kids Are People offered way beyond what I could even have imagined. I found myself under the wing of Katie and Mary Blenk who taught me, along with the student population, what it means to give oneself so wholeheartedly to something that a day doesn't go by that I didn't think, quite honestly, "Am I insane?" The day-to-day challenges of certain children, and the day-to-day responsibilities and expectations as a teacher, are so unique that I learned a great deal about myself as a teacher and as a person. The children have pushed me and demanded a great deal from me that I have had to work extremely hard. I have always felt that if it weren't for Katie and the children, I would not have realized my potential as a teacher.

I think the reason for the intensity of this integrated environment isn't just due to the hard work of the teachers and to the challenges of these kids, but it is also due to the interactions and the feelings the children have created among each other. I get such an overwhelming feeling of pride for the typical kids who enter Kids Are People without having been exposed to a friend in a wheelchair and, after a few days at school they are running up to a teacher and asking if they can help someone get their lunchbox or help another child draw a picture. As a teacher trying to promote exactly these kinds of feelings and interactions, there is no greater moment. All of the frustrations of working hard and feeling exhausted are worth it when I see these friendships evolve.

The special characteristic of Kids Are People that I have admired over the past few years is that it is a non-judgmental, positive, and nurturing place. The typical kids help the special needs children and the special needs kids help the typical kids learn a valuable lesson in life — that being different is what we are all about, and that everybody deserves the same opportunities in life. These values are so fundamental to the greater picture in our world. Every night I would go home feeling exhausted, but I would have with me the knowledge of what Katie and the staff and children at KAP are creating each day. What valuable lessons to learn at such a young age! If only the rest of the world could do the same.

Through the course of my life at KAP, I think I've grown a little smarter and more accepting. But even more poignantly, the children reminded me of a crucial thing for a teacher to remember: what it is like to be a child. It is this reminder that makes me want to dig way deep into a child who I am faced with who may not talk or walk, or has enormous temper tantrums because I have asked him to "please sit down." There are few people in this world who have the desire to dig down and pull out what may lie inside these kids and is struggling to get out. However, the people who do want to do it are the ones who really know what "rewarding" means. There is no greater reward than seeing a child who had so many obstacles to get over make huge amounts of progress and succeed at being a child.

I'm happy to have proved myself wrong over the years after having spent that 45 minutes in the classroom in Philadelphia. Without question, we all love the kids, which is why we do what we do every day at Kids Are People and what makes it the powerful and unique place that it is.

Cydney Dundon
Teacher at Kids Are People School for four years

When Katie first asked me to come teach at her new elementary school, I said I had to think about it. I knew I wanted to teach art, and I knew I wanted to be at the elementary level. What I said to Katie was that I wasn't sure if I could do it — my concern was that I wouldn't be able to work with all the different children with special needs. I could teach art to just about anybody — but I was having trouble picturing how I would teach art to children that couldn't talk or didn't have complete use of their hands. I told Katie all these concerns. I said I wasn't sure how to teach something that was so physical and sensory-oriented to children who were hampered in these particular areas. I wasn't quite as concerned about the children with behavior problems or attention deficits, because they didn't present a physical barrier to me. I just needed a different and varied approach with these children. Keeping this in mind, though, I realized that the same must be true for the more physically challenged children. Katie confirmed this, and presented me with some books to read, and also told me that I would be their hands, or their teachers would be their hands, but they could make their own choices, or work on making their own choices with us, and so be mentally involved with the process we were physically helping them with.

Once I decided to definitely accept the job, I realized I had opened up a new world for myself. Not only would I be presenting the children with art projects, but each project would be broken down to as many steps as possible, so the children and teachers could all approach the projects slowly, keeping in mind any special modifications the children might need — help cutting, special questions about what colors they would like to use, help gluing, and holding hand over hand while working with clay. Not only were the teachers glad to help the children with special needs with each art project, but their friends also volunteered continuously for the privilege of helping their friend do his or her project. That is without a doubt the best part of the art classes. Watching all the children smile and laugh as they paint or glue, and especially watching the pairs of children — one helping the other complete the project or painting, and the laughter they share, and the sense of satisfaction they share as they look at each other when they finish what they have set out to do.

For me this illustrates how the world should be: one person helping the other — filling in for each other where help is needed — to accomplish things and feel good about each other. When I teach all these children, I not only get a sense of satisfaction in seeing their completed art projects, but I get an even better feeling when I see them all working together — making sure each child gets to do the project, and taking as much pride in their friend's project as they do in completing their own. Just the little day-to-day accomplishments of all the children with special needs, along with their peers' appreciation of those accomplishments, account for the greatest amount of satisfaction I could possibly get in life.

Nina Wellan
Teacher at Kids Are People School for three years

I am taking this opportunity to share my experiences working at Kids Are People School. For the past twelve years I have had the pleasure of engaging my teaching skills in an integrated program. Some of the kinds of special needs the children have had are problems associated with cerebral palsy, speech problems, deafness, Down Syndrome, and learning disabilities. Kids Are People School offers children education by both therapists and teachers. The assistance the children receive is in the classroom and also in small groups or one-on-one supervision. I have found not only do other children learn in a positive way how to help their peers, but parents are receiving an education that only an integrated program could offer. Children with and without special needs learn to relate with one another without embarrassment, fear, or intolerance. Children without special needs learn to see the children with special needs as peers with gifts and abilities. The openness, flexibility, and individualization of Kids Are People School provide a natural environment, encouraging all children, including those with special needs, to achieve and find success.

Some of the components I have viewed at Kids Are People School is that children are seen as individuals; a child with a special need is first of all a child and, like all children regardless of background, physical characteristics or abilities, has the same basic needs for food, shelter, warmth, nurturance, competence, and love. Every child needs to be in the least restrictive environment: an environment that enables each to foster his or her physical, emotional, and intellectual development. All children do learn, although each may learn at a different rate or in different way. I have recognized that the needs of some children may require more time, skill, and energy, but the overall result is rewarding. I have personally seen children as infants with major gross motor delays grow into children with only minor gross motor problems. One of the services I have found most helpful is at staff meetings we attend service-training sessions that are designed to help teachers examine and understand their own attitudes toward children with special needs and to develop positive attitudes toward children with special needs. A teacher must convey positive, realistic attitudes toward all children in order to facilitate positive peer interactions and motivate all children. For example, teachers have increased the use of visual aids such as flannel boards, pictures, puppets, and sign language pictures which help teachers, children, parents and therapists communicate.

Children who are physically challenged do benefit from the regular activities. All of these experiences in large and fine muscle work, socialization, and the language and art activities are beneficial. Physical therapists offer activities in which the child and the other classmates can participate.

Children with many different types of behavior problems are included, and teachers find the techniques of behavior modification are helpful.

Teachers are able to teach other children how to help or assist the child with special needs and encourage all to work together. Activities such as simple circle games, building blocks, painting, and computers can be developed to involve all children successfully.

Many have asked me why I stay in the same occupation for such a lengthy time. My answer is that I believe in what I am doing. Inclusion has had its impact on me, and I feel it has reached far beyond the child and the immediate situation. As an educator, I feel a responsibility to help children develop the outlook and skills which enable them to function effectively in spite of their special needs. I look forward to the future of Kids Are People School and hope that other schools can become more diverse when dealing with children.

Karen A. Dolan
Teacher at Kids Are People School for twelve years

I have worked at Kids Are People School for four years. During these four years I have learned a lot about inclusion and how it works in the classroom. When I was in college we learned about inclusion. However, they made it seem like it was so easy to do. But when you actually get out into the real world and work in an inclusive program, you find it's not as easy as the textbooks make it out to be. Sometimes it can be very hard. For example, when you are doing a lesson, you might have a child who is unable to focus because of attentional problems and hyperactivity. You have to be prepared to deal with these problems and find a way to help the child refocus as well as maintain the group's attention without disruption. Or you might have a child who doesn't have muscle control and can't do a writing lesson by herself, so you need to hold her hand as well as help the other children. While you can always enlist the help of the other children, in these instances it wouldn't be appropriate. And while therapists also help, they aren't in the class all day every day, so it really does come down to the teacher. It takes a great deal of organization, planning, energy and time to make inclusion really work.

Teaching in an inclusive setting is not perfect; you have your ups and downs (on a particularly bad day you can end up being tackled to the floor by an overly upset child). However, I believe the ups outweigh the downs. For example, when a child who has Down Syndrome says the word "please" for the first time, or a child whose doctors said he would never read reads his first sentence, it means a great deal.

If it wasn't for inclusion and the love, support and dedication of the staff and administration, some of these children might not have made the gains they have made.

I firmly believe in inclusion because I have seen it work.

Elizabeth A. Walsh
Teacher at Kids Are People School for four years

There seems to be a great deal of speculation currently as to whether the concept of total inclusion is an educationally feasible one. Initially, I think, it is easy to dismiss the concept altogether, simply because it seems too lofty or too idealistic. People tend to think of it along the same lines as world peace or the Red Sox winning the World Series: a good idea in theory, but hardly workable on any practical level.

Being a Yankee fan, I will not comment on the Red Sox' chances this year. I can, however, say with a great deal of confidence that total inclusion in theory and application is alive and well and flourishing across the street from Fenway Park, at Kids Are People Elementary School. Students who, a short time ago, were isolated or segregated into completely homogeneous groups are now side by side with children of varying abilities.

During free-time, a child with an IQ of 165 coauthors a play with a student who tested at an IQ of 75. A young girl who is confined to a wheelchair is helping a boy who is speech-delayed record an audio version of his favorite story. That same girl gets out of her wheelchair and into her walker to join dance class on Friday afternoon. All the while, a staff of infinite ability is tangibly and ideologically orchestrating the entire process.

There are no limits set on what we feel we are capable of accomplishing. Nor do we, in turn, accept limits which society has placed on children with special needs, *our* children. We possess the mindset necessary for total inclusion to not just work but work wonders. Children labeled as emotionally disturbed, who may have gotten into a great deal of trouble in other schools, come to Kids Are People with a clean slate. No self-fulfilling prophecies for children who may need nothing more than a fresh start and exposure to an open mind.

Kids Are People is a school full of success stories. Children who had in the past gotten what they wanted by simply screaming are being encouraged and taught to "use their words" or point to a picture on a communication board. They are encouraged not only by their teacher but by their peers — peers who attend Kids Are People because the elementary school which they attended previously would not teach a seven-year-old geometry, or had classes of thirty children to one teacher, or did not provide adequate physical or speech therapy.

Regardless of the circumstances surrounding their decision, many parents in the Boston area are looking to Kids Are People, not as an alternative but as the ideal. The ideal atmosphere for their children to learn to their full potential in the least restrictive environment. An environment fueled by encouragement, positive reinforcement, and genuine concern for the well-being of the children. An environment which could never truly exist in a non-inclusive, segregated classroom.

James Sheehan
Teacher at Kids Are People School for one year

CHAPTER TEN

Summary: Where Do We Go From Here?

On August 10th, 1994, I knew beyond all doubt that inclusion was definitely working at Kids Are People School.

Now I already knew it: kids had made incredible gains — even tragically serious diagnoses had been changed due to gains children had made that, according to the medical profession, they shouldn't have made. Children who were supposed to be dead were alive; children who weren't supposed to walk were running; children who weren't supposed to talk were talking; and children who were supposed to be locked forever in their own little worlds, never to care about others, were laughing at jokes, wrestling their friends to the ground, and screaming at me for attention.

And there was a sense of community at the school that only love and caring for one another could bring out. Children were automatically helping one another. Kids with special needs were helping other kids. Children without special needs were jumping up without being asked, helping their friends with special needs with positioning issues. And teachers were friends, parents and educators all rolled into one for the kids. The staff had developed an easy way with one another, supporting each other and using humor to get through difficult times. Everyone, staff and children alike, was growing and learning; inclusion was working.

But August 10th was the day that I first brought the oldest group of children up to the third floor to see what we had been working on for hours, daily, for several weeks. We had rented the third floor to accommodate an additional 36 children and to add a large motor room, science lab, art room and drama room to the school. In our motor room, I wanted enough space to play outdoor games and for a large climber. The winter of '93 had been the worst. We were locked inside for months, and I wanted the kids to have more exercise if last winter was the beginning of a trend.

I searched every equipment catalog I could get my hands on, looking for an outdoor climber I could put indoors. These climbers were wonderful. They were ADA accessible; transfer stations had been designed so children in wheelchairs could get from their chairs onto the climber independently. I wanted one of these climbers, but I couldn't put any of them inside. I called places begging them to adapt their outdoor climbers so I could put one indoors. But all the climbers were designed to be stabilized in the ground with cement.

I finally found a climber from Lakeshore which could be put indoors or outdoors, only it wasn't accessible. It didn't even have a set of stairs. All entrances to the climber represented a physical feat for children — which, by the way, was great for our typical kids. I believe in general that the typical kids shouldn't lose out because of their friends who are physically challenged, and the climber would be excellent for motor development for the typical kids, even the oldest ones. It was a challenging climber, and I loved it for our typical kids. I bought it determined to make it accessible.

The climber arrived. It was supposed to take two people one day to put it together. It took six people more than three weeks. Nina Wellan, one of our teachers, and I designed a transfer station from a picture in a catalog of a transfer station on another climber. We had to give up a slide to make room for the transfer station. We had to add several fencelike structures to prevent unsteady walkers from losing their balance and falling off. We had to move openings, fit beam 1 into beam 10 even though it was supposed to go into beam 2, and so on. The climber looks nothing like its picture; a little of its beauty was lost in the redesign, but a little magic was added, because now all the children can use it safely and, for the most part, independently.

On August 10th, when I brought the oldest crew of kids upstairs, we had put the climber together, but the transfer station wasn't completely built.

On the elevator ride up to the third floor, I could feel the excitement of the group. It was a riot. They were so cute imagining what would be on the "new floor". The entrance to the third floor space opens into the large gross motor room with the climber. When we stepped in, there were literally screams of delight when they saw the climber. "Look at that!" "I can't wait!" "When do we get to use it?"

Now every once in a while an incident happens in your life that hits you in the stomach and makes you feel like you've been kicked. I was looking at all the kids, and they were all talking at once, including Jammie, who is in a wheelchair. She was as excited as the rest, not seeing the climber as an obstacle. Everyone was talking except one little girl who just kept staring at the climber. She wasn't smiling; she looked upset. She finally turned to me and said, "But how is Jammie going to get on there with her wheelchair?"

Sitting here writing this, reliving that moment, brings tears to my eyes, because her comment meant that somehow we as a community had gotten through to these kids. We had changed their way of looking at the world. All eyes turned to me; dead silence hit the room. The kids looked horrified. Something had to be done to fix their climber so Jammie could get on it. I quickly explained about the transfer station and how it would work. This was acceptable to the group, and the tour continued.

About a week later, the same group was once again taking a trip to the third floor, this time for Jammie to try out the transfer station, which was completed. Now maybe the kids at our school are very special individuals (which I do believe), but kids will be kids and there isn't any way I can believe that the whole group wasn't dying to get on the climber. But we were really pressed for time and needed to have Jammie try out the transfer station in case we needed to make adjustments. The group really surprised me. They all sat down to watch Jammie get on at the transfer station by herself, crawl across the climber to the slide, and slide down the slide to the feet of the group. Kids were yelling, "Come on, Jammie, you can do it! Good job, Jammie!" Jammie then proceeded to get into her wheelchair from the bottom of the slide, totally unassisted. This was a first. What was great was that those children were completely delighted with the accomplishments of their friend. They vicariously enjoyed her first trip to the climber. None of them sulked or demanded a turn. They were just happy that their friend could join them on the climber in the future.

This experience that the children are living has changed their lives, and I hope it is something these children will carry with them into adulthood. Inclusion, when done right, has the ability to change the world a bit. For these children at least, prejudice has a difficult time existing as part of their understanding of how to deal with people. Once again it was reaffirmed to me that what started in our program as an accident 14 years ago, and has been an uphill battle, is good, is right, and is the only way to educate.

Inclusion is working at Kids Are People School and in other little niches across the country. But what about the future of inclusion? When I look into the future, I know that we will continue to do what we can to foster inclusion, and as long as I'm able and willing to run our program it will remain an inclusive setting. But I have three sets of fears about the future of inclusion.

The first one I have already discussed: that if the programs which are only superficially "doing inclusion" continue to be the model, which is what I see happening, then inclusion will be a failed idea. The decision makers in each district will slowly revert to a segregated model to "protect" children with special needs. This is what happened in the aftermath of the "failure" of mainstreaming. There was a marked increase in the number of mainstreamed classes that included children with special needs in Massachusetts in the years after 1974, when the special education reform was implemented. When a study was done in 1987, the record of the 1980s showed that the number of special segregated classes had dramatically increased (Landau, 1987). It is hard to see the same decision makers suddenly working to make meaningful inclusion happen in the 1990s, when inclusion is a far more radical and complex process of integrating children with special needs in regular classes.

I haven't been able to figure out if our state department of education is really working to make inclusion happen or not. In several discussions we've had, they *say* they're for inclusion, but that position is not clearly evident in the programs I have visited over these past years as a consultant on inclusion. Further, they are adamant they will only support inclusion in public schools, saying they are opposed to private education.

This position bothers me because we are a private school. It is private schools like the Kids are People School that often provide the best models for how to practice inclusion, as we can innovate without the bureaucracy of the public schools.

As a reult of our Kids Are People experience, I have helped adults understand and accept inclusion and change how they see children with special needs through classes and lectures. The typical children at our school might not have learned anywhere else to care about such things as whether a friend can get on the climber. For that matter, these children might not have *had* friends with special needs.

The typical private schools for children with special needs are officially certified as special education schools; they are usually placements that only serve children with special needs. Kids are People School is an exception which recognizes the good work that can be done with children with special needs in a mixed student setting. As a private school we not only provide instruction appropriate to the child's special needs, but the care and training that enables complexly involved students to manage more effectively, and sometimes return to public school programs.

It is widely recognized now that public schools have a minimal capacity for innovation. Reduced budgets diminish this limited capacity since they mean larger average class sizes and fewer teaching staff, even while the schools are being flooded with new students. In urban areas where schools are most stressed, many new students require extra expensive treatments directed at the effects of bilingualism and poverty.

Further, public schools have enormous bureaucratic inertia and staff that works hard to protect turf. The separate system of special education has no history of talking with regular educators about collaboration; it has independent monies from federal and state funds which it spends to educate students with special needs separately. State and federal financing practices enshrine this separateness. Either or both bureaucracies often resist the changes inherent in a move to inclusion, especially without a history of working together at the central district level, much less at the school building. At the building level, special educators must redefine their roles to work primarily in the regular classroom. They often resist this practice, having lost "their students." The long-term impact of this separation is that few of these students ever leave the special needs system. The separateness is maintained.

The generally conservative inclinations of an often oppressive non-supportive bureaucracy work against radical innovative practices. Inclusion is a radical innovation even in school districts responsive to innovation. Historically, public schools have been resistant to meaningful change. It is a well-documented fact that when public schools engage in experimental programs, almost no districts make successful programs a regular part of the district's offerings. Even "good" school systems are afflicted by these pressures. There is an absence of opportunities and creative energy to develop innovative practices and make them an intrinsic part of the school district's practices. This is a matter of extreme concern at the federal level when new legislation attempts to steer schools to new practices.

Can the complexities of inclusion as we have described them in this book be thought through and then carried out by teachers who are overwhelmed by larger class sizes, with less help as assistant teachers and aides are laid off, and with little or no time for consultation with their colleagues, or opportunities to work together to improve their collaboration in the classrooms? There is much talk of collaboration among teachers; little reality about how to enable the collaboration to occur within the working day. Little, if any, leadership is evident from the state department on these matters.

Thus, while many districts mouth the slogans of inclusion, they have few ideas about how to engage their teaching staffs in the dialogues needed to make inclusion work, or to support their efforts at dialogue and collegial work that are likely to make inclusion happen in positive ways for all the students involved. Special education staffs still do not talk easily or regularly with their regular education colleagues about the collaborative efforts to make these concepts work. And as with mainstreaming in the prior decade, regular education teachers feel they are being dumped on — only now there are fewer hands than before to help them even accommodate the children with special needs, much less provide them with appropriate instruction.

Worse, under the banner of inclusion, too many children with special needs are being underserved since inclusion is being used to deny children services so as not to stigmatize them in the regular classroom. There is currently much rhetoric and mostly poor practices, and probably much more denial of services than the law allows and we should tolerate. In too many ways, the realities that discredited mainstreaming practices are being reenacted in the rhetoric and practices surrounding inclusion, aided and abetted by the budgetary pressures.

Against the context of this sad tale, there needs to be recognition of the singular role that private schools can serve.

The inertia or resistance to change in Massachusetts is illustrated by the attempt to encourage school districts to develop programs that would enable all students with special needs to be served in their local school. More than a decade ago, the state department sought to discourage placements in private schools by offering the districts a 50% credit for the out-of-district tuition costs if the district created a program appropriate to the child's needs within their district. Placements in private schools continue, even with this inducement. The public schools have enormous financial incentives to bring these students back and educate them appropriately within the district but have largely failed to do so.

It is widely recognized that practices around inclusion have arisen in the private school sector, especially those schools with diverse student populations containing both typical children and those with special needs. The reason these practices have arisen from the private sector is that committed people like myself have been free to try new ideas and make them work, while the efforts of our colleagues in the public schools get stifled by the bureaucracy of their school and central office. When public school people do make these positive changes, these people do not get credit for what they do but are made to jump through additional hoops. Taking our ideas and using them to demonstrate to schools how *they* can make these changes happen is a compliment, but credit should be given to the private school sector as innovators. We can help train them, or simply provide collegial support to the public school programs, as recognized by my serving as a state department consultant.

At this time, recognizing these realities of public schools, and with disillusionment with public education's capacity for change, there is now a widely shared perception that public education needs considerable help in changing its practices. The move toward school choice reflects this sentiment. It is recognized by the current strong trend to put public monies into charter schools and other non-public school enterprises, e.g., the Edison Project, which are to serve as living experiment stations in education.

It is an anachronism for the state leadership in education to be opposed to private school education. What is called for here and now is *support for all quality educational programs* which are doing a good job of educating America's children. All state departments of education need to search out their quality programs, public *and* private, and join all educators together to utilize the ideas and practices, to turn around the educational failures in this country as a joint effort of both sectors. The private vs. public education conflict is immature, and built out of fear, the same fear that encourages racial tension, segregates children with special needs, and teaches female children that they are weak and useless. This impetus needs to start at each state department of education with a change in attitude and practice. They are the State Department of Education, not the State Department of *Public* Education!

What state departments, as educational leaders, can and should do:

- All state departments must adopt a leadership stance, facilitating the efforts of districts to plan and implement inclusive programs. This seems to be a very difficult expectation for them.
- State departments have to declare publicly the desirability of promoting public-private partnerships between schools, recognizing public education's past failures in many communities, and the capacity of private schools to innovate and serve as learning sites for public school staffs. In fact, these partnerships can be beneficial and stimulating, as a field for discourse and exchange between private schools working at implementing inclusive practices and public schools who may not be as far along. And if the private/public partnerships are fostered by the State Department of Education, it needs to be done without preconceived hidden agendas. The only acceptable agenda is to improve education for *all* children. Private–public school partnerships can enrich both systems since each has knowledge and practices the other may benefit from. It is the flexibility of a private school, within the context of firm commitment, that has enabled us to develop the practices we discuss in this book.
- Concurrently, the state department must cultivate private schools with only typical children to enroll children with special needs, providing a process by which they can be certified to accept these students. This can dramatically expand the opportunities for inclusion of these students,

much as it has increased the possibilities of preschool children with special needs attending schools with typical students.

- Develop a roster of public and private schools who are doing inclusion well across the state. Develop a plan to use these "accredited inclusion school" programs as training sites for public and private schools. They can provide demonstration lessons and hands-on training to staff from schools in their surrounding communities. The state should attach actual funds so the training is conducted without penalizing communities that wish to move forward. This "experiment station" model can enable practitioners in both sectors to learn from each other by viewing inclusive classrooms and working in inclusive classrooms along side their teachers.

- In parallel, a leadership program for schools interested in implementing an inclusion strategy should be developed by the state directly, or more likely, by these demonstration schools. The leaders and senior staff members of interested schools would learn about inclusion. In a second stage, school staffs should be encouraged to develop an implementation plan for their school. With help from the "experiment station" staff, they could be helped to implement it. Federal funds directed to the state could be directed toward these purposes.

- Develop an inclusion policy group that will talk about and develop suggested policies for reorganizing schools' practices to enable inclusion programs to be developed. These should be developed for preschool, kindergarten and elementary schools, middle/junior high schools, and high schools. They would include such issues as ways to allot time for consultation and common planning among the regular, bilingual and special education staffs as part of a teacher's schedule; for additional training; for providing administrative support to teachers working in inclusive settings, etc.

But there should be a limit to how much time and money is spent on this. Time is of the essence for our children, and people ready to move ahead need to be given that opportunity, not made to wait for other, more resistant groups to catch up. In addition, groups who are already saying "we can't do it because of this or that reason" should not be chosen for funding and training. Too much time has already been wasted for our children on convincing groups to change who don't want change. Only groups ready to plunge in and dramatically change what education currently looks like should be the initial participants. It is better to add a few more great programs that are educating appropriately than to spread monies, talent and time thinly to get nowhere. These new sites could then become new training sites.

And it is important to listen to what people *say they need* to make the changes necessary. There was no greater frustration to me when I was a consultant than to have people buy into the dream only to have the school or department of education say, "*Oh, no! We can't do that.*" No wonder so many teachers in public schools have resigned themselves to believing, "It can't be done. Nothing ever changes."

- Begin to collate, and develop when necessary, curricula that school staffs should be encouraged to use to prepare students and staff for inclusion programs.

Above all, the state departments have to get off the rhetoric and help out in positive ways, not bureaucratic and regulatory ways (their favorite way of showing their power), to facilitate inclusion practices.

These proposals address our second fear — *the situation of the students we have seen who are not in either the few really good inclusive programs or the good segregative programs.* In the last 14 years I have visited many programs. I've seen some wonderful programs and some awful programs. The awful programs at best are segregated, provide institutional care, not education, and the care is of poor quality. They sometimes lack warmth. The rooms are very quiet because the teachers don't talk with the children; the teachers are doing maintenance care/babysitting of children they don't see as capable people. There is no excitement, no expectation, only a set attitude that this, and only this, is what these children are capable of. Jammie, who gave us "Just Once A Week" (p. 177), was one of these children. I want to know why and how this could have happened!

I feel so badly about the children out there for whom it's too late. I often meet children that I know would be different people now if only we had gotten them four years ago. What we are doing at Kids Are People School is a drop in the bucket. When I look at the whole picture of all children with special needs getting quality inclusive education, I feel overwhelmed.

Our last concern about the future of inclusion is about the future of the students at our school, because I want to know *who will provide a positive program for our kids where they can get the same caring education*, with the same sense of community and the same appreciation for them and their individual abilities.

We have already determined we need to go through the eighth grade, because we don't think the children should have to make the transition to a middle school and then two years later to high school. The Kids Are People Elementary School came out of a need for an inclusive elementary school based on our experiences placing these students from our preschool. We have figured out some key components which make inclusion work at the elementary school level. What would a program look like for true inclusion at the high school level? Until the Elementary School existed, this was not our problem. But now it is, because in three or four years we will have children needing an inclusive high school.

KEY COMPONENTS OF A *TRUE* INCLUSIONARY PROGRAM

For anyone starting an inclusive program or working in one that's not working, let me reiterate what we have come to see as the key components or characteristics critical for true inclusion. Anything less is a feeble attempt at meeting a legal requirement.

The teacher is the most important component of quality education for children in any setting. The teacher should:

- be warm and caring,
- not predetermine how much the child can accomplish,
- see the child as having as-yet untapped potential, and
- be willing to be creative and appreciate small gains with praise and encouragement.

The typical children play a critical role for those with special needs. They provide support, encouragement and models of appropriate behaviors, all of which moves the process of change along faster.

The classroom. The students with special needs who are part of a class are viewed as valuable members of the school community who do not stand out and look or feel different. In general, all the students are learning at their own rate and level, are happy to be learning, and are being challenged.

The administrator. Inclusion has to start at the top if it is going to work.

The community of support. This begins with the parents of your students, who obviously wish to have their child in your program. Additionally, a crucial activity for every program, after it has recruited its staff, is to identify and recruit qualified and experienced professionals in the related services staff who can evaluate your students' strengths and needs *and* also help your school staff translate their findings into good programming decisions. These persons must be experienced working with the needs of young children — from pre-school through the primary grades, or higher if your school program includes older students.

A more difficult issue for all programs, but especially when they include students with unusual problems, is finding competent specialists: resources in their community, or the larger area, to help them deal with the children's special needs in the context of a school program. This outside consultation is especially critical for getting the most up-to-date information in new areas of specialization, such as augmentative communication. Other specialists you should locate include a speech and language therapist, physical and occupational therapist, nurse and other medical personnel, counsellor, psychologist and social worker. These professionals contribute not only to the progress of the child but to the working strength of your staff. They can explain the child's and family's strengths and problems and can review and reassure staff about their efforts. *The consultation and help of these professionals becomes a major support system!*

But most importantly, they should be able to help you and your teaching staff translate their findings into good, workable program practice that can be integrated into the inclusion program in the class-room to the greatest extent possible. You want persons who will talk practically, not exotically and esoterically, about the child. Because it is the teaching staff who spend the most time working directly with the child, *they* are the ones who have to be able to understand the information gained from the specialist in order to implement it on a daily basis. The more the staff understands about a given child's strengths and needs, the more they can utilize them in planning programs appropriate for that child, and the more they can figure out novel ways to help the child fit into the total program.

The Keys to Making Inclusion Happen:

1) Well-trained, caring individuals who want to work in the program because they firmly believe in inclusion as the best method of education.
2) A mix of typical students and students with special needs, with the ratio being about one-third children with special needs.
3) There are a variety of children with different special needs issues in each program, but no child is a pioneer. All the

children with special needs should have peers with similar special needs to identify with so they don't feel unique or different than everyone else.

4) Class sizes are small, and there are additional teachers available to facilitate small-group work.

There is a mythology that inclusion practices can save dollars because integrating special needs students in regular classes means eliminating the old "special education" programs. Given the budgetary pressures, this is a seductive fantasy that school districts will encourage to save money, but it will insure the failure of these programs. Inclusion does *not* mean moving the children with special needs into existing classes of twenty-five typical children! There aren't meaningful educational activities available to the mainstreamed students with special needs in those understaffed and under-funded settings.

Inclusive classes are more complex, have a broader range of diversity among the students, and will usually — probably always — require extra adults to ensure that each child's strengths and needs are addressed.

5) Classes are multi-aged so that all the children are always working on different projects throughout the day and no one is segregated within the class.

6) Individualized education is planned around all children so that no one is held back and no one is passed over.

7) Cooperative education is stressed, where children problem-solve together and peer teaching is ongoing. Teachers facilitate education by helping the cooperative process.

8) Therapies are not deleted and turned into consultations, but staff and parents are trained so that everyone can facilitate the progress being made in therapy at the times appropriate for each child.

9) Typical peers are invited whenever possible for therapies if a child needs more one-on-one therapy, so that children are not segregated. Small-group therapy is done within the classroom whenever possible.

10) There is time built into the teaching day that allows the teaching staff to consult with each other and plan programs. This is a key — and often missing — element in the school design!

A word of advice to teachers: Do not be forced into having to work in an inclusive setting if you don't want to do it. It doesn't mean you're an awful person.

Advice to the Program Developer: If you create programs, don't force staff who are unwilling or uncomfortable with an inclusion focus to work in these types of programs. It won't work for the students, and the staff will not be happy either.

It takes people who believe in it heart and soul to make inclusion work. If you force it on others, or allow yourself to be forced into working in an inclusive setting when you don't want to, you are morally wrong and doing a disservice to the cause and to the children. Mandating people to be kind, caring and appropriate doesn't work; if it did, most of what is negative in society today would not exist. Expecting teachers who enjoy working as loners in their own classrooms to work with other teachers in an inclusive setting will also make true inclusion a rare and difficult outcome. True inclusion with a diversity of students in a class requires teachers who must work together with colleagues to make the opportunities happen for each child, whether the child has severe special needs, is from a bilingual background, is from a disorganized family or just is poorly prepared for school work.

So Where Do We Go Now?

Seeing the positive outcomes for true inclusion, our nightmare is that the majority of the current methods being used by the majority of programs under the banner of inclusion will provide negative results. In five to ten years, inclusion will come to be seen as a pipe dream. Schools, to appease those mandating inclusion, will continue to place students in classrooms where they are never really a part of the group, where optimal learning is not taking place for them — with the result that the health, education and welfare of the children with special needs will be at risk.

Quality inclusion cannot be done in large classes, without support, without appropriate equipment and materials, and without trained staff who have time allocated as part of their work day to consult and plan with each other!

In my opinion, if it's not going to be done right, I don't think inclusion should be done at all. If we aren't going to do it the best way, then it would be better for these children to get the more individualized one-on-one attention they can receive in segregated classrooms, with a strong after-school/weekend socialization program to allow them to make friends and play with their agemates.

The law says, and I agree, that children should be included wherever possible, and I have fought for this principle for years. And I feel that, for the most part, all children have a right to be included. But as strongly as I believe these things, I am very worried about these children being hurt by not receiving appropriate services in classrooms for the sake of the rhetoric of inclusion. So I honestly think that people need to stop and look at what they are doing.

Evaluating What We Have Done

Every school department in each city or town should have someone overseeing the programs which already *call* themselves inclusive. That person should be someone who has directly worked with children with special needs; equally as important, it should be someone who *truly* believes in inclusion — not someone it was forced upon. Good choices would be people who have been advocates for children with special needs for several years, not the heads of special education departments. These people are more likely to be on the side of the children regardless of what other people want.

Next I think they should spend a *lot* of time in each program, observing the interactions in the classrooms, following around behind the children with special needs to see what the quality of the program is for each child. They should interview the teacher, asking specific leading questions, to get a real sense of how the teacher *really* feels about inclusion. Principals and administrators should also be interviewed to see how it came to be that they are including children with special needs. Was it their idea? Was it something they wanted? Was it forced upon them? And this inclusion monitor should help any teacher to leave who does not feel comfortable and positive in the inclusion classroom, without harm to their career. They should be replaced by someone who *wants* to do it.

For teachers and other staff who are doing a bad job with inclusion, even though they want to do it, because they do not have the knowledge, material, equipment, or program setup, immediate training and support should be offered them along with the materials, equipment and program changes in a timely fashion. We need to stop and see what we are doing — What isn't working? What is? — instead of just muddling through hoping everything will be fine.

Our Wish List for Making Inclusion Work Better

We also have some wishes for the here and now of inclusion, for our program specifically, and as they relate to other programs and children.

- That we would be paid in a timely fashion by all agencies responsible for funding us.
- That doctors and other medical personnel who feel they

have the right to label a child would talk to us first before putting in writing their opinion of a child's behavior, abilities or needs. Their assessment of their limited interaction with the child could be much more beneficial to the child if they had some insight from the people who know the child. They need to remember that parents and schools don't always see the child in the same manner or observe the same behaviors. Most individuals act differently in various situations and environments.

- That all therapists out there working with children would (a) realize that a wheelchair is not the end of the road therapeutically for a child and (b) take it upon themselves to set aside time every six months to evaluate the equipment needs of the children they work with. Children grow — equipment doesn't.

- That colleges and universities would open programs for the training of new pediatric therapists and child evaluators. There aren't enough.

- That colleges and universities would stress the importance of inclusion as a technique while training pediatric therapists, and that for all students they train to work in one capacity or another with children, they stress the importance of professionalism and responsibility to the program and to the children.

- That medical schools stress to future doctors the importance of communication between themselves and the schools that educate their patients.

- That Medicaid and insurances would stop delaying approval of requests for equipment needs. I don't know what they are thinking, but someone's not going to request a wheelchair if it's not needed. This again just comes down to money. In Massachusetts, Medicaid has only one person to review all these requests. I wish more people would be hired specifically to review equipment requests. Six months is too long to wait. Two weeks would be more appropriate.

- That politics would be removed from the placement evaluation of children.

- That team meetings would be fairly balanced so that a true team recommendation could be made.

- That public school personnel would feel free to give their real opinions about placement; their own job future shouldn't be part of the equation.

- That the Powers that Be would recognize not only that

public school education is often failing our children, but that throwing money at the same system and the same people isn't going to change things. Lawmakers need to ask themselves, why are *so* many parents turning to private school education? If the reason is that the quality of the education is superior, then maybe a hard look needs to be taken at why it is better. The question needs to be asked, why don't all children *deserve* this kind of superior education? If the answer is that all children do deserve it, then the next question is if and when the public schools are going to provide it. The fact is there are some good public schools, but why are there just some? A school is a school. What goes on in a school determines if the education is quality education or not. What goes on in a school is determined by the money, the teachers and the persons running the program — those are the three components — so where does the problem lie?

If most of these wishes came true, my job would be a lot easier. I don't expect changes — in fact, I see things getting more difficult. As discussed in Chapters Two and Three, if inclusion continues in the direction it is going, where real inclusion isn't taking place, then segregation of children with special needs will become the status quo again to "protect" the children. And there will even be "evidence" to support those opposed to inclusion in their endeavors to hide our children with special needs away from society.

And out of the mouths of babes:

All Together, All Apart
We are all different
Everyone knows
But we can be alike
In many ways.
For we have a day
When we all celebrate:
We are all together,
We are all apart.

— Benjamin Moody, age 8
Kids Are People School

Just maybe things will change and we will be "All Together", but not apart. For the future improvement of education and the spread of inclusion, may this book be meaningful. This is our last wish.

References

Batshaw, M.L., & Perret, Y.M. (1986). *Children with Handicaps: A Medical Primer* (2nd ed.). Baltimore: Paul H. Brookes.

Bickenbach, J.E. (1993). *Physical Disability and Social Policy.* Toronto: University of Toronto Press.

Bleck, E.E., & Nagel, D.A. (1989). *Physically Handicapped Children: A Medical Atlas for Teachers* (2nd.ed). New Jersey: Prentice Hall.

Capute, A.J., & Accardo, P.J. (1991). *Developmental Disabilities in Infancy and Childhood.* Baltimore: Paul H. Brookes.

Dorland's Illustrated Medical Dictionary, 26th ed. (1981). Philadelphia: W.B. Saunders Co.

Gilfoyle, E.M., Grady, A.P., & Moore, J.C. (1981). *Children Adapt* (p. 58). Thorofare, NJ: Charles B. Slack, Inc.

Landau, J.K. (1987). *Out of the mainstream: Education of disabled youth in Massachusetts.* Boston: Massachusetts Advocacy Center.

Lewis, E.G. (1991). *Terms and Phrases Related to Disabilities.* Newton, MA.: New England Resource Access Project, Education Development Center, Inc.

Meisels, S.F., & Wasik, B.A. (1990). Who should be served? Identifying children in need of early intervention. In S.J. Meisels & J.P. Shonkoff (eds.), *Handbook of Early Childhood Intervention.* Cambridge: Cambridge University Press.

Moffett, J., & Wagner, B.J. (1991). *Student-Centered Language Arts, K-12* (4th edition). Hanover, NH: Boynton Cook Publishers.

Salisbury, C.L. (1991). Mainstreaming During the Early Childhood Years. *Exceptional Children, 58*(Oct/Nov), 146-155.

Taylor, S. (1988). Caught in the Continuum: A Critical Analysis of the Principle of the Least Restrictive Environment. *The Journal of the Association of Persons with Severe Handicaps, 13*(1), 41-53.

Thomas, C.L. (1989). *Taber's Cyclopedic Medical Dictionary* (16th ed.). Philidelphia: F.A. Davis.

Umphred, D.A. (1985). *Neurological Rehabilitation.* St. Louis: C.V. Mosby.

From Segregation to Integration: A Brief History of Special Education and Inclusion

The history of inclusive education for children with special needs involves thousands of individuals who have fought on various fronts to ensure that *being different* stops being synonymous with *being excluded*. Those fighting to turn this principle into real practice have included parents, children and adults with special needs, educators, human service professionals, lawyers and legislators, and many concerned citizens who viewed exclusion on the basis of disability as an unacceptable social injustice. The discussion of the practices at Kids are People School serves to demonstrate how these practices can be implemented in an ordinary school.

History, of course, does not stop; social movements do not have a specific end point. To maintain the forward motion of this transformation in practices, and to enable them to move forward in ever-expanding ripples, each new generation of educators must understand where we have come from so as to develop new visions of where they might go and learn from where we have previously been.

The purpose of this chapter is threefold.

1. A brief history reviews how we got here from the period prior to the revolution in practices and conceptions related to children with special needs and/or with disabling conditions. This background serves as a context for understanding the logic and the practices we have presented in this book. The story and reality of the practices developed over the past decade at Kids are People School provide a lesson in what can be done in the present and what we might all strive for in the future.
2. We discuss what data is available that describes the effects

of integration and inclusion on children, their parents and
teachers.

3. We propose some answers to such questions as "Where
are we now ?" and "Where do we think we might go?"

In 1954, the U.S. Supreme Court decision *Brown v. Board of Education* barred "separate but equal" as a principle for organizing education and recognized that "in these days it is doubtful that any child
may reasonably be expected to succeed in life if he is denied the
opportunity of an education" and that "such an opportunity, where
the state has undertaken to provide it, is a right which must be made
available to all on equal terms" (Beyer, 1983, p. 364). Chief Justice
Warren wrote, "In the field of public education the doctrine of 'separate but equal' has no place. Separate educational facilities are inher-
ently unequal" (Goodwin, 1985, p. 269). Although this decision applied at the time to racial segregation, it established the principle that
public education had to be provided equally to all children, with no
exceptions for race, class, and later on, physical or mental status.

In the early 1970's in two class action lawsuits, *Pennsylvania Association for Retarded Children (PARC) v. Pennsylvania* and *Mills v. Board
of Education*, the courts set forth the legal principles establishing that

1. all children can benefit from education and training,
2. all children are entitled to free public education and training appropriate to their needs, and
3. all children are entitled to as normal an educational placement as possible.   (Beyer, 1983, p. 365)

All three principles later appeared in state and federal legislation
mandating special education reform.

In 1973, *Lau v. Nichols* considered the plight of 1800 children in
San Francisco of Chinese ancestry who did not speak English. The
children received no supplemental help as they sat in all English
classes, and the Court "acknowledged that the children were being
'effectively foreclosed from any meaningful education' and ruled that
the school system's practices amounted to illegal discrimination"
(Beyer, 1983, p. 366). Advocates for children with special needs used
this decision to establish the right of all children to education that is
appropriate, meaningful and designed to meet their individual needs.

During this period, state and federal legislation was also changing the practice of special education in communities throughout the
country. This legislation addressed two areas, the civil rights of all
people with special needs to ensure equal access to education, housing and jobs, and specific legislation for education and programs for
children with disabling conditions. In January, 1972, Senators Hubert

Humphrey and Charles Percy introduced a bill in Congress to amend the Civil Rights Act of 1964 to add "physical or mental handicap" to race, color, and national origin as illegal grounds for discrimination in any program receiving federal support (Scotch, 1984). Section 504 of the Rehabilitation Act of 1973 was a single sentence that read, "No otherwise qualified handicapped individual in the United States, as defined in Section 7(6), shall, solely by reason of his handicap, be excluded from the participation in, be denied the benefits of, or be subjected to discrimination under any program or activity receiving Federal financial assistance" (Scotch, p. 52). That sentence became the legal foundation for ending the exclusion of children with special needs from public education.

During the 1960's and early 1970's, federal legislation expanding services to children with special needs provided for special programs and change in special education. The history of this legislation is long and complex, with early childhood education receiving the bulk of attention in the early years. Hebbler, Smith, and Black (1991) summarize this legislative history; we review some of the highlights which set the stage for inclusionary education for all children.

P.L. 89-10, the Elementary and Secondary Education Act of 1965 (ESEA), which provided federal money to schools, libraries, and various agencies serving poor children, was amended to include children with special needs in 1966. In 1968 P.L. 90-538 established the Handicapped Children's Early Education Program, which funded model early childhood education programs for children with special needs. The Education of the Handicapped Act (EHA), authorized in 1970, provided grants to universities and state and local education agencies for research and training in special education.

By the mid-1970's there was a growing acceptance that the education of young people with special needs needed to move from the band-aid approach of scattered non-unified programs to federally mandated services which would be designed, regulated, and implemented by state and local education agencies. The first real step in this direction came in 1974. Public Law 93-380, amendments to the Education of the Handicapped Act of 1970, provided new, specific requirements for state education agencies to provide services at the preschool, elementary, and secondary level. For the first time the terms *least restrictive environment, non-discriminatory testing, child identification*, and *full services* appeared in federal legislation.

These amendments were the forerunner of P.L. 94-142, the Education for All Handicapped Children Act of 1975 (renamed the Individuals with Disabilities Act [IDEA] in 1990), and marked the first time the educational needs of children with special needs warranted a comprehensive, nationwide policy with specific guidelines for local education programs.

P.L. 94-142: The Path from Legislation to Reality

Public Law 94-142 was signed into law in November, 1975. The law established a broad outline of principles for the development of appropriate educational services for children to assure all handicapped children a free, appropriate, publicly funded education and related services designed to meet each child's special needs. The Act protected the rights of handicapped children and their parents or guardians and ensured knowledgeable participation and consent of the latter in their child's education. The states were made responsible for assuring the delivery of these services and the protection of child and parent rights by the local education agency. The law, and the regulations which followed, spelled out very specific guidelines for the provision of educational services to students with special needs 3 through 21 years old.

For the first time in United States history, the federal government took a firm stand in setting criteria and procedures for the provision of public education for children with special educational needs. The law called for sweeping reforms in the way special education services were delivered. Its eventual impact on both special and regular education has led many to call it a "Bill of Rights" for students with special needs. The law has massively influenced how we view and deliver public education to all children (Singer & Butler, 1987).

The requirements of the law include:

1. Identification of all children with special needs in the local school district.
2. Assessment of each identified child, using nondiscriminatory assessment instruments, in the language of the child's home, with the prior and informed consent of the parents.
3. Creation of an individualized education plan (IEP).
4. Notification of parents or guardians of the prospective identification and assessment; a request they approve of same, and participate in the assessment and the development of the program plan for their child. They have a right to reject the plan and have clearly identified grievance and appeal procedures.
5. Assurance of placement of children with special needs in the "least restrictive environment"; and
6. The provision of "related services," including therapies, transportation, aides, etc., deemed necessary for the student's successful educational program.

Several features have had a powerful and direct impact on public education for all children. P.L. 94-142 mandated that every child needing special services must have an Individualized Education Program (IEP). The plan must include

A. a statement of the present level of educational performance of such (handicapped) child,
B. a statement of annual goals,
C. a statement of the specific educational services to be provided to such child, and the extent to which such child will be able to participate in regular education programs,
D. the projected date for initiation and anticipated duration of such services,
E. appropriate criteria and evaluation procedures and schedules for determining, at least on an annual basis, whether instructional objectives are being achieved.

The IEP was intended to serve as a tool to ensure that each child received an appropriate and individualized program, that the process included parents, teachers, administrators, and the student, especially when she was older, and that everyone had a written document which could be used to measure progress and weigh accountability. The examining and planning team were required to be multidisciplinary and include the parents. The parents had to agree to the plan as it was finalized in writing following the planning meeting.

Though the IEP has accomplished some of these goals, it is an expensive document to develop, and it often *is not used* as a planning document or guide by the service providers — though the special services the student requires, for the amount of time he requires them, must be delivered as specified in the IEP. There is continuing uncertainty as to the status of the document and whether it constitutes a contract, in a legal sense, between the parents and the school district. When parents disagree with its recommendations or its implementation, they may appeal, and the document and its content becomes the basis for the appeal. Since each plan is intended for a full year, it may freeze the student's program once he has accomplished the goals of the plan. As Chapter 7 of this book pointed out, the current IEP process can result in plans written by a team which does not actually work with a child, behavioral objectives outgrown within months or even weeks — not the year that IEPs formally cover — and objectives so specific as to compel teachers and therapists to 'teach to the objective' rather than to the child.

For example, as a physical therapist I was asked to work with a 7 year old boy who progressed from crawling, to standing and walking in 6 months, but one of the three sensorimotor behavioral objectives in his IEP was "Child will catch a 12-inch ball 80% of the time." There was nothing about walking in that list of behavioral objectives. I also remember thinking, "Eighty percent of what time?" The child's teacher was concerned that we continue to meet the ball-catching goal even though the very limited time I had with the child dictated that I work with him, his parents, and teachers on his newly developing walking skills. The issue was resolved, but not without several telephone calls, a meeting, and much time wasted by everyone — particularly the child.

The IEP was an idea and a tool which has served a useful purpose on several levels. Goodman & Bond (1993) suggest several changes for bringing the IEP back to the original function for which they feel it was intended — "that of reviewing, not structuring, priorities" (p. 418).

1. Create a looser construction, with several annual goals backed up by alternative behavioral objectives and tentative intermediate objectives.
2. Measure progress by portfolios of work, with assessments of the final product and comparisons within time. Taping and narrative descriptions of behaviors could be used to document changes.
3. Periodic narratives could describe specific areas of behavior, with comparisons to past observations which follow a common theme. For example, describe the frequency with which a child initiates interactions with typical classmates.

Adrienne Asch, who has written extensively on the experience of living with a disability, suggests that the IEP is a tool of segregation, that by appointing one group of students the need for an IEP, we penalize and separate them from the majority.

> In thinking about today's education for disabled students I have argued that either every child (disabled or not) needs an IEP, or that no one does. If the spirit of Section 504 animated the educational system, professionals would develop plans not for individual disabled children but for bringing schooling environments into conformance. It is not so much that the child needs individualized evaluations and goals with which to measure progress, but that the school environment needs evaluations and goals with which to measure its ability to serve all its students, including those with disabilities. I would therefore urge educators to construct what I am coining Programs for Educational Accessibility (PEAs) and to locate the problem where it belongs: in program accessibility and in the attitudinal barriers of teachers, not in the disabilities and deficits of students. (Asch, 1989, p. 190)

The IEP has helped the education community formulate ideas for programs and establish the need for some form of team work and method of accountability. It has become cumbersome, and may actually hinder the movement toward inclusion of disabled students into the regular classroom. It is time to rethink the purposes and uses of the IEP and create a system which recognizes the special needs of all children.

As local school systems rushed to meet the new requirements of the law, especially the priorities of serving children who had been systematically excluded from public education or underserved there, the most immediate result was a substantial increase in the number and diversity of students with special needs entering public schools. Reports issued by the Office of Special Education and Rehabilitation Services (OSERS) for 1983, 1984, and 1985 documented a 16.2% increase in the size of the special education population in this country from 1976-77 to 1983-84 (Walker et al., 1988).

These increases were attributed to a number of factors, including reclassification and broadening of definitions of special needs populations, increased identification of students with special needs, and increases in the actual numbers of some categories of students with special needs due to improved survival of sick and premature babies (Kochanek, Kabakoff, & Lipsitt, 1990). Regardless of the cause, special education had to accommodate increasing numbers of students who for one reason or another were placed outside the regular education system.

As the number and diversity of students in special education increased, some special education leaders became concerned that this unchecked growth was not leading to improved educational services. They saw increasing numbers of children moving into special education and out of the mainstream, and a chance at full participation in a normalized society of the school. As administrators, teachers, and parents struggled to find the right placements for students, provide appropriate related services and programs, and stay within reasonable legal and financial boundaries, the debate about where special education was going accelerated. Some argued it was going nowhere and that the entire educational system needed a complete overhaul (Lipsky & Gartner, 1989; Reynolds, Wang, & Walberg, 1987; Stainback & Stainback, 1984).

The first rumblings of dissatisfaction with the status quo in special education were actually heard in 1968, almost a decade before P.L. 94-142. In his presidential speech to the Council for Exceptional Children, Lloyd Dunn (1968) warned that

> This expensive proliferation of self-contained special schools and classes raises serious educational and civil rights issues which must be squarely faced. It is my thesis that we must stop labeling these

> deprived children as mentally retarded. Furthermore we must stop
> segregating them by placing them in our allegedly special programs.
> (p. 6)

He proceeded to critique homogeneous special education classes and
diagnostic and labelling procedures, suggesting that

> These procedures have probably been doing more harm than good
> in that they have resulted in disability labels and in that they have
> grouped children homogeneously in school on the basis of these
> labels. (Dunn, p. 8)

In its stead, he detailed a blueprint for change in the structure and
function of special education. He made specific recommendations for
changes in school organization which would lead to more integration
of students with mild special needs within the regular school program, and suggested changes in curriculum design, in the increased
use of related school personnel, and in environmental and techno-
logical adaptations. He particularly emphasized the need for prescrip-
tive and diagnostic teaching, with resulting individualization of programs.

> Existing diagnostic procedures should be replaced by expecting
> special educators, in large measure, to be responsible for their own
> diagnostic teaching and their clinical teaching. In this regard, it is
> suggested that we do away with many existing disability labels
> and the present practice of grouping children homogeneously by
> these labels into special classes. Instead, we should try keeping
> slow learning children more in the mainstream of education, with
> special educators serving as diagnostic, clinical, remedial, resource
> room, itinerant, and/or team teachers, consultants, and develop-
> ers of instructional materials and prescriptions for effective teach-
> ing. (Dunn, p. 11)

Dunn appears to have been a seer, although he was expressing
concerns others had also expressed in the debates about what is special
about special education, and in the repeated findings that separate classes
for mildly mentally retarded students had not benefited them to any
serious degree. Almost twenty years later, with special education accommodating students with far more complex and significant special
needs in the public schools, his speech became the seed for a new movement in the evolution of special education programming.

The Regular Education Initiative

In 1984 the first calls for cooperation and even the "merger" of
regular and special education were made. Madeline Will, then Assistant Secretary for the Office of Special Education and Rehabilitative
Services of the U.S. Department of Education, talked of a "second

stage" of an educational revolution in which "the concept of excellence in education applies to all students, and excellence means striving to reach one's utmost potential" (Will, 1984). She suggested that special education commit itself to breaking down four barriers to the integration of people with special needs:

1. The barrier between special and regular education.
2. The barrier to full integration of handicapped individuals in a heterogeneous society.
3. The barrier between the nursery and the school.
4. The barrier between the school and the work place.

(Will, 1984, p. 12)

In a later speech, Will suggested that real educational reform had to begin at the individual school building level.

> Building level administrators must be empowered to assemble appropriate professional and other resources for delivering effective, coordinated, comprehensive services for all students based on individual educational needs rather than eligibility for special programs. This means special programs and regular education programs must be allowed to collectively contribute skills and resources to carry out individualized education plans based on individualized education needs. (Will, 1986)

During the 1980's the Regular Education Initiative (REI) emerged as a federal effort to seek ways to more generically link special and regular education programs. While the critics agreed about the problems within the special education system, strong disagreements emerged about the direction of the "solutions," and two distinct camps emerged about the deeply felt philosophical differences relating to the segregation versus integration of students with special needs in regular programs.

The initial debate centered on students with mild, or high prevalence, disabilities, in which Reynolds, Wang, and Walberg (1987) argued for a merger of the two systems and total inclusion of these students in regular education. Lieberman (1985) argued, however, that regular education was not even significantly involved in the REI debate, leading him to warn advocates for a full merger between regular and special education that

> We cannot drag regular educators kicking and screaming into a merger with special education. The daily evidence on mainstreaming is too overwhelming. This proposed merger is a myth, unless regular educators, for reasons far removed from "It's best for children," decide that such a merger is in their own best interests. (p. 513)

Others have suggested extreme caution and opposition to this merger. Though full integration was a worthy goal and ideal, they pointed out that a merger of the two systems could result in a loss of educational services for students with more moderate and severe disabilities (Kaufman, Agard, & Semmel, 1988; Lieberman, 1985). Kaufman et al. (1988) pointed out that a majority of students identified as mildly handicapped were receiving most of their education in integrated settings anyway, and that a clearer identification of students with special needs led to a clearer delineation of specialized, individual services.

Lipsky and Gartner (1989) moved the debate toward a radical restructuring of the entire educational system. They claimed that

> It is not special education but the total educational system that must change... whatever the rationale or the benign purpose claimed, children with disabilities have been denied access to public education, or, when given access, have received an education that is not equal to that given other children. (p. 382)

Stainback and Stainback (1984) argued that the dual system of regular and special education had been a good idea whose time was over. They accused the dual system of creating "an unnecessary and expensive need to classify students," and further criticized classification of any kind as setting up artificial barriers between special and typical students. They called for the total inclusion of all students in regular education programming and classrooms, especially the more severely disabled students who had, until this time, been largely served in separate classrooms or schools (see also Hanline, 1993a, 1993b; Hunt et al., 1993; Cole & Meyer, 1991; Rynders et al., 1993).

The inclusion of students with severe physical and/or cognitive special needs in regular classrooms represented an enormous leap in the evolving theoretical debate and in real educational practice. Students who must be trained in basic self-care skills, who are capable of self-injurious behaviors, or who need to have lunch served through a feeding tube, present to teachers an entirely new set of challenges from students identified as having mild learning and behavior problems.

Their needs do not place them outside the human family, and a few model programs like Kids Are People School have demonstrated that these children can be successfully integrated into regular classrooms. However, if inclusion of these students is to have positive outcomes, they must have teachers and administrators highly committed to their participation in the classroom, all the necessary related support services, physical accommodations for specific needs, family support and involvement, and added monies (Hunt et al., 1993; Fuchs & Fuchs, 1994; Martin, 1994). This integration takes tremendous energy, imagination, and dedication to the ideal of inclusive education for all students. Teachers must reconsider the "normal" duties they must address in their classrooms, and probably re-think and expand what they view as educationally relevant in their classrooms. In school systems already stretched to include services for increasingly needy and diverse student populations, we need to move with great care and attention to a balance between reality and quality, if students with severe special needs are going to be success-fully and truly included in regular education.

What Parents Think About Integration

Carol Briggs Ayres's son, Andy, has Down Syndrome and was integrated into the local public school kindergarten when he was six years old (Ayres, 1988). Ayres reveals her rollercoaster feelings as she and Andy move through his — and her — first year as a "just like everybody else" kindergarten family. She describes Andy's graduation day:

> My proof of Andy's success in kindergarten came at the end of the year when parents were invited to attend the kindergarten gradu-ation. As I entered the room (by now I felt I had a right to be there), the sight of my little boy sitting quietly with the others in his construction paper mortar board reduced me to tears. "There's my Mom!" he cried out with pride in his voice. The girl sitting next to him smiled. Her mother was there too.... Integration does not deny disability, but it does acknowledge personhood. Andy is about to become a first grader who happens to have a disability, instead of being "one of the special ed kids." I will always stay in close touch with the parents of children with disabilities. We band together like Conestoga wagons around a campfire when we are united on an issue unique to our children. But our place, as well as our children's, is in the regular education classroom too. (Ayres, p. 25)

Studies have compared the attitudes of parents of children in integrated and segregated programs (Turnbull & Winton, 1983), re-sponses of parents of typical and disabled children to integration (Miller et al., 1992), and the reactions of teachers and parents in integrated programs. In one of the largest studies of its kind, Miller et al. (1992) surveyed the parents of 304 children. Two hundred and thirty two parents formed four groups according to their children's program type and whether or not their child had special needs. The four groups consisted of 68 parents of children with developmental delays in inte-grated settings, 35 parents of children with delays in segregated set-tings, 70 parents of typical children in integrated programs, and 59 parents of typical children in settings with no children with special needs. The parents were surveyed along two central measures, their attitudes toward integration for children with special needs and their satisfaction with their own child's placement. Parents of children with special needs in integrated settings felt their children "were more involved with typical children and they were more satisfied with their children's opportunity for involvement with typical children than were their counterparts who had children in segregated arrangements" (p. 241). Parents of typical children in integrated settings also expressed more satisfaction with socializing opportunities than did their counterparts in settings with no special needs students.

Parents have been among the strongest advocates for quality education which also recognizes the right of all children to be included in the regular public school experience (Hasazi et al., 1993). Parents of children with special needs and typical children who have experienced integration value the life-lessons which grow from environments in which diversity is welcomed and valued (Peck, Carlson, & Helmstetter, 1992). Perhaps one of the most positive outcomes of the integration movement is the recognition that the feelings, opinions, and ideas of parents matter greatly in the education of their children.

What Teachers Think About Integration

Teachers are the front line soldiers in this march toward a new educational culture. If they are well trained in what to expect, given the time and tools to develop new skills, and provided the support needed to cope effectively and creatively with the broader range of children who inhabit integrated classrooms, they will make it work. On the other hand, teachers who are already feeling overwhelmed by increasing numbers of children with complex problems, a perception that they are undervalued by the communities they serve, and the stark reality of the same money for more work, are not likely to do a good job managing the changes required for integrated classrooms. Though researchers generally recognize the pivotal role of teachers in the integration movement (Strain, 1990), relatively few studies have investigated their responses, particularly in elementary and secondary schools (Haynes & Gunn, 1988; Peck, Carlson, & Helmstetter, 1992; Giangreco et al., 1993).

Giangreco et al. (1993) interviewed 19 general education teachers who worked in 10 Vermont public schools in kindergarten through grade 9. All of these teachers had a severely disabled student in their classroom full time within the past three years. Only two of the teachers had any in-service training to prepare them for these students, and all the teachers had aides assigned to the classroom and ongoing support from special education personnel and related service personnel (e.g., physical and speech therapists). The teachers were asked which approaches worked best for them and why, what related ser-

vices were the most effective, and what they felt the benefits of integration were, or if there were any perceived benefits.

None of the 19 teachers had significant previous experience with
severely disabled students. All but two of the teachers described positive changes in their attitudes and perceptions of the students. The
authors of the study call this slow change a 'transformation,' and
attribute it to a wide range of factors. "Teachers also reported beginning to view the child as a person rather than a disability, and they
established a personal relationship with the student" (p. 365). Teachers used a number of approaches in the classroom, but a common
theme was the decision to "treat him like any other kid in the class"
(p. 366). The majority of teachers also favored strategies that encouraged the children to learn actively, and in small problem-solving
groups.

The transformed teachers felt that benefits accrued to the students with and without special needs, and to themselves in both the
personal and professional spheres. The students with special needs
improved in awareness and responsiveness to the environment and
people, gained specific skills, and appeared to enjoy the struggle to
meet new challenges. Typical classmates were described as becoming
more accepting of differences, and displaying "an increased level of
social/emotional development, flexibility, and empathy" (p. 369). Some
of the teachers saw themselves as role models for the children and
developed a sense of increased confidence and pride that they had
met a new challenge and changed in positive and productive ways.
They accepted and embraced the spirit and reality of including students with severe special needs in the classroom, and proved to themselves and the community that inclusion works.

What Happens to the Children?

Researchers have evaluated the effects of mainstreaming and
integration on young children with mild to moderate special needs
and on their typical peers (Buysse & Bailey, 1993; Esposito, 1987;
Fenrick, Pearson, and Pepeinjak, 1984; Cole et al., 1991; Odom, Deklyn,
& Jenkins, 1984). Some studies were more concerned with determining whether there would be negative developmental effects on typical children (Esposito, 1987); more recent research has addressed the
potential needs and benefits for all the children (Kohl & Beckman,
1990). The common conclusion of these authors is that integration
has no negative effects on the developmental progress of typical children. When programs are based on a shared philosophy of inclusion
for all children, with a clear understanding of the developmental needs
of individual children, and with the necessary supports in place, chil-

dren, parents, and teachers report positive experiences.

A smaller number of studies have considered the more complex issues involved in the inclusion of children with severe and profound disabilities (Cole & Meyer, 1991; Ferguson, 1985; Hanline, 1993a, 1993b; Hunt et al., 1993). These authors have looked at the effects of the inclusion of these students in public schools on teachers, typical peers, and the students themselves. As very few students with severe special needs have yet had significant, long term experience in integrated or inclusive classrooms, the results of this research represent a very small beginning in assessing the outcomes for everyone concerned.

The survey of teachers who had included students with severe special needs (Giangreco et al., 1993) revealed that teachers felt that the disabled and typical students had gained from the experience in a number of ways. Much of the current research focuses on structural and administrative adaptations in the classroom (Hunt, Haring, Farrin-Davis, Staub, Rogers, Beckstead, Karasoff, Goetz & Sailor, 1993), or on the social interactions of the students with severe special needs and their typical classmates (Hanline, 1993a, 1993b). Both groups of students make gains in social awareness and ability to interact with their peers (Hanline, 1993a, 1993b). Katie Blenk, in her descriptions of students at Kids Are People School, provides plenty of anecdotal evidence that carefully structured curriculum and a real commitment to the potential of every student to learn new skills results in positive, and sometimes miraculously positive outcomes for children with special needs and their typical peers.

Salisbury (1991) used qualitative research methods to find and describe the context and practices of an elementary school as it became a more inclusive setting over a 30-month period. The most visible changes were structural alterations in staffing patterns, with special education teachers moving into regular classrooms, increased information sharing among staff, physical changes to remove functional restrictions on students, and reassignment of students and teachers to reflect natural proportions of students with and without special needs.

Teachers became aware of the need for changes in how they structured learning when they realized that though students with special needs were in the classroom, they were usually clustered at the rear of the room, working in parallel, but not *with* the rest of the class. New strategies the teachers found useful in bringing all students together to learn included shared planning and teaching between regular and special education staff, cooperative learning groups, attention to physical accessibility to all class activities, and emphasis on attitudinal changes regarding equity for all students in the classroom.

Preparing Students with Special Needs for the Future: How Are We Doing?

Kids Are People School and other inclusive programs around the country are pioneers in a new vision of education which recognizes the need to prepare all children for a cooperative future in a nation where diversity is becoming the common standard. Children with special needs are in many ways just one more group of students who, once recognized as having been unfairly excluded are now challenging the system to include them. They are themselves as diverse as any other group of children. Each must be viewed as bringing individual needs and gifts into the classroom. Some of their needs can be met with a bit of flexibility and imagination; others require significant adaptation and reorganization of classrooms and curriculum. Below we ask you to consider some issues related to the history and the future of inclusive education.

Special education has evolved into a "curriculum of exclusion" (Rubenfeld, 1993), serving thousands of students in separate, non-flexible tracks which often lead to dead ends in economic and social adult life. Special education served many students through the development of curriculum which balanced individual student needs which included academic and functional skills, but these strengths were often offset by the negative impact students and their families felt as an isolated and often denigrated minority. Phyllis Rubenfeld spent 9 years in a special education program in New York City. She eventually earned her doctorate at Teachers College of Columbia University and is now a professor at Hunter College of the City University of New York, where she focuses on the cognitive and emotional effects of special education on children with special needs. She argues that special education separated her and her classmates from the chance to explore their own possibilities, and to wrestle with real social and intellectual issues which lead to growth and maturity. She calls these losses the hidden casualties of special education:

> It is my central thesis and deepest conviction that without a drastic alteration of teaching methods and classroom conditions, special education cannot possibly succeed in its ostensible goal of preparing students with disabilities to lead an independent, productive life. As it exists now, and as our experiences demonstrate, special education serves neither the psychological nor normative needs of students with disabilities. It fails on three fronts, the academic, the social, and the psychological. Scholastically, the curriculum is most often repetitive and unchallenging. Socially, the segregated classrooms are restrictive and isolating. These two failings contribute to the psychological pitfall of segregated classes; special education

often fails to instill, and sometimes actively discourages, the ambi-
tion and self-esteem essential to success in life. When special education means separate education, it is more of a handicap than a
help. (Rubenfeld, p. 122)

The Individuals with Disabilities Education Act, originally P.L.
94-142, will be 20 years old in 1995. One generation of students with
special needs has grown to adulthood in the special education system
spawned by P.L. 94-142. Their collective report card raises some serious questions about the effectiveness of their education.

Edwin Martin (1994), the head of the Office of Special Education
Programs at the U.S. Department of Education at the time of the
passage of P.L. 94-142 and instrumental in its passage and implementation, recently summarized data from a study of 8,000 high school
graduates who have a variety of special needs. The results indicated
that 60% had failed at least one of the regular education courses in
which they enrolled, 53% did not receive special services such as
therapy, and only 16% out of high school for three to five years attend any college. Most who do attend go to two-year schools.

These results reflect not only on the special education program,
but on the total public education system which, in its past and current form, has failed the majority of students with special needs.
Public Law 94-142 ensured the movement of thousands of students
into public education programs, but special education kept them a
segregated minority. The next phase of educational change, integration and inclusion, will hopefully lead to a more promising future for
students with special needs.

Children with special needs become adults with special needs. Just as
regular education has historically prepared children for adult plea-
sures and responsibilities, schools must do the same for students who
have special needs. Education policy reflects the concerns and priorities of the society in which it evolves. The Americans with Disabilities Act, civil legislation designed to protect people with special needs
from discrimination, was passed in 1990. That same year, the National Association of Developmental Disabilities Councils published
a report based on findings from a nationwide survey of 14,000 people
with developmental disabilities and their families (National Association of Developmental Disabilities Councils, 1990). The report, entitled "Report on the 1990 National Consumer Survey," focused on
areas in which supports and services determine quality of life: coordination and access to services, education and learning, work, income,
housing, health, transportation, and civil rights.

In each of these areas there were reported deficiencies and lack
of funding and coordination of service between various and complex

service delivery systems. For example, more children were found to have access to public education, "but segregation in school programs is still the most common experience, especially for children with severe disabilities" (National Association of Developmental Disabilities Councils, p. 20). More people were living in independent housing, but needed more support. Inadequate transportation was named as a significant barrier to independence in all areas, and nearly one out of every five individuals or families said they lacked health insurance.

A common theme in the report was the desire of individuals and families for independence, the right to choose jobs, housing, and social life, to participate in life on their own terms in their own communities. The report covers almost every aspect of the lives of individuals with developmental disabilities and their families. It concludes with recommendations for guidelines for decisions which affect lives into the next century. Respect for individuals and their families, the right to make decisions and live independently, and the need to recognize disability policy as an integral part of national social, health, and education policy are some of the key values suggested in the report.

The National Council on Disability published *The Education of Students with Disabilities: Where Do We Stand?* (1990), which reported the results of a year long study which included a review of research and testimony of 50 witnesses in formal hearings. The report credited P.L. 94-142 with changing the landscape of education for students with special needs and establishing parents and students as a participating force in that change, but the overall report card indicated a need for improvement in all areas. Among the 27 findings laid out in the report were:

1. Parent and professional relationships were often strained and adversarial.
2. Many parents still find it difficult to locate appropriate services for their children.
3. Parents and students felt that many programs continue to have lowered expectations for students with special needs.
4. Services for students with special needs in rural, minority, and disadvantaged families lag behind others.
6. Families perceive that outcomes of due process hearings favor schools.
16. Evaluations and diagnostic classifications vary across states and local school districts often not addressing the individual needs of students.
18. Special education is essentially a separate program within regular school districts.

Findings 19-27 take on the federal role in funding and monitoring programs and the somewhat dismal outcomes for further education and employment that continue to be the lot of adults with special needs. If the purpose of education is to prepare students to work, live, and play together and fulfill their individual potential for productive, rewarding lives, then the two key words, *together* and *individual*, should guide program planning and implementation from preschool through high school.

Inclusive education, when it is done right and incorporates appropriate supportive services, can work well for all children, including those with severe special needs. Research done over the past twenty years tells us that young children with mild to moderate special needs benefit across all developmental areas in integrated settings (Herink & Lee, 1985; Peck & Cooke, 1983; Bricker, Bruder, & Bailey, 1982; Guralnick, 1990) and that young children without special needs continue to thrive in integrated settings (Esposito, 1987; Jenkins, Speltz, & Odom (1985); Kohl & Beckman, 1984; Odom, Deklyn & Jenkins, 1984). When appropriate services, positive attitudes, and structured programs are in place, students with severe special needs benefit from inclusion in regular programs (Cole & Meyer, 1991; Hanline, 1993; Rynders et al., 1993).

Students with severe special needs present parents and teachers with complex and what may often appear to be overwhelming challenges. Alternatively, the rewards and gifts these students can offer those who interact with them often surpass all expectations. Giangreco et al. (1993) offer the results of a study which describes the experiences of teachers who had students with severe special needs in kindergarten through grade 9 placed in their classrooms for one year. The teachers relate positive outcomes for students with and without special needs and themselves. Students with special needs became more aware and responsive, gained specific skills, and appeared to enjoy and interact socially with their classmates. Teachers felt the typical students gained an awareness and increased acceptance of significant differences, and "an increased level of social/emotional development, flexibility, and empathy" (Giangreco et al., p. 369). The teachers themselves reported a sense of pride in their ability to accept and meet new challenges and feelings that the experiences changed their perspective and skills for the better in significant ways.

As integrated education for students with severe special needs is a relatively new phenomenon, research which will help clarify what works and what is needed. Hanline (1993a, 1993b) explored the nature of peer social interactions in a preschool program in which children with severe special needs were totally included. Though the findings have to be viewed tentatively, as only three children with profound special needs were observed interacting with typical classmates, the author credited the positive and consistent social interactions to the fact that the program was inclusive all day, the ratio of children with special needs to typical children followed natural population proportions (about 10%), and the interactive focus of the curriculum supported inclusion of all the children in activities.

The future success of inclusive education rests on universal recognition of the need to rethink and restructure traditional educational models of service delivery. Kids Are People School represents a new vision for truly inclusive education. Critics and skeptics might point out that many of the innovative practices there, smaller teacher-student ratios, multi-age groupings, cooperative and peer teaching, and individualized and interactive programs are simply not feasible in the financially restricted, overcrowded public schools. But similar programs have worked around the country (Lipsky & Gartner, 1989; Stainback, Stainback, & Forest, 1989).

Family support and advocacy has been the foundation of change and will continue to provide an essential push toward the creation of universal, inclusive education (Ayres, 1988; Bailey & Winton, 1987; Dybwad, 1990; Miller et al., 1992; Turnbull & Winton, 1983; Winton, 1986). Teachers and parents have always been partners in the education of children. When children have special needs, often including complex and sometimes life-threatening medical and other problems, this partnership takes on increased importance. Parents of children with special needs often spend disproportionate amounts of time with their children, becoming experts in the management of behaviors, medical/technical procedures, and equipment adaptations which are often completely new areas to teachers and administrators. Public Law 94-142 made the recognition of the essential role of parents one of the cornerstones of the legislation. Twenty years later national studies find parents still complaining of having to battle for respect in their dealings with school personnel (National Council on Disability, 1990). Creating inclusive educational environments is a complicated, often frustrating, and demanding job. Parents are in some ways the most experienced members of any individual child's educational team; they have a complete history, knowledge of present skills and needs, and an intense and very real stake in assuring their child's attaining their maximum potential independence through education and training. Listen to them.

The creation of inclusive educational programs is a step toward the creation of an inclusive society. Most of us seem to agree that in theory it is a good idea. However, lots of good ideas have been born, thrived for a while, nurtured by good people and good intentions, and then faded away due to lack of success and loss of interest. We cannot, at least legally, go back to the bad old days of hiding people with special needs in back rooms and human warehouses. It is possible, however, that segregation, and the inevitable continuation of a second-class group of people doomed to failure by attitude and design, will continue and possibly grow if we do not accept that creating an inclusive society is very hard and sometimes painful work. The children, staff, and parents of Kids Are People School and a few other programs across the country form a microcosm of what can happen when ideas and philosophy are translated into reality. Better societies begin in better schools. We have begun to meet the challenge; the future is up to all of us.

REFERENCES

Asch, A. (1989). Has the law made a difference? What some disabled students have to say. In D.K. Lipsky & A. Gartner, *Beyond separate education: Quality education for all* (pp. 181-205). Baltimore: Paul H. Brookes Publishing Co.

Ayres, C.B. (1988). Integration: A parent's perspective. *Exceptional Parent, September*, 22-25.

Bailey, D.B., & Winton, P.J. (1987). Stability and change in parents' expectations about mainstreaming. *Topics in Early Childhood Special Education, 7*(1), 73-88.

Beyer, H.A. (1983). A free appropriate public education. *Western New England Law Review, 5*, 363-389.

Bricker, D., Bruder, M.B., & Bailey, E. (1982). Developmental integration of preschool children. *Analysis and Intervention in Developmental Disabilities, 2*, 207-222.

Buysse, V., & Bailey, D.B. (1993). Behavioral and developmental outcomes in young children with disabilities in integrated and segregated settings: A review of comparative studies.

Cole, D.A., & Meyer, L.H. (1991). Social integration and severe disabilities: A longitudinal analysis of child outcomes. *The Journal of Special Education, 25*(3), 240-351.

Cole, K.N., Mills, P.E., Dale, P.S., & Jenkins, J.R. (1991). Effects of preschool integration for children with disabilities. *Exceptional Children, 58*, 36-45.

Davis, W.E. (1989). The regular educational initiative debate: Its premises and problems. *Exceptional Children, 55,* 440-446.

Dunn, L.M. (1968). Special education for the mildly retarded: Is much of it justifiable? *Exceptional Children, September,* 5-22.

Dybwad, R.F. (1990). *Perspectives on a parent movement: The revolt of parents of children with intellectual limitations.* Cambridge, MA: Brookline Books.

Esposito, B.G. (1987). The effects of preschool integration on the development of non-handicapped children. *Journal of the Division of Early Childhood, 12*(1), 31-46.

Fenrick, N.J., Pearson, M.E., & Pepeinjak, J.M. (1984). The play, attending, and language of young handicapped children in integrated and segregated settings. *Journal of the Division of Early Childhood, Winter,* 57-67.

Ferguson, D.L. (1985). The ideal and the real: The working out of public policy in curricula for severely handicapped students. *Remedial and Special Education, 6*(3), 56-60.

Fuchs, D., and Fuchs, L.F. (1994). Inclusive schools movement and the radicalization of special education reform. Exceptional Children, 60, 294-309.

Giangreco, M.F., Dennis, R., Cleninger, C., Edelman, S., & Schattman, R. (1993). "I've counted Jon": Transformational experiences of teachers educating students with disabilities. *Exceptional Children, 59*(4), 359-372.

Goodman, J.F., & Bond, L. (1993). The individualized education program: A retrospective critique. *The Journal of Special Education, 26*(4), 408-422.

Goodwin, R.J. (1985). Public school integration of children with handicaps after Smith v. Robinson: "Separate but equal" revisited? *Maine Law Review, 37,* 267-299.

Guralnick, M.J. (1990). Social competence and early intervention. *Journal of Early Intervention, 14*(1), 3-14.

Hanline, M.F. (1993a). Inclusion of preschoolers with profound disabilities: An analysis of children's interaction. *Journal of the Association for Persons with Severe Handicaps, 18,* 28-35.

Hanline, M.F. (1993b). Learning within the context of play: Providing typical early childhood experiences for children with severe disabilities. *Journal of the Association for Persons with Severe Handicaps, 18*(2), 121-129.

Hasazi, S.B., Johnston, A.P., Ligget, A.M., & Schattman, R.A. (1994). A qualitative policy study of the least restrictive environment provision of the Individuals with Disabilities Education Act. *Exceptional Children, 60*(6), 491-507.

Haynes, K., & Gunn, P. (1988). Attitudes of parents and teachers toward mainstreaming. *The Exceptional Child, 35*(1), 31-37.

Hebbler, K.M., Smith, B.J., & Black, T.L. (1991). Federal early childhood special education policy: A model for the improvement of services for children with disabilities. *Exceptional Children, 58*, 104-112.

Herink, N., & Lee, P.C. (1985). Patterns of social interaction of mainstreamed preschool children: Hopeful news from the field. *The Exceptional Child, 32*(3), 191-199.

Hunt, P., Haring, K., Farrin-Davis, F., Staub, D., Rogers, J., Beckstead, S.P., Karasoff, P., Goetz, L., & Sailor, W.L. (1993). Factors associated with the integrated educational placement of students with severe disabilities. *Journal of the Association for Persons with Severe Handicaps, 18*(1), 6-15.

Jenkins, J.R., Speltz, M.S., & Odom, M.L. (1985). Integrating normal and handicapped preschoolers: Effects on child development and social interaction. *Exceptional Children, 55*, 420-428.

Kaufman, M., Agard, J.A., & Semmel, M.I. (1986). *Mainstreaming learners and their environment.* Cambridge, MA: Brookline Books.

Kochanek, T.T., Kabacoff, R.I., & Lipsett, L.P. (1990). Early identification of developmentally disabled and at-risk preschool children, *Exceptional Children, 56*, 528-538.

Kohl, B., & Beckman, P.J. (1984). A comparison of handicapped and nonhandicapped preschoolers' interactions across classroom activities. *Journal of the Division of Early Childhood, Winter*, 49-56.

Levine, E.L., & Wexler, E.M. (1981). *P.L. 94-142, An Act of Congress.* New York: Macmillan Publishing Company.

Lieberman, L.L. (1985). Special education and regular education: A merger made in heaven? *Exceptional Children, April*, 513-516.

Lipsky, D.K., & Gartner, A. (1989). *Beyond separate education: Quality education for all.* Baltimore: Paul H. Brookes Publishing Co.

Martin, E.W. (1994). Inclusion: Rhetoric and reality. *Exceptional Parent, April*, 39-42.

Miller, L.J., Strain, P.S., Boyd, K., Hunsicker, S., McKinley, J., & Wu, A. (1992). Parental attitudes towards integration. *Topics in Early Childhood Special Education, 12*(2), 231-246.

National Association of Developmental Disabilities Councils (1990). Forging a new era: The 1990 reports on people with developmental disabilities. *Journal of Disability Policy Studies, 1*(4), 15-42.

National Council on Disability (1990). The education of students with dis-abilities: Where do we stand? A report to the President and the Congress of the United States, September 1989. *Journal of Disability Policy Studies, 1*(1), 103-132.

Odom, S.L., Deklyn, M., & Jenkins, J.J. (1984). Integrating handicapped and nonhandicapped preschoolers: Developmental impact on nonhandicapped children. *Exceptional Children, 51*(1), 41-48.

Peck, C.A., Carlson, P., & Helmstetter, E. (1992). Parent and teacher per-ceptions of outcomes for typically developing children enrolled in integrated early childhood programs: A statewide survey. *Journal of Early Intervention, 16*(1), 53-63.

Peck, C.A., & Cooke, T.P. (1983). Benefits of mainstreaming at the early childhood level: How much can we expect? *Analysis and Interven-tion in Developmental Disabilities, 3,* 1-22.

Reynolds, M.C., Wang, M.C., & Walberg, H.J. (1987). The necessary re-structuring of special and regular education. *Exceptional Children, 53,* 391-398.

Rubenfeld, P. (1993). The more things change, the more they stay the same: A call for a new drive to integrate students with disabilities. *Journal of Disability Policy Studies, 4*(1), 117-130.

Rynders, J.E., Schleien, S.J., Meyer, L.H., Vandercook, T.L., Mustorien, T., Colend, J.S., & Olsen, K. (1993). Improving integration out-comes for children with and without severe disabilities through cooperatively structured recreation activities: A synthesis of re-search. *The Journal of Special Education., 26*(4), 386-407.

Salisbury, C.L. (1991). Mainstreaming during the early childhood years. *Exceptional Children, 58,* 146-155.

Scotch, R.K. (1984). *From good will to civil rights: Transforming federal disabil-ity policy.* Philadelphia, PA: Temple University Press.

Singer, J.D., & Butler, J.A. (1987). The Education for All Handicapped Children Act: School as agents of social reform. *Harvard Educational Review, 57,* 125-152.

Stainback, S., Stainback, W., & Forest, M. (1989). *Educating students in the mainstream of regular education.* Baltimore, MD: Paul H. Brookes Publishing Co.

Stainback, W., & Stainback, S. (1984). A rationale for the merger of special and regular education. *Exceptional Children, 51,* 102-111.

Strain, P. (1990). LRE for preschool children with handicaps: What we know, what we should be doing. *Journal of Early Intervention, 14*(4), 291-296.

Turnbull, A.P., & Winton, P. (1983). A comparison of specialized and main-streamed preschools from the perspectives of parents of handi-capped children. *Journal of Pediatric Psychology, 8*(1), 57-71.

Walker, D.K., Singer, J.D., Palfrey, J., Orza, M., Wenger, M., & Butler, J (1988). Who leaves and who stays in special education: A 2-year follow-up study. *Exceptional Children, 54*(5), 393-402.

Will, C.M. (1984). Let us pause and reflect, but not too long. *Exceptional Children, 51*, 11-16.

Will, C.M. (1986). Educating children with learning problems: A shared responsibility. *Exceptional Children, 52*, 411-415.

Winton, P.J. (1986). The consequences of mainstreaming for families of young handicapped children. In C.J. Meisel (ed.), *Mainstreaming handicapped children: Outcomes, controversies, and new directions* (pp. 129-147). Hillsdale, NJ: Lawrence Erlbaum Associates.

Glossary

Abduction Joint movement away from the midline, or center, of the body.

ADA (Americans with Disabilities Act) A federal law which extends to all Americans with disabilities civil rights and legal protections in housing, employment, education and use of public social, recreational, and transportation facilities.

Adaptive Equipment Devices used to assist children and adults in functional activities, including specially designed eating utensils, seating, walking or other mobility aids.

ADD (Attention Deficit Disorder) Defined by the APA (American Psychiatric Association) as due to minimal brain disorder and consisting of a cluster of symptoms including short attention span and impulsive behavior.

Adduction Joint movement toward the midline, or center, of the body.

ADHD (Attention Deficit and Hyperactivity Disorder) Defined by the APA as due to minimal brain disorder and consisting of a cluster of symptoms including short attention span, impulsive behavior, and hyperactivity.

ADL (Activities of Daily Living) Daily self-care activities including dressing, bathing, toileting, and eating.

AIDS (Acquired Immune Deficiency Syndrome) An immunodeficiency syndrome caused by HIV (human immunodeficiency virus) transmitted through sexual contact, tears or saliva into blood, or blood into blood. The virus permits infections, malignant cancers, and neurologic disease.

Ankle/Foot Orthosis (AFO) A brace designed to be worn on the foot and lower leg below the knee; sometimes called a short leg brace.

Apgar Scores Numbers based on a scale to measure a baby's general condition at birth and 5 minutes after birth. Baby is observed for (1) heart rate, (2) respiratory effort, (3) muscle tone, (4) reflex irritability, and (5) color. Each area gets a 1 or 2, for a maximum score of 10.

Aphasia A loss or impairment of the ability to understand or express language symbols in either written or spoken form, caused by central nervous system dysfunction.

Apnea A temporary cessation of breathing. Cause can be a number of medical conditions or unknown.

Arnold-Chiari Malformation A deformity in the central nervous system in which the medulla and pons (lower parts of the brain) are small, and the cerebellum (lower back part of the brain) extends into the spinal canal. Occurs in some children with spina bifida and contributes to hydrocephalus (excess collection of fluid in the space between the brain and skull).

ASL (American Sign Language) Considered the native language and primary source of communication by many in the deaf community.

Asthma A condition caused by spasmodic contractions in the bronchi of the lungs. Is triggered by allergies, exercise, or environmental conditions and results in wheezing, coughing, and loss of breath.

Ataxia Muscle incoordination which occurs only with purposeful movement. Can be a form of cerebral palsy.

Athetosis Movement disorder marked by slow, uncontrollable sinuous movements usually of the fingers, toes and feet. Can be a form of cerebral palsy.

Audiologist A specialist in the evaluation and rehabilitation of people with hearing loss and deafness.

Augmentative Communication Systems of adapted technology and programs which encourage and enhance verbal and non-verbal communication. The type and complexity is determined by physical, cognitive, and social-emotional needs of the child and financial constraints.

Autism A childhood disorder characterized by withdrawal from people, perseveration, minimal purposeful spoken communication, and echolalia.

Balance The ability to maintain the body in an upright posture against the forces of gravity. Depends on mature reflex reactions, strong postural muscles (neck and trunk for sitting and neck, trunk, and hips for standing), and good spatial awareness.

Blindness A loss of sight which is either hereditary or acquired, due to congenital or traumatic injury.

Body Image A child's self concept of his/her body parts, an integrated sense of where they are, relationship to each other, feeling of movement, positions, and internal and external spatial relationships.

Braces See **orthotic devices**

Bradycardia A slow heartbeat marked by a pulse rate under 60 beats per minute.

Catheter A thin, hollow tube for withdrawing fluids from the body. Commonly used by children with spina bifida to withdraw urine from the bladder through the urethra.

Central Nervous System (CNS) The part of the nervous system consisting of the brain and spinal cord, and cranial nerves; the command center of the nervous system.

Cerebral Palsy A disorder of movement and coordination caused by damage to the central nervous system before, during, or within two years of birth. Damage is non-progressive and results in various types and degrees of muscle weakness, muscle tone imbalance incoordination, and developmental delay.

Cerebrospinal Fluid (CSF) Liquid surrounding the brain and spinal cord (CNS). Protects against trauma and sudden pressure changes and helps provide nutrition.

Cleft Palate A condition in which the palate (roof of the mouth) does not close during fetal development, resulting in an open space. Causes difficulty with nursing, eating, and speaking and often requires multiple surgeries during childhood.

Colostomy A surgical transfer of the lower opening of the large intestine to a small surgically created opening from the abdomen. A bag is attached outside the abdominal hole for the collection of waste material.

Communication Board An augmentative communication device consisting of a board on which letters, objects, and/or actions are represented. Can be manual or electronic; use and size are determined by a child's individual needs.

Congenital Amputation Failure of part or all of a limb to grow during fetal development; child is born missing part or all of a limb.

Contracture A permanent shortening of muscle at a joint. Most often the joint is pulled into a flexed (bent) position resulting in weakness and functional limitations. Effects can be reduced or controlled by consistent exercise, functional movement, and appropriate positioning.

Cystic Fibrosis A hereditary childhood disease caused by defective enzyme production in the pancreas. Results in excess mucous in the lungs, causing severe respiratory problems.

Deafness A loss of hearing which results in deaf children becoming members of a distinct linguistic minority.

Developmental Delay (DD) A condition marked by a difference between a child's actual development and the expected age of reaching developmental milestones. Includes measures of sensorimotor, cognitive, social, emotional, and adaptive behavior.

Developmentally Appropriate Practice (DAP) An educational program based on age appropriate, developmental, and individual needs of each child, emphasizing learning as an interactive process.

Diplegia A motor disability marked by muscle weakness and tone imbalance, and incoordination of either both legs (most common) or both arms (unusual).

Disability A limitation in a person's ability to perform an activity considered typical for (his/her) age and general circumstances.

Down Syndrome A genetic disorder caused by abnormal cell division during fetal development. Results in variable degrees of developmental delay, medical problems, and mental retardation.

Dyslexia A learning disability in which a child has difficulty interpreting and processing written language.

Echolalia An involuntary parrotlike repetition of words spoken by others, sometimes seen in children with emotional disorders.

EEG (Electroencephalogram) A test used to measure electrical activity in the brain.

EMG (Electromyogram) A test used to measure the electrical activity produced by a muscle contraction.

Encephalitis An inflammation of brain tissue.

Encephalopathy Any dysfunction of the brain, sometimes used to describe conditions of brain damage in which the cause is unknown and there is no specific diagnosis.

Expressive Aphasia A condition in which a person can understand written or spoken language but cannot give appropriate responses.

Extension Joint movement which results in the straightening of a joint.

Fetal Alcohol Effects (FAE) A cluster of developmental problems arising from fetal exposure to alcohol. Can include mild to moderate mental retardation, asymmetrical and other atypical facial characteristics, and behavioral problems.

Fetal Alcohol Syndrome (FAS) A more severe and definitive cluster of developmental problems arising from fetal exposure to alcohol. Can include delayed developmental milestones, moderate to severe mental retardation, atypical facial characteristics, inappropriate social behavior, and attentional problems.

Fine Motor Skilled movement and hand manipulation of small objects, including eye-hand coordination skills.

Flexion Joint movement which results in the bending of a joint.

Form Discrimination Tactile discrimination and recognition of various sizes, shapes, textures, and sequenced qualities of different objects.

Free Appropriate Public Education (FAPE) Concept stated in P.L. 94-142 referring to the civil right of all children, regardless of degree or type of disability, to a public education.

Gastrostomy Tube A tube placed through a surgically created hole in the abdominal wall for the purpose of getting liquid nourishment directly into the stomach. Used in cases of serious eating and/or swallowing disorders.

Grande Mal Seizure A convulsion lasting several seconds to minutes involving involuntary muscle contractions of the whole body.

Gross Motor Movement skills or development involving the large muscles. Includes postural and balance activities, crawling, sitting, walking, and running.

Handicap Any disadvantage that limits or prevents a person from performing age appropriate activities. Term is often used to emphasize environmental barriers to activities.

Hemiparesis/Hemiplegia Motor dysfunction of one side of the body, including muscle weakness, muscle tome imbalance, and incoordination.

Hemophilia Hereditary blood disease characterized by prolonged coagulation time. Results in failure of blood to clot and abnormal bleeding.

Hydrocephalus A condition in which excess cerebrospinal fluid accumulates in and around the brain. Often occurs with spina bifida and is treated by shunting the extra fluid from the brain to another body cavity, often the stomach.

Hypotonia Muscle tone marked by very low tension. Can result in extreme muscle weakness, incoordination, and delays in motor milestones in children.

IDEA (Individuals with Disabilities Education Act) The federal law originally passed by Congress in 1975 as the Education of All Handicapped Children Act, P.L. 94-142. Establishes the legal right of all children to appropriate public education in the least restrictive environment possible.

Orthotic Device Braces or mobility equipment (wheelchair, walker, prone stander) which give support to muscles and joints to encourage and/or support independent movement.

Orthotist A specialist in the design, development, and use of braces and adaptive devices for the support of the musculoskeletal structures of the body.

Osteogenesis Imperfecta A congenital condition marked by imperfect bone formation and resulting in brittle bones which break easily. Sometimes called 'brittle bone disease' and treated with careful exercise, braces for joint protection.

Otolaryngologist A physician who specializes in the evaluation and treatment of the eyes, nose, and throat.

Paraplegia/Paresis Paralysis or extreme weakness of the lower trunk and legs caused by congenital or traumatic spinal injury.

Peripheral Nervous System (PNS) The part of the nervous system consisting of the sensory and motor nerve pathways connecting the spinal column and all the muscles of the trunk, arms, and legs.

Perseveration Constant repetition of meaningless words, phrases, or movements.

Pervasive Developmental Delay (PDD) A childhood condition in which there is delay across all areas of development, speech and language, cognitive, fine and gross motor, social, emotional, and adaptive behaviors.

Petit Mal Seizure A seizure lasting several seconds and not usually observable to the casual onlooker.

Phasic Reflexes Primitive, automatic responses to stimuli normally seen in newborn and very young infants. Examples are rooting, in which the head turns toward touch on mouth, and flexor withdrawal, in which the leg pulls up in response to pressure on the sole of the foot.

Pronation In reference to twisting motion at the wrist, muscles of the forearm turn resulting in the palm of the hand facing downward.

Prone Position A person is lying on his stomach, face down.

Prone Stander An assistive device designed to fully support a person in the standing position for significant amounts of time. Is often used with non-independent walkers to give them the experience of prolonged standing and help strengthen joints and muscles.

Proprioception Perceptual awareness of where body parts are positioned in space.

Prosthesis/Prosthetic device An artificial replacement for all or part of an arm or leg.

Protective Reactions Automatic movements in which the arms and/or legs extend outward to support a person whose base of support has suddenly shifted.

Psychiatrist A physician who specializes in the evaluation, diagnosis, and treatment of mental illness.

Psychologist A specialist in the study, analysis, and treatment of behavior and relationships. Certified to do behavioral and educational testing.

Physical Therapist A specialist in the evaluation, analysis, and treatment of sensorimotor delay and disorder with emphasis on gross motor, balance, walking, and general mobility and functional skills.

Quadriparesis/Quadriplegia Paralysis or extreme weakness of the neck, trunk, leg, and arm muscles caused by congenital or traumatic injury to the spinal cord.

Range of Motion (ROM) Measured degrees or amounts of motion in joints. Each joint in the body has particular movement patterns and typical, measurable degrees of motion.

Receptive Aphasia A person cannot understand or process language written or spoken for appropriate interpretation.

Reflex Behavior An involuntary motor response to a stimulus. Sensorimotor development depends in part on growth from the simple reflex movements of a newborn to complex postural reflexes which support sitting, standing, walking and running. See also **phasic reflexes, tonic reflexes, righting reactions, protective reactions, equilibrium reactions**.

Rett's Syndrome A condition with onset at 6 months to 10 years with identification based on the following criteria: EEG abnormalities, breathing dysfunction, seizures, spasticity, scoliosis, growth retardation (physical and developmental), extremely small feet.

Righting Reactions Automatic movements in which the head and neck realign with the trunk when the body is moved off balance. Flexible movement rotation of muscles is a key to these responses.

Rotation In reference to joint movement, turning motion which is possible at ball-and-socket joints (such as the hips and shoulders) and at the truck of the body.

Scoliosis A lateral or side-to-side curvature of the spine, in the shape of a long 's'. If severe, can cause problems for internal organs, pain, and imbalance of muscle strength and control in sitting and standing.

SEA (State Education Agency) Any agency directly related to statewide education activities, i.e, State Department of Education.

Seizure Disorder A neurological condition in which there are abnormal brain waves, measured by encephalogram and treated with medication.

Sensorimotor Adaptive behavior which reflects the integrated function of sensory input, fine and gross motor skill, and functional activities, i.e. self care.

Sensory Integration The internal organization of all sensory input, including sight, hearing, touch, proprioceptive, kinesthetic, and vestibular. A developmental process which leads to the channeling and use of sensory information to adapt behaviors into increasingly complex activities.

Shunt A thin tube going from the cranial cavity (space around the brain) into another body cavity (often the stomach) to drain excess cerebrospinal fluid from the brain and prevent hydrocephalus.

Sickle Cell Anemia A hereditary form of anemia mainly affecting African Americans. Causes red blood cells to produce abnormal hemoglobin, resulting in abdominal and bone pain and leg ulcerations.

Spasticity Muscle tone marked by very high tension. Interferes with voluntary movement and can lead to stiffening of muscles around a joint and contractures. Effects controlled by exercise, positioning, and bracing.

Speech and Language Therapist A specialist in the evaluation, analysis, and treatment of disorders of speech articulation and communication, including receptive and expressive language.

Spica Cast A full body cast extending from the chest to the legs. Often put on children after hip surgery.

Spina Bifida A congenital condition which occurs when the bony spinal column does not completely close, allowing a protrusion of part of the spinal cord and/or meninges. Multiple effects can include variable paralysis and loss of sensation in the trunk and legs, bony deformities, bowel and bladder dysfunction, and hydrocephalus. Treatment includes immediate closure of the spinal opening, shunt for the hydrocephalus, sensorimotor and other therapy, medical treatment and/or therapy for bowel and bladder function.

Stereognosis The ability to recognize shapes, sizes and weights of objects through touch only, with no visual input.

Strabismus Failure of the eyes to converge when focusing on an image, resulting in squinting or 'cross-eyes'.

Supination In reference to twisting motion at the wrist, muscles of the forearm turn resulting in the palm of the hand facing upward.

Supine Position Person lies on his back, face up.

Syndrome Used to describe a group of symtoms or characteristics which are descriptive of a particular condition, i.e. Down Syndrome, Rett's Syndrome.

Tactile Sensation Messages into the central nervous system from sensory stimulation on the skin, i.e. hot, cold, sharp, dull, wet, dry.

Tonic Reflexes Primitive, automatic changes in muscle tone resulting in positional changes in the limbs, occuring in response to body position or head movement. In the asymmetrical tonic neck reflex (ATNR), head turning results in bending of the arm and leg on the face side, and straightening of the arm and leg on the skull side. In the symmetrical tonic neck reflex (STNR), bending the head forward results in arms bending and legs straightening, with the reverse occurring when the head goes back.

Tourette's Syndrome A syndrome of facial and vocal tics with onset in childhood, progressing to generalized jerking movements in any part of the body. Also known as Gilles de la Tourette's Syndrome.

Tuberous Sclerosis A hereditary disease marked by tumors on the central nervous system and sometimes on the eye, heart and stomach muscle. Results in progressive deterioration of cognitive and social-adaptive skills and seizures.

Vestibular Refers to the sense of balance which is mediated through a system located in the inner ear.

Visual Motor Coordination The ability to coordinate vision with movements of the body or parts of the body.

Sample Evaluation Checklist: Daily Living Skills

Chapter 7 discussed the cumbersome and unresponsive nature of the annual IEP system currently in place. More regular evaluation of the student's progress is absolutely necessary to carry out truly individualized education. To facilitate this kind of dynamic evaluation, we have developed a set of checklists in all areas of the curriculum, which the teacher can use at any time to inventory a student's skill attainments. Here we present one such checklist for Daily Living Skills. To use the checklist, place the appropriate mark in the box next to each skill: a check mark for an attained skill, check-minus for a skill which is being worked on, and a minus sign for a skill which the student has not yet achieved. These evaluations should be done at least three times a year.

Kids Are People Elementary School

Kindergarten – Grade Six
Multicultural, Inclusive Program
Therapeutic Services

656 Beacon St., 2nd floor
Boston, MA 02215
(617) 266-0028
(617) 266-0423

DAILY LIVING SKILLS

✓ -means accomplished
✓̄ -means working on
— -not yet accomplished

EATING SKILLS	SEPT	JAN	MAY
Student will suck and swallow liquids with out spillage			
Student does control drooling			
Student can pick up and feed bite-size pieces of food with out continuous dropping			
Student does feed self without messing table, self, others, etc...			
Student does chew food and swallow with mouth closed			
Student holds own cup			
Student does lift cup and drink contents without spillage			
Student can use utensils correctly without messing self, table, others, etc...			
Student feeds self entire meal without assistance and without considerable mess			
Student can serve self food without assistance			
Student can pour liquids without spillage			
Student can choose necessary utensils and dishes for meal			
Student can spread food with knife			
Student can cut sandwich with knife			
Student will grasp a napkin to clean mouth			
Student can appropriately use wet wipe/ face cloth to clean hands and face after meals			
Student can communicate need for more food or drink			
Student can clean up place after eating : i.e. put away materials from lunch box, wash table, throw away garbage, put away lunch box			
Student has acceptable table manners			
Student uses " Please" and " Thank-you" when asking for food			

TOILETRY	SEPT.	JAN.	MAY
Student is toilet trained			
Student will communicate by signing, or other method, need to use toilet			
Student can undo clothing for toileting			
Student knows to and does wipe self during toileting			
Student knows to use toilet paper			
Student can get toilet paper for self			
Student can sit self or stand self appropriately at toilet without accident			
Student does not wet or soil self constantly			
Student does not need reminding to use bathroom			
Student knows to wash hands after toileting			
Student knows can turn water on and off			
Student knows how to get soap			
Student knows to rinse soap off hands before drying			
Student knows to dry hands after washing them			
Student washes hands after toileting only with reminder			
Student toilets only when given a timed schedule			
DRESSING SKILLS			
Student can take off shoes and socks			
Student can put a hat on			
Student can take off hat on command			
Student can put on socks			
Student can put on shoes			
Student can remove pullover garment			
Student can put on pullover garment			
Student can remove coat			
Student can put on coat			
Student can remove mittens and gloves			
Student can put on mittens and gloves			

DRESSING SKILLS CON'T	SEPT.	JAN.	MAY
Student can put on boots			
Student can remove boots			
Student can unzip clothing			
Student can zip clothing			
Student can unsnap clothing			
Student can snap clothing			
Student can unbutton clothing			
Student can button clothing			
Student can unhook clothing, unlatch, etc...			
Student can hook clothing,latch, etc...			
Student can unbuckle clothing			
Student can buckle clothing			
Student can identify front and back			
Student can identify inside and outside of clothing			
Student can turn clothing from inside out and knows when to this			
Student can assist dressing oneself			
Student can put legs correctly in pants			
Student can pull up pants unassisted			
Studen can put arm in button shirt/sweater correctly			
Student can tie laces			
Student can hang-up coat			
LEISURE TIME			
Student will play with balls, dolls, trucks, etc...			
Student will play with climbing structure			
Student can change channel on t.v. and make program selection			
Student does not disrupt others watching t.v.			
Student does follow rules in simple games			
Student does participate in sports without direct constant intervention from adults			
SAFETY			
Student knows not to touch hot things			
Student knows not to run into traffic			

SAFETY CON'T	SEPT.	JAN.	MAY
Student is cautious about jumping off high objects			
Student knows not to fool around on or to push others while on the stairs			
Student knows to exit building during fire alarm			
Student knows to recognize and obey traffic signs and lights			
Student does understand safety rules for crossing street			
Student understands not walking into others and objects on a sidewalk			
HYGIENE/MANNERS			
Student knows to wash hands : Before eating			
After toileting			
After messy art project			
After playing in sand, dirt, etc...			
Student can use brush or comb to comb hair			
Student can brush own teeth			
Student knows to put toothpaste on brush			
Student can open toothpaste container			
Student knows to cover mouth when coughing			
Student knows to cover nose when sneezing			
Student knows to cover mouth when yawning			
Student knows when to blow nose			
Student can blow own nose			
Student can sit straight			
Student can stand straight			
Student knows face is dirty and needs washing			
Student knows shoes are untied and ties them or requests assistance			
Student knows clothes are twisted and straightens them or requests assistance			
Student knows he/she has cut self and asks assistance or shows teacher			

HUMAN BODY	SEPT.	JAN.	MAY
Student can draw a person			
Student can touch parts of body when modeled			
Student can touch parts of body when named			
Student eats adequate amounts of nutritional food without assistance			
Student sleeps an adequate amount of time to be rested for daily activities			
Student can follow simple gross motor games, skills, etc...			
SOCIAL SKILLS			
Student can show affection by hugging, kissing, etc...			
Student accepts affection of hugging, kissing, etc...			
Student can follow 1 part direction			
Student can follow 2 part direction			
Student can follow 3 part directions			
Student can follow 3 or more set of directions			
Student can show anger without aggression			
Student does not bite			
Student does not hit			
Student does not kick			
Student doe not scratch			
Student does not scream or throw temper tantrums			
If student can not or will not talk,student attempts one of the following: Signing			
Communication board			
Communication book			
Choosing objects			
Using eye gazing			

Resources for the Classroom

Science Resources: Books of Experiments

Abruscato, Joseph. *Teaching Children Science.* 1992: Allyn & Bacon.

Brandenberg, Aliki. *Digging Up Dinosaurs.* 1981: Harper Collins Publishers.

Chisholm, Jane, and David Beeson. *Biology: An Usborne Introduction.* 1984.

Dennard, Deborah. *How Wise is an Owl? The Strange Things People Say about Animals in the Woods.* 1993: Carolrhoda Books, Inc.

Dickinson, Terence. *Exploring the Sky by Day: The Equinox Guide to Weather and the Atmosphere.* 1989: Camden House.

Evans, David, and Claudette Williams. *Let's Explore Science: Water and Floating.* 1993: Dorling Kindersley.

Ford, Adam. *Weather Watch.* 1981.

Gibbons, Gail. *Recycle: A Handbook for Kids.* 1992.

Johnson, Rebecca L. *The Great Barrier Reef: A Living Laboratory.* 1991.

Kerrod, Robin. *The Simon & Schuster Young Readers' Book of Science.* 1990: Simon & Schuster.

Maki, Chu. *Snowflakes, Sugar and Salt: Crystals Up Close.* 1988: Lerner Publications Co.

McVey, Vicki. *The Sierra Club Kids' Guide to Planet Care and Repair.* 1993.

Mutel, Cornelia F., and Mary M. Rodgers. *Our Endangered Planet: Tropical Rain Forests.* 1991: Lerner Publications Co.

Prochnow, Dave, and Kathy Prochnow. *How? More Experiments for the Young Scientist.* 1993.

Rosen, Sidney. *Which Way to the Milky Way?* 1992.

Souza, D.M. *Powerful Waves.* 1992.

Van Cleave, Janice. *Physics for Every Kid.* From the Science for Every Kid Series. 1991: John Wiley and Sons.

Walker, Sally. *Water Up, Water Down: The Hydrologic Cycle.* 1992.

Yamashita, Keiko. *Paws, Wings and Hooves: Mammals On the Move.* 1993: Lerner Publishing Co.

Zubrowski, Bernie. *Bubbles: A Children's Museum Activity Book.* 1979: Little, Brown & Co.

Zubrowski, Bernie. *Tops: Building and Experimenting with Spinning Toys.* 1989: Morrow Junior Books.

Mathematics Resources: Everyday Mathematics

In our mathematics curriculum, we make extensive use of the Everyday Mathematics materials developed by the University of Chicago School Mathematics Project (UCSMP). For product and ordering information, contact:

Everyday Learning Corporation
P.O. Box 1479
Evanston, IL 60204-1479
(708) 866-0702
(708) 866-0748 fax

Augmentative Communication Materials

KidPix, Boardmaker, Speaking Dynamically, Kenex, touch windows, keyboard letters (called ZoomCaps), switches and other materials:

Don Johnson Incorporated
1000 N. Rand Rd.
Wauconda, IL 60084-0639
(800)999-4660
(708)526-4177 fax

Picture Communication Symbols, SuperPaint, Boardmaker, Speaking Dynamically, and other materials:

Mayer-Johnson Co.
P.O. Box 1579
Soloma Beach, CA 92075-1579
(619)550-0084
(619)550-0449 fax

Sign language books, videos, and letter charts; visual notification devices (flashers for phones, doorbells and fire alarms), TV decoders, and other materials.

Harris Communications
6541 City Unit
Eden Prairie, MN 55344-3242
1-800-825-6758 voice
1-800-825-9187 TTY
(612)946-0924 fax

Communication aids for children and adults:
Crestwood Co.
6625 N. Sidney Place
Milwaukee, WI 53209

Touch Talker, Light Talker, and other communication equipment:
Prentke Romich Co.
1022 Heyl Road
Wooster, OH 44691
1-800-262-1984
(216)263-4829 fax

Deaf and hard-of-hearing educational books and materials:
Gallaudet University Bookstore
800 Florida Ave. NE
Washington, DC 20002-3695
(202)651-5380
(202)651-5489 fax

Fine and Gross Motor Materials

Accessibility devices, self-help equipment (cups and utensils), therapy balls, swings and bolsters, toileting chairs, tables, chairs, prone standers, walkers and other materials:

Adaptability
P.O. Box 515
Colchester, CT 06415-0515
1-800-266-8856
1-800-566-6678 fax

Equipment Shop
P.O. Box 33
Bedford, MA 01730
(617)275-7681
(617)275-4094 fax

Fred Sammons Inc.
P.O. Box 32
Brookfield, IL 60513-0032
1-800-323-5547
1-800-547-4333 fax

Kaye Products Inc.
535 Dimmocks Hill Road
Hillsborough, NC 27278
(919)732-6444
1-800-685-5293 fax

Smith & Nephew Rolyan Inc.
N93 W14475 Whittaker Way
Menomonee Falls, WI 53051
1-800-558-8633
1-800-545-7758 fax

Preston Rehab Catalog
P.O. Box 89
Jackson, MI 49204-0089
1-800-631-7277
1-800-245-3765 fax

Therapro
225 Arlington St.
Framingham, MA 01701-8723
1-800-257-5376
(508)875-2062 fax

Rifton
P.O. Box 901
Rifton, NY 12471-0901
1-800-374-3866
(914)658-8065 fax

Able Generation, Inc.
1465 Woodbury Ave., Ste. 9, Box 320
Portsmouth, NH 03801-3210

Other Computer Software

The Magic Reading Library and many other wonderful products.
  Tom Synder Productions
  80 Coolidge Hill Rd.
  Watertown, MA 02172-9718
  1-800-342-0236
  (617)926-6222 fax

Storybook Weaver:
  MECC
  6160 Summit Drive
  N. Minneapolis, MN 55430-4003

Living Books, The Play Room, The Tree House:
  Broderbund
  500 Redwood Blvd.
  Novalo, CA 94946

Multicultural Education on Special Needs

One commercially available kit to teach typical children what it feels like to have various kinds of special needs is called *What If You Couldn't...? An Elementary School Program About Handicaps*. It was developed by the Children's Museum of Boston in conjunction with WGBH-Boston. For product and ordering information, contact the distributor:

Burt Harrison & Co., Inc.
P.O. Box 732
Weston, MA 02193-0732
(617)647-0674
(617)647-0675 fax

Below is the curriculum I designed for our program.

THE WHAT IF I COULDN'T SERIES

What if I Couldn't Talk
A. This is called being mute; what can cause this?
B. Interview people who are mute and ask them what their world is like. Put together quotes from them to write a book for kit.
C. Activity Cards
   a. Have children put kerchief across mouth to see what it is like. (Teacher-directed; make sure parents know about these activities ahead of time.)
   b. What couldn't you do or would you have trouble doing if you were mute?
   c. Have children draw pictures of what it would be like to be mute—get specifics from them about their drawings and their feelings.
D. Develop materials to go with this: puzzles, books, dolls, sequencing cards.
E. How do mute people tell others what they think, want or need?
F. Make up sign sentences under pictures the children drew. Create this into a book for the kit.
G. Different methods of communication.
   a. Teach children to eye gaze.
   b. Teach children signing.
   c. Teach children to ask question for hand raising if mute person is significantly involved physically, e.g., "If you want/need/feel this raise your hand. I'll count to five."

What if I Couldn't Walk

(Important to indicate equipment which can help people walk.)
A. Explain
   - Sometimes people have weak muscles.
   - Sometimes people have muscles which are too strong.
   - Sometimes people are paralyzed and can't feel to walk.
B. Interview people who need help to walk. Put together quotes from them to write a book for the kit.
C. Activity Cards
   a. Borrow a wheelchair, crutches, and braces from local Easter Seals, a hospital, families, or children in program. Have children try out different equipment
      - using one leg
      - with legs taped together, etc.
   b. What couldn't you do, or would you have trouble doing if you couldn't walk? (make a list)
   c. Have children draw pictures of what it would be like to not be able to walk unassisted. How does it make you feel?
   d. Develop material to go with this, i.e., puzzles, books, dolls, sequencing cards.
   e. Go for a walk in the neighborhood. Do two things:
      1) Have children imagine they are in a wheelchair and have them look for places that the wheelchair couldn't go — if possible, use a wheelchair while on your walk.
      2) Have children look for places provided for people with special needs, i.e., parking spaces, and explain about respecting these.
D. Materials: walker, wheelchair, crutches, braces, dolls, puzzles, books, sequencing cards.

What if I Couldn't Use My Hands
A. Explain how sometimes people have
   - only one hand or arm
   - or very strong or weak muscles so it's hard for them to use their hands and arms
   - or sometimes no feeling at all in their arms
B. Have children try to
      button
      zip
      tie their shoes
   with only one hand.
C. Have the children draw a picture about what it would be like to be unable to use their hands.

   a. Draw with only one hand (opposite of their handedness; other hand behind back)
   b. Have them paint a picture using their mouth to hold brush.
D. Develop materials to go with this: puzzles, dolls, sequencing cards, books, posters.
E. Have a person without upper body use come to talk to the children.

What if I Couldn't See
A. This is called being blind — what can cause blindness?
B. Interview people who are blind and ask them what their world is like. Put together quotes from them to write a book for the kit.
C. Activity Cards
   a. Blindfold children, let them see what it's like.
   b. What couldn't you do or would you have trouble doing if you were blind? Have children make a list.
   c. Have children draw pictures of what it would be like to be blind.
   d. Develop materials to go with this, i.e. puzzle with blind person, books, dolls, sequencing cards.
   e. How do blind people read?
   f. Make up Braille sentences under pictures children drew of what it is like to be blind. Create this into a book for the kit. Have children who are blind as part of the group so they can read it.
   g. Have a person who is blind come in and talk to the group.
D. Materials: walking stick, dolls, puzzles, books, Braille cards, sequencing cards.

These are just a few examples of activity kits which can be created and ways your students can create the written and oral materials. When you conduct this program, make sure the parents know about the activities in each of these units at the time you conduct them with your students.

Index

ABOUT THE AUTHORS

Katie Blenk holds a dual undergraduate degree in Early Childhood Education and English from the University of New Hampshire, and Master's degrees in Early Childhood Education from Wheelock College and in Counseling Psychology for Children and Adolescents from Boston College. She is a validator for the National Association for the Education of Young Children. She opened Kids Are People School on February 19, 1980, at the age of 25. The first child with special needs was "included" in 1981.

Katie and her sister Mary run the Kids Are People Preschool and Elementary School programs. Katie has lectured extensively on inclusion. She has been a consultant on inclusion to the State Department of Education and a member of the State Office for Children Special Needs Task Force. She currently resides in Rockport, Massachusetts.

Doris Landau Fine holds a Bachelor of Science and Master of Science in Physical Therapy from Sargent College of Allied Health Professions at Boston University. Since 1971 she has worked with children in a variety of community settings, including early intervention programs, Head Start, and public schools, and has lectured at Northeastern University, Boston University and the University of Massachusetts at Boston. She has trained staff in early childhood and Head Start programs and published in these areas. She currently consults to Kids Are People School and is completing her doctorate at the Florence Heller School, Brandeis University. She lives in Newton, Massachusetts.